Reshaping Museum Space

Architecture, Design, Exhibitions

Edited by

Suzanne MacLeod

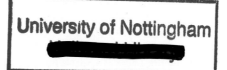
 Routledge
Taylor & Francis Group

LONDON AND NEW YORK

1005669764

First published 2005
by Routledge
2 Park Square, Milton Park, Abingdon, Oxon OX14 4RN

Simultaneously published in the USA and Canada
by Routledge
270 Madison Avenue, New York, NY 10016

Reprinted 2006 (twice)

Transferred to Digital Printing 2008

Routledge is an imprint of the Taylor & Francis Group, an informa business

Typeset in Sabon by
Florence Production Ltd, Stoodleigh, Devon
Printed and bound in Great Britain by
TJI Digital, Padstow, Cornwall

British Library Cataloguing in Publication Data
A catalogue record for this book is available from the British Library

Library of Congress Cataloging in Publication Data
MacLeod, Suzanne.
Reshaping museum space: architecture, design, exhibitions/
Suzanne MacLeod.
p. cm. – (Museum meanings)
Includes bibliographical references and index.
1. Museum architecture. 2. Space (Architecture). 3. Museum buildings.
4. Museum exhibits. 5. Museums – Information technology.
6. Museums – Technological innovations. 7. Cultural property – Protection.
8. Museums – Philosophy. I. Title. II. Series.
NA6690.M37 2005
727'.6–dc22
2004026855

ISBN 10: 0–415–34344–5 (hbk)
ISBN 10: 0–415–34345–3 (pbk)
ISBN 13: 978–0–415–34344–2 (hbk)
ISBN 13: 978–0–415–34345–9 (pbk)

Richard Toon is Senior Research Analyst, Morrison Institiute for Public Policy, Arizona State University, Tempe, Arizona. He was previously Education and Research Director at the Arizona Science Center, in Phoenix, Arizona, US. He completed his PhD in Museum Studies at Leicester University in 2003 and has been a programme evaluator and public policy consultant for over 20 years.

Jon Wood works at the Henry Moore Institute in Leeds, UK, where he co-ordinates the research programme and curates exhibitions. He is an Associate Lecturer at Leeds University, where he teaches on the 'MA in Sculpture Studies' course. He specializes in sculpture from 1850 to the present and is currently writing a history of the artist's studio.

Acknowledgements

This book emerged out of a conference held at the University of Leicester in April 2004 and would not have been possible without the support of the University of Leicester, Haley Sharpe Design and the staff of the Department of Museum Studies. I am grateful to Dr Simon Knell, who enthusiastically supported the idea for the conference and the book, and to Professor Eilean Hooper-Greenhill, who has taken a keen interest in the content of the book and provided much-needed direction and advice. I am grateful to Richard Sandell for his ongoing support and to Catherine Bousfield at Routledge, who has provided clear and helpful instructions throughout. Thanks should also go to the contributors to the book, all of whom worked to make the production process as simple as possible – something which I greatly appreciate – to Jim Roberts for his technical assistance, and to Jocelyn Dodd, Mark O'Neill, Richard Toon and Richard Sandell, who provided thoughtful feedback on chapters. Finally, I would especially like to thank my husband Lee Ridsdale, who continues to take an interest in my work and to act as a constant source of encouragement and humour.

Picture credits

Introduction

Suzanne MacLeod

At no other point in their modern history have museums undergone such radical reshaping as in recent years. Challenges to create inclusive and accessible spaces open to appropriation and responsive to contemporary agendas have resulted in new architectural and spatial forms for museums. One result of this large-scale and varied remaking of museum space is that the space of the museum is increasingly recognized as an environment created through a complex of practices and systems of knowledge. Museum professionals are beginning to recognize the constitutive character and transformative possibilities of museum space as well as the ability of museum users and museum professionals to reshape museum spaces through practices of appropriation. Museum space is now recognized as a space with a history of its own, a space active in the making of meaning and, most importantly, a space open to change.

This recognition is undoubtedly linked to the substantial new building projects that can be identified internationally and that have begun to challenge traditional concepts of museum architecture and suggest new possibilities for display and experience. However, the rethinking of museum space relates to more than the physical structure and exhibition hardware of the museum. Many museums are working to reposition both collections and visitors in order to generate new spatial forms, without large-scale architectural developments. These shifts are variously characterized as creating spaces for lifelong learning, spaces of mutuality and inclusive spaces, where physical, intellectual and cultural barriers to access may be overcome.

Reshaping Museum Space: Architecture, Design, Exhibitions takes aspects of these recent museum developments as its focus. Pulling together the views of museum professionals, architects, designers and academics the book highlights the complexity, significance and malleability of museum space and provides an opportunity for some preliminary reflections upon recent developments in museum space and for the detailed analysis of specific case studies. In particular, the chapters concentrate on the processes and practices of museum building and exhibition design, focusing on the nature, character and possibilities for museum space through an understanding of the complex ways in which it is made.

A recurring issue across a good number of the chapters in *Reshaping Museum Space* is the tension between iconic architecture and the agendas of access and inclusion that form the central tenets of the modern museum. Often criticized as architectural indulgences, iconic buildings can compound the separation between the building, its contents and its context, ensuring the persistence of a rather limited and partial understanding of architecture as the aesthetic outcome and privileged activity of the architect – a view that ignores the complexity and difficulty of any architectural project. As Richard Toon notes in Chapter 2, architectural texts devoted to the museum tend to concentrate on images of specific architectural features such as staircases, entrances and lighting solutions, the assumption being that the architecture exists in its ideal form before the communities of use move in.[1] Similarly, architectural histories of the museum privilege the museum as an architectural object, celebrating some museums, ignoring others and obscuring from view the complex histories of practice through which the space of the museum has been continually recreated (Chapter 1).

The chapters in *Reshaping Museum Space* suggest a broader understanding of architecture based upon a recognition of the range of professionals and stake-holders involved in the architectural production process and the complexity of navigating these often-contradictory agendas and aspirations towards the building of a new museum. As Moira Stevenson suggests in Chapter 5, for many museum professionals directly involved in capital development projects, achieving the aims and vision of their institutions and turning development plans and ideals into a reality have demanded stringent planning, nerves of steel and a commitment to ongoing evaluation and change. With this in mind, a good number of the chapters in *Reshaping Museum Space* concentrate on the *process* of architectural and spatial reshaping in order to highlight the various 'negotiations' through which architecture gets built and the problems and inconsistencies that can creep into the architectural structure of the museum as a result of this complexity (see, for example, Chapters 5, 6, 7, 8 and 16).[2]

As museums have come to be consciously recognized as drivers for social and economic regeneration, the architecture of the museum has developed from its traditional forms into often-spectacular one-off statements and architectural visions. High-profile examples include Frank Gehry's Guggenheim Bilbao and Daniel Libeskind's Jewish Museum in Berlin. While recognized as often drawing mass appeal and admiration, such buildings may also fight against the other agendas of the museum, confirming to a broad public that museums are not for them (see Chapters 2, 4, 8 and 15). For example, Helen Rees Leahy (Chapter 8) notes a tension between the spectacular space of distraction and disorientation in a number of recently built and renewed art museums, and the agendas of learning and inclusion to which the institutions are fully committed. Similarly, in Fabienne Galangau-Quérat's account of the creation of the Grande Galerie de l'Evolution at the National Museum of Natural History in Paris (Chapter 7), the language of spectacle and the successful incorporation of architectural scale and splendour into the exhibition experience would seem to have been achieved at the expense of a content-rich experience.

Iconic architecture can place a city or town on the cultural map. It can, as in the case of Bilbao, raise the profile of a place or region and work in an incredibly positive way to challenge preconceptions and encourage economic investment. It can add enormously to the pleasure of museum visiting, creating a visual feast and sense of occasion that is rarely experienced in other building types. The challenge, however, is to achieve this alongside the integration of site, architecture and exhibition. Fighting against the iconic tendencies in museum architecture, a number of the chapters describe ways of working that stem from the visions and agendas of the museum and may potentially result in three-dimensional design solutions that form a direct relationship between context, content and spatial experience (Chapters 9, 16 and 17). Within the approaches described here, visitor experience is privileged over the design of beautiful objects and narrative plays a key part in structuring space and anchoring content to context. Here, the architecture and other design features become part of a range of elements, macro and micro, arranged and orchestrated to create possibilities for interaction and experience. As Peter Higgins notes (Chapter 16), museums built in this way can also become an 'anchor attractor' when master-planned into the commercial activities of a given location.

Common to all of this is a repositioning of the museum as a flexible space, open to change, responsive to visitor needs and in touch with contemporary issues and agendas (see Chapters 10, 11, 12, 13 and 14). Lawrence Fitzgerald's description of the rationale behind the redisplay of Kelvingrove Museum and Art Gallery in Glasgow (Chapter 10) charts a shift in conceptions of museum space where permanency has given way to a system of changeable modules enabling 60 per cent of the display to be changed over a six-year period. And, in Chapter 12, Jon Wood describes the innovative and inspiring *Close Encounters: The Sculptor's Studio in the Age of the Camera* at the Henry Moore Institute in Leeds, which re-evoked the sculptor's studio in the gallery without recourse to 'mock-ups with turntables, tools, stone and sawdust'. These and the other examples offered in *Reshaping Museum Space* point to some of the sophisticated techniques being utilized in a range of exhibition formats at the present time. Such examples challenge the notion of 'dumbing down' in museum displays, pointing instead to a myriad of possibilities.

A common characteristic of many of the examples of museum space cited by the contributors is the recognition on the part of the exhibit designers of the need for didactic exhibition elements that ground the user and enable some level of engagement with the subject matter, while at the same time providing space to imagine, contemplate and reflect. In Chapter 13, on the cross-overs in spatial characteristics between the worlds of the museum and the gallery, Christopher Marshall differentiates between the essentially 'projective space' of the museum and the 'reflective space' of the gallery. Museums, he argues, are more 'projective' in the way that they pull together exhibitionary elements in order to convey a message. Galleries on the other hand offer, in the main, a more 'reflective' space based upon the contemplation of individual works. Marshall concentrates his attention on the ways in which museums have begun to utilize the reflective space of the gallery through the incorporation of aesthetic elements in museum displays. Citing a range of examples, including the Grande Galerie de l'Evolution, where reflective space is considered to have overwhelmed the didactic content-rich projective space of the museum, Marshall identifies a general trend towards the incorporation of reflective space in museums. Here, art-inspired elements open the space of the museum up to a more evocative and experiential form of communication. For Marshall, this provision of what he terms the 'free space' of the gallery, the space of open-ended communication, in the traditionally more linear and didactic displays of the museum, is changing the character of museum space.

The shift in museum space that Marshall identifies seems to share a great deal in common with the characteristics of other museum and gallery spaces described in *Reshaping Museum Space*. For example, in Jon Wood's description of *Close Encounters: The Sculptor's Studio in the Age of the Camera* (Chapter 12), one senses a move towards Marshall's projective space within the confines of the gallery through the clever manipulation of space, photographs and sculpture. Similarly, in Stephen Greenberg's description of the *Holocaust exhibition* at the Imperial War Museum (Chapter 17), he refers to an additional layer of exhibition, planned in to respond to the gravity of the subject, as 'the space to imagine'.

Marshall's ideas also reverberate with Richard Sandell's consideration of the social agency of museum space and the social responsibility of those actively involved in the shaping of museum space (Chapter 14). Sandell cites the example of the *Out of Line* exhibition at the exit to the Anne Frank House in Amsterdam. In this multi-media presentation, visitors are faced with a series of real-life dilemmas and are asked to vote on each in favour of 'freedom of expression' or 'the right to protection against discrimination'. The choices are reflected in the gallery space as the results of the vote are displayed on the gallery ceiling.

All of these examples seem to effect some kind of balance, albeit through very different techniques, between an object and content-rich display and provision for user-led meaning-making, creation of content and content organization. Central to this is the role of new technologies and the possibilities offered for user-led experiences through the incorporation and use of new media (Chapters 3 and 9). *Reshaping Museum Space* highlights these changes, drawing attention to the malleability of museum space and the need for all those involved in the process of making museum space to shift their attention from object- to experience-making.

The chapters are ordered into four overlapping parts. Part I includes four chapters, all of which focus on the nature of museum space. In Part II, the chapters are broadly concerned with the architectural reshaping of museums and galleries, and in Part III a group of chapters discuss specific exhibition design solutions and approaches. Finally, Part IV includes three chapters that cut across the key themes of the book. Such structuring devices can tend to gloss over the detail and differences between individual chapters and *Reshaping Museum Space* is no exception to this. The real worth of the book lies in the detail of individual contributions and the sometimes slight, and sometimes major, differences in approach and judgement that each chapter contains.

Notes

1 This has been usefully theorized by Jonathan Hill. J. Hill (ed.), *Occupying Architecture: Between the Architect and the User*, London and New York: Routledge, 1998.
2 I. Borden and J. Rendell (eds), *InterSections, Architectural Histories and Critical Theories*, London: Routledge, 2000, p. 5.

Part I

On the nature of museum space

1

Rethinking museum architecture

Towards a site-specific history of production and use

Suzanne MacLeod

Introduction

> If you could distil the essence of pure modern architecture, and remove all traces of the usual compromises and cut corners and clumsy details and flash populist moves, then you would get a strange, unsettling, austere, but rather beautiful building. Such absolute purity is of course impossible to achieve. But the New Art Gallery in Walsall comes closer than any new cultural landmark built in Britain for years. It is both extraordinary and extraordinarily good. It repays attention: this is emphatically not a one-liner building.[1]

> A building for people in which to experience art? Not in my book. This is an architectural indulgence which allows enthusiasts to experience an impressive building but where nowhere near enough thought has been put into how a wider public will use that building. It is a traditional gallery in new clothes. It gets nowhere close to the essential 'feelgood' relaxing atmosphere needed to make people love it. Why are there no production facilities, no crafts, no film. There aren't even areas to sit.[2]

These two statements were both written about the New Art Gallery, Walsall, on its opening in 2000. They offer just two examples of the kinds of narrative that have circulated around the programme of new museum building and expansion that has taken place on an international scale over the last three decades. Where Hugh Pearman is relieved that, on this occasion, the usual 'dirtiness'[3] of architecture (compromise, populism and economy) has been avoided by the architects, John Stewart-Young speaks only of missed opportunities and partial responses to the making of a new museum. While Pearman sees an architectural masterpiece, Stewart-Young sees an architectural indulgence and castigates the architects of the building for omitting the most obvious of architectural elements necessary in a museum fit for the twenty-first century – places to sit.

Such statements point towards some of the perceived 'problems' of museum architecture that have become evident in the wake of the large-scale reshaping of museums. A recurring criticism of many new and renewed museums is that the vision and desire of the architect to create a signature building have ridden roughshod over the needs and aims of the museum. Such buildings may work very well as icons and cultural landmarks without achieving the levels of accessibility, usability and relevance for both visitors and staff, promised during their conception.

These frustrations of museum architecture expose its complexity. Here, personal agendas and goals mix with institutional ambitions and visions, economic development plans, the expectations of funding bodies and the broader social ideals and expectations for the museum's role in society. Making architecture involves a large number of people from different fields and 'communities of practice' who speak different languages and hold different aspirations and priorities, values and beliefs, so much so that the varying judgements on architecture can seem difficult, if not impossible, to reconcile.[4] There seems to be little shared ground between them. Yet such diversity of perception and priority is not uncommon, often characterizing even the smallest of capital development project teams.

What seems to cloud the issue here, but does also perhaps offer some common ground, is an underlying understanding, or notion, of what architecture is – an assumption that architecture is the aesthetic outcome and activity of the architect. This dominant and powerful understanding, it is argued here, sits behind many of the debates surrounding museum architecture and is the cause of many of the problems associated with working with architects in museums: the seeming lack of control of the building process on the part of the museum, the inability of the client to communicate the institutional vision to the architects, the fear of interfering with the architectural process and hoisting too many compromises on to the architect, the fear of being perceived as a philistine by questioning a design concept, and so on . . .

Taking its lead from a body of architectural theory that has emerged in the gap opened up by Henri Lefebvre's work on the production of space,[5] this chapter sets out to oppose this underlying and dominant definition of architecture and to argue instead for a fuller reading of museum architecture[6] as a social and cultural product, continually reproduced through use. Such a broadening of our understanding of what architecture is would enable us to begin to consider the contexts within, and processes through which, museum architecture is continually reproduced. In this way, we might begin to explore the complexity of museum architecture and understand more about how it gets made.

While the key aim of this chapter is to challenge underlying and reductive notions of architecture, it is also concerned with architectural histories of the museum – the stories through which we learn about museum architecture. Architectural histories of the museum tend to be based upon and reinforce the dominant understanding of architecture as the aesthetic outcome or activity of the architect. Such histories can be recognized as legitimizing current practice and contributing to some of the problems associated with museum architecture. With this in mind, the chapter begins from existing architectural histories of the museum and suggests the need for a new type of site-specific museum history – one based on architectural production and use. An understanding of architecture as set forward here begins to set an agenda for that research towards a greater understanding of the 'multifaceted negotiations'[7] of architecture.

The ideas set forward in the chapter are explored through my interest in England's regional museums and galleries. In the last decades of the nineteenth and first decades of the twentieth century, a phenomenal number of museums and galleries appeared across the towns and cities of England, particularly in the industrial north and midlands. At the present time, many of these same museums and galleries are undergoing significant architectural and spatial change. In the wake of over two decades of museum building and with the input of significant capital expenditure from the Heritage Lottery Fund, the significance of the large-scale reshaping of these museums and galleries has not gone unnoticed. The changes are hailed as dragging modernist museums based on outdated notions of knowledge and understanding into the twenty-first century, where transparency, collaboration and notions of visitor-centred learning are key. Of course, the specific histories of these sites are far more complex and interesting than such notions of large-scale epistemic change suggest.

Since it was founded in 1877 and a purpose-designed building was erected on Upper William Brown Street, the Walker Art Gallery[8] in Liverpool has undergone a series of architectural and spatial transformations. In the late nineteenth century, the 1930s, the 1950s, and again recently, the museum has been the subject of significant architectural rearrangement and expansion. Inside, the space of the museum has shifted continuously. Sometimes this change has been slow and imperceptible and, at other times, especially at times of architectural development, change has been dramatic. In this chapter, selected episodes from the Walker's past will be taken to illustrate the social and cultural character of museum architecture and to begin to explore what an architectural history of the museum based on production and use might include. This brief consideration of the Walker also suggests that important spatial (and hence social) changes are often made according to the beliefs and motives of those who control the space of the museum. The architecture of the museum was, in the final decades of the nineteenth century, and continues to be, at the beginning of the twenty-first century, a contested site, formed through the contradictory and often conflicting visions and agendas of those directly involved in the architectural and spatial reshaping. Thus, the chapter also touches upon the plays of power involved in the making of museum architecture.

Rethinking museum architecture

The Walker Art Gallery opened to the public in 1877 and, by 1901, the Curator, Charles Dyall, was able to list 43 art galleries, 'mostly under Municipal control', which had opened in the provinces and which had, according to Dyall, sought advice from, and precedents in, the Walker.[9] The dramatic rise in the number of museums and galleries across the towns and cities of England is well documented. As Alma Wittlin suggested in 1949, around 295 museums were built in the UK between 1850 and 1914, taking the total number of museums in Great Britain to over 350.[10] While a good amount of attention has been given to a consideration of the social conditions driving such developments forward, little attention has been given to the architecture of the provincial museums – a fact that can be accounted for, in large part, by the dominant understanding of architecture that continues to shape the ways in which we think about the physical and spatial structure of the museum.

A good number of texts have been written on the history of museum architecture, but none of these core historical texts considers the ongoing history or process of change that has been, and continues to be, the reality in most museums. Existing histories of museum architecture tend to approach buildings as objects and architecture as describing the practice and activities of the architect. Architects, and architects alone, make architecture. Architecture is complete when the final door handle is added and when the snagging list is resolved. It exists, in its idealized architectural state, as a pure object, not yet tainted by the impure communities of use.[11]

The histories based upon this definition take us on a journey from Durand's 1803 design for an art museum, to Leo von Klenze's Glypothek in Munich (1816–30), Schinkel's Altes Museum in Berlin (1823–30) and John Soane's Dulwich Picture Gallery, London (1811–14), each architect adding something new to the museum as a building type. For the majority of architectural historians, these architects established a typology of museum design and formal solutions in lighting and circulation that prevailed until the mid-twentieth century, and that modern architects continue to refer back to.[12] This stress on the progressive development of the museum as a building type consigns the museum buildings of Mies van der Rohe to the category of misguided interruption, properly redirected by Louis Kahn at Kimbell and Yale.[13] Such readings of the museum welcome the return to historicism in the museum architecture of the late 1970s and 1980s, as it continues the historical narrative so rudely interrupted by the modernist architecture of the 1950s and 1960s. Here the stress is, in the main, placed on the shell of the 'finished' museum and on the skills of the canon of star architects.

As the museum has come, in the later decades of the twentieth century, to be consciously recognized as a driver for urban regeneration, so new demands have been placed on architects to create one-off individual pieces of architecture and high profile landmarks. Architectural solutions as diverse as The Pompidou in Paris (Richard Rogers and Renzo Piano 1972–7) and Guggenheim Bilbao (Frank Gehry 1994–7) have challenged the established canon and led to a number of architectural historians attempting the development of alternate typologies.[14] Many of these new typologies appear forced and restrictive, illustrating the complexity of museum types and the difficulties of classification.

Architectural histories, as described above, tend to take us from one megamuseum, one architectural precedent or exemplar to another, reinforcing the dominant notion of architecture and blocking off any view of the complexity of architecture and the subtle histories of site-specific change in the process. The outcomes of the dominant conception of architecture as the privileged activity of the architect and as an aesthetic work are also evident in museums in numerous ways. Many museum professionals, understandably, find it very difficult to engage with architecture – after all they don't speak the specialist language of architecture and can feel ill-equipped to hold an opinion. Related to this is the tendency of museums to assume that the architect will lead building projects, resulting in museums which may be beautiful and 'architecturally strong', but don't necessarily provide the requisite spaces expected by the museum staff or in line with the longer-term plans for development. In addition to this, the view of architecture as a product that other people make compounds the separation between the building and its contents that manifests itself in the much-quoted examples of architects and visitors valuing the museum building for its own sake.

A number of sources begin to provide a more useful way of thinking about the architecture of the museum. A growing literature can be identified that looks beyond the definition of architecture as the activity and creative output of the architect towards an understanding of the built environment as a social and cultural product, continually (re)produced through use. From this literature, four key overlapping observations concerning the production of architecture may begin to suggest an alternate reading. In the following sections, the four observations are explored through selected episodes from the architectural past of the Walker.

Architecture as a social and cultural product

Research has shown that architecture can be conceived as the outcome of a perceived social need, located in the specifics of time, space and site.[15] As society changes and new social needs arise, new building forms will be produced in order to fulfil that social need. Similarly, architectures, the physical structures of buildings and the uses to which they are put will change shape over time as needs and priorities shift. As Anthony King noted in 1980, buildings are informed by a society's ideas, its forms of social organization, the beliefs and values that dominate at a particular moment and its distribution of resources.[16] Understanding buildings as social and cultural, rather than physical entities, means building some level of understanding of the society of which they are a part.[17]

The Walker has changed shape many times as its social contexts have shifted. Existing research into the social conditions that led to the establishment of museums and galleries in the industrial towns and cities of the north and the midlands begins to provide a context for the perceived need for a gallery of art in Liverpool.[18] Towns like Liverpool had grown exponentially over the course of the eighteenth and early nineteenth centuries – changes that had dramatically altered the organization of society.[19] By the early nineteenth century, the social problems brought about by industrialization and urbanization were signalling the need for civic reform. High mortality rates, slum housing and poor sanitation characterized the poorer quarters of the industrial towns and civil unrest had erupted in cities such as Liverpool, Nottingham and Bristol. By the mid- to later decades of the nineteenth century, governance in the provinces was shifting from local councils with relatively few powers following the 1835 municipal reforms, to increasingly powerful and interventionist councils actively involved in municipal development.[20] In the second half of the nineteenth century, town councils cleared slum housing, established higher sanitary standards and regulations, installed sewers and fresh water supplies, improved education provision and opened public parks. The development of public museums and art galleries was one part of this municipal development. Culture had come to be recognized by central government as one possible solution to the country's increasingly difficult social problems.[21]

In Liverpool, severe poverty, the highest mortality rates of any town in the country, including London, lack of sanitation and no reliable water supply were the main causes for concern.[22] Liverpool had grown dramatically over the eighteenth and nineteenth centuries; the population of 7,000 in 1710 had, according to P. J. Waller, increased elevenfold by 1801 and a further threefold by 1841.[23] By the nineteenth century, a large proportion of the country's cotton and other trades passed through Liverpool and, for an entrepreneurial few, fortunes were made. The majority of Liverpool's population however comprised the labouring classes, mostly unskilled, in a market chiefly devoted to distribution rather than manufacturing, the concomitants of which were, as Waller phrased it, 'irregular wages and irregular ways'.[24] Crime was high and alcohol abuse a cause for concern; in 1874 Liverpool could boast 1,929 public houses, 383 beer-houses . . . and 272 off-licences and refreshment houses, outnumbering the combined total of all the other types of shop in the town.[25]

As the problems of Liverpool were publicized,[26] and as the Conservative council followed a programme of public health improvements actively taking an interest, albeit at a distance, in the public health of its citizens,[27] Liverpool Liberals focused on the temperance campaign. The temperance movement emphasized education and 'counter-attractions' such as free libraries and friendly societies. Over the course of the 1870s numerous missions and other public spaces opened where the poor could rub shoulders with the middle classes – exposure that would encourage them to resist the temptations of drink and the forms of social behaviour associated with it. A gallery of art offered yet another form of alternative recreation.

If the perceived social need for a gallery of art in the town linked into fears over social unrest and a genuine philanthropic drive to improve the lot of the working classes, the architectural and spatial form of the gallery was linked directly to the desire on the part of a number of prominent Liverpool men, across the political spectrum, to raise the cultural profile of Liverpool. With this in mind, the gallery was based upon already existing precedents for what made good museum architecture, both in London and on the Continent. Like many early museums and galleries in the northern towns and cities, the Walker was established upon the enfilade of galleries, albeit on an exceptionally small scale. The new building, set on the site next to the public library at the top of William Brown Street, comprised an entrance hall, ten galleries and a few small spaces around the staircase for lavatories, cloakroom and the newly appointed Curator, Charles Dyall. The building was constructed from polished sandstone with a pedimented portico supported by six Corinthian columns. On top of the building was placed a colossal female statue of commerce, representing

Figure 1.1 The Walker, National Museums Liverpool. Courtesy of National Museums Liverpool.

15

Liverpool, and to the sides of the entrance large sculptures of Raphael and Michelangelo made a claim to a prestigious artistic heritage. Bas reliefs were placed along the front and sides of the gallery representing King John granting the Charter to Liverpool, William III embarking at Hoylake for Ireland, Queen Victoria's visit to Liverpool and the laying of the foundation stone of the Art Gallery by H. R. H. the Duke of Edinburgh,[28] further signalling the history and royal associations of the town.

Inside, where almost the entire space was given over to display, the entrance vestibule, off which led the lower galleries, was richly decorated with a Minton tiled floor, heavy marble pilasters and dark woodwork. A central staircase led from the enclosed entrance vestibule to the galleries on the first floor. Early photographs of the galleries show deep-coloured walls with a close and at times cluttered hang. The opportunity to view the pictures attracted a broad audience and visitor figures reached 2,349 a day in 1880, a figure not exceeded since.[29]

By the 1920s, the fortunes and popularity of the Walker seem to have diminished somewhat as the gallery lost its traditional core audiences and became the subject of a good amount of criticism in the press. Liverpool was a very different place and was suffering from the downturn in the economy and declining trade resulting in high unemployment, strikes and civil unrest.[30] The political ground had shifted dramatically since the Walker's foundation, with liberal values of free trade, individualism and philanthropy giving way following the war to increased state control and higher taxes. The introduction from the early twentieth century of national assurance schemes had, in part, alleviated some of the extreme poverty issues and 'the drink question' had diminished in importance as restrictions were put on licensing hours, as the alcoholic content of beer was reduced and as taxes were placed on spirits.[31] As the political ground shifted, so did the organization of Liverpool society. Liverpool's genteel social elite diminished in power following the war, a trend marked by the reinvention in 1922 of the Wellington Rooms, previously a focal point for the Liverpool social season, as a venue for more popular entertainments.[32]

Between 1925 and 1938 the council built over 22,000 new homes which housed one-eighth of Liverpool's population by 1931.[33] The majority of this housing was built in the suburbs, enforcing the exodus, aided by the motor car, of much of the inner-city population.[34] As the standard of living increased for a good proportion of the working population, new spaces for leisure opened in Liverpool, including ballrooms and purpose-built cinemas such as the opulent Forum on Lime Street, which opened in 1931.

It was in response to and as part of these shifts and as increasing amounts of public money went into their running[35] that museums and galleries across the country began to take on a more public-oriented role.[36] The profession was becoming more organized and a body of professional knowledge concerning the educational role of museums was increasingly sophisticated. New expectations were placed on the Walker in April 1931 when a series of letters were exchanged in the *Daily Post* accusing the gallery of failing to fulfil its true function and calling for it to take a more active part in the life of the city. The

Walker was also criticized for the now outdated practice of the gallery being led by a group of local councillors and aldermen and the letters called for the appointment of a professional museum director. The exchange ended with a petition to the City Council, signed by 80 or 90 prominent citizens of Liverpool.

The renovation and expansion of the gallery (1831–3) by Liverpool architect Sir Arnold Thorneley and the decisions to create a more open, public space in line with the architectural precedents of the day must be understood within this context. In the entrance, which had, as the *Museums Journal* pointed out in 1933, resembled the entrance to the Royal Academy,[37] the main staircase was demolished, along with the small ancillary rooms, to create a spacious entrance hall. As shown by the recent changes at the Walker, which have returned the entrance hall to its 1930s' colour scheme, the entrance hall was transformed from an enclosed and somewhat forbidding space into a bright, open public circulation area. From 1933, under the direction of the newly appointed director, Frank Lambert (previously Director at Leeds City Art Gallery), it became policy to appeal to areas of broad public interest and offer a wide range of temporary exhibitions.[38] Loan cases of exhibits from the V&A were introduced in 1934 and in that same year musical concerts were offered in the gallery. The balance had shifted from an architecture more suited to a gentlemen's club, to an architecture increasingly allied, in form and in use, to the creation of a public space.

By 1939, the Walker Art Gallery had closed once again as it was taken over for the duration of the war and beyond by the Ministry of Food. The gallery would not reopen until 1951 and only then after significant refurbishment. As Lambert commented on the gallery's reopening, the Walker was a very different gallery to that 'which we all knew before September 4, 1939'.[39] Once again, a significant spatial, and hence social, reshaping of the gallery had taken place.

The boundaries and possibilities of architecture

As this selective and schematic consideration of the architectural history of the Walker begins to suggest, however, the shaping of our built environment is not an arbitrary process dependent upon broad social and political structures and this brings us to our second observation. Specific associations and organizations are active in the setting of agendas and the establishing of boundaries and possibilities for the making of architecture.

At the present time, it is possible to think broadly about organized groups and bodies, such as local councils, and government bodies such as the Heritage Lottery Fund, English Heritage and the Museums Association, as impacting upon the decision-making process through the setting of specific agendas and priorities for museums. Each of these groups may differ in their perception of the roles of museums – of what a museum should be – and the institutional/client vision will gradually sharpen or shift as these various bodies and groups are negotiated. We might also include here the myriad of consultative documents from access consultants, architectural planning consultants and lighting consultants, to name just a few.

When the Walker was first built, however, there were no specific museum bodies or government organizations responsible for the setting of guidelines and agendas for museum building. In 1877, a small group of councillors and aldermen, passionate about the progress and development of their towns, set out to emulate existing galleries of art that had been established in London and on the Continent, erecting buildings based on the museums and galleries they most admired and which would meet their basic requirements of access, circulation and display.

By the 1930s, the emergence and acknowledgement of a museums profession had certainly impacted upon the power of the aldermen and councillors. Once again, precedents for the alterations were sought in the nationals and other prestigious galleries, including the new Duveen galleries at the National Gallery and the Fitzwilliam galleries at Cambridge. This time, however, the latest museum techniques were of consequence and importance.

Individual agendas and questions of power

As Carla Yanni has pointed out, and this leads us to our third observation, each architectural and spatial solution to a particular social, institutional or professional need is only one of many possible answers. At the level of the specific building project, a range of individuals, often with conflicting visions, agendas and values, will inform the decision-making process and the final design.[40] Recognizing that many museum buildings were the 'architectural products of multifarious committees', Yanni exposed the ambiguity of specific science museum architectures and their inability to communicate a clear scientific message through an analysis of the sometimes conflicting conceptions of science held by those with the power to influence the museum's design.

We can explore this idea further though Adrian Forty's work on the modern hospital:

> Of the several studies of the history of hospital architecture, none deals specifically with the problem of why the form of hospital buildings has changed over time. The customary explanation is that their development resulted from advances in medical and scientific knowledge, but this seems inadequate for several reasons. In the first place, it ignores the question of why scientific knowledge develops at all. Moreover, there is no reason why scientific knowledge should be applied to buildings, or to anything else, unless it is in someone's interest to do so. In the history of society, knowledge matters less for what it is than for the use that is made of it. In the development of hospital buildings, some scientific discoveries led to changes in their design but others did not; equally, changes occurred independently of any revision of prevailing scientific beliefs. This lack of a clear causal relationship between scientific discovery and innovation in building form suggests that more attention should be given to the motives of those who controlled hospitals than to the development of science.[41]

Forty's concentration on the motives of those who controlled the modern hospital allows for a site-specific reading of buildings as well as allowing for more than one function. Just as an effective cure was not always the sole or most important function of the modern hospital, so the modern museum's functions have been multiple and varied, across a range of stakeholders, since its foundation in the nineteenth century.

The personal agendas of those directly involved in the shaping of the Walker at various moments in its history remain unrecorded. However, evidence of the political tendencies of key movers and shakers, as well as commentaries in the local press and the occasional text written by the individuals themselves, do begin to offer a sense of some of the agendas guiding their involvement. For example, although driven by increased state involvement in the arts, the early history of the Walker was dominated by two individuals, both of whom seem to have held multiple understandings of the function of the gallery: the Gallery Chairman, P. H. Rathbone, well known for his Ruskinian philosophy of art and Liberal politics, and local brewer and financier of the new gallery, Andrew Barclay Walker. Both seem to have played very different roles in the gallery's establishment and both seem to have held distinct and possibly oppositional understandings of the function of the gallery.

On Rathbone's part, concerns over the social conditions of the working classes informed his belief in the need for civic architecture that would act as a constant incentive to Liverpool's inhabitants to emulate the deeds of past times and become better citizens.[42] Rathbone came from a family of Unitarians who regarded social service as a part of their religion and who were actively involved in the temperance movement.[43] His belief in the political value of art also informed the acquisitions policy whereby paintings recognized as holding popular appeal were selected over more esoteric works.[44] This was not an issue of equality, of course, but was as much a concern over social unrest and his desire to 'enable the individual to realize that he is a requisite element in a living organic whole [where] every man should feel that he had his defined place and use in the world'.[45]

Where there is power there is also self-interest and the royal associations signified so obviously on the outside of the gallery were to become tangible for those directly involved in the Walker's development as members of the royal family were invited to mark special events at the gallery. For Walker in particular, funding the building of a gallery of art in the town perhaps consolidated the already strong support he received from the council in his business affairs. Such assertions are, of course, fraught with dangers of reading too much into, or taking out of context, the statements and events of the time.

Architecture's continual remaking through use

Finally, if architecture can be understood as a social and cultural product, it must also be recognized as continually reproduced through occupation and use. As Jonathan Hill has argued:

The architect and user both produce architecture, the former by design, the latter by use. As architecture is experienced, it is made by the user as much as the architect. Neither are the two terms mutually exclusive. They exist within each other. Just as the architect is also a user, the user can be an illegal architect.[46]

In the museum then, a range of users – professionals, researchers, families, tourists, organized groups, repeat visitors and so on – must also be recognized as continually remaking the architecture of the museum through the uses to which it is put. Such uses are, to a great extent of course, closely controlled by the individual and organizational visions of museum space dominant at any particular moment. This said, most of us could probably call to mind a memory of a museum space suddenly transformed through the uses to which it was put, even if it did return to its established character with its requisite spatial practices soon afterwards.

In 1877 there was no perceived need for the visitors to the Walker to feed their thoughts and needs into the architectural and spatial development process. Similarly, possibilities for the appropriation of museum space through use were tightly controlled as specific behaviours and uses of space were programmed into the architecture and management of the institution. In the current re-developments at the Walker, however, considerable public consultation has been undertaken in the development of the plans for the gallery. The boundaries and possibilities for how that information is used will of course be influenced by the institutional visions, organizational expectations and personal agendas of those involved in the gallery's future reshaping.

Taking these four observations into account, dominant definitions of architecture as the creative output and activity of the architect can be recognized as limited to, and in the interest of, one very specific community of practice.

> Professionals protect their territories by deriding incursions from 'outside' as ignorant or mistaken, implying there is a truthful and correct interpretation of a fixed body of knowledge, to which they alone have access. For the purpose of economic and social self-protection, the architectural profession provides the products and practices of its members with an iconic status and cultural value, in order to suggest that only the work of architects deserves the title of 'architecture'.[47]

Clearly, to begin to understand museum architecture, we must move beyond this partial view and shift our attention towards the relations between social organization, government and professional bodies and the motives of individuals involved in the production of museum space at specific historical moments. Working to our newly expanded definition of architecture, the architecture of the museum is, in fact, the result of the actions of a whole host of groups, organizations and individuals. Here, the architecture of the museum is no longer limited to a static physical building, but expanded to include the physical structure, the layout of functions in space, the layout of collections in space, the management, the programming and so on, in a constant state of (re)production through use.

Returning to Charles Dyall's list of art galleries established between 1877 and 1901, and bearing in mind the dominant definition of architecture as the creative product and activity of the architect, it is perhaps now possible to see why existing histories of museum architecture tend to ignore all but the high-profile, 'architecturally important' examples. Provincial museums and galleries in Britain are rarely considered at all, reduced as they are to 'municipal' inter-pretations of real architecture – mean and parochial versions, often designed by the town architect, of the real thing. As Walter Benjamin's observations on the Paris arcades have shown, however, stylistically, the replica arcades developed across other cities may have shared certain characteristics with the Parisian 'originals' but each replica is bound to its particular time and location, that is, to the lived complexity of place.[48]

Conclusion

Since the first architectural histories of the museum were written, a definition of architecture as an aesthetic object and as the privileged realm of the architect has dominated in museums. The problems associated with this understanding of museum architecture have become particularly pronounced in recent years as new museums have been built and as existing museums have undergone significant architectural expansion and change. Clearly, we need to understand more about the ways in which (museum) architecture gets built.

Identifying existing underlying conceptions of architecture as unhelpful, this chapter has argued for an understanding of the architecture of the museum as a social and cultural product, whose need is created through the social and political exigencies of the day and whose form is influenced through the various government organizations and professional bodies active in setting the bound-aries and definitions of the museum at that particular historical moment. These visions may not overlap exactly and may, indeed, be oppositional.

The production of the architecture of the museum must also be recognized as taking place at the level of the individual, and here we are concerned with the plays of power between architects, designers, project managers, directors, cura-tors, users and all those involved at an individual level in the production of a specific site. Importantly, this production does not stop when a new building is complete and before the doors of the museum open; rather, production is continual and ongoing through occupation and use.

As the fragmentary glimpses of the Walker's architectural past begin to suggest, such an understanding of the architecture of the museum could potentially rewrite the architectural history of the museum, producing instead: a history which exposes the social contexts, relations and practices through which archi-tecture is produced; a view of the space of the museum as contradictory and encapsulating many, sometimes oppositional, values and beliefs; and an understanding of (museum) architecture as a complex and contested activity, far from the pure ideal of architecture that has dominated our thinking for so long.

If the rethinking of architecture set forward in this chapter seems to reduce the importance of the architect, this is not intentional. Museums are reliant at times of architectural development, as the chapters in this book attest, on the knowledge and expertise of the architect. However, as Jeremy Till has stated:

> Architecture is open to a much wider range of influences and possibilities than the monolithic professional view would have us believe; the community of architects is as impure as the community for which they are designing. The importance is to see this not as a sign of weakness, but as an opportunity for a more expansive definition of roles.[49]

There is no such thing as a pure space of occupation; 'accident, dirt, politics, tension, selfishness, social structures – all besmirch the purified ideal.'[50] For museums, a greater critical awareness of the range of forces and motives active in the shaping of museum space may enable museum practitioners to act intentionally, rather than reactively, creating museums which are of their place and designed to fulfil a number of uses and roles.

This chapter only begins to scratch the surface of this subject and its author is well aware that it is all too easy to make statements and judgements at a schematic and theoretical level that are not borne out in practice. Much research remains to be undertaken into the ways in which those actively involved in the reshaping of specific museum spaces, now and in the past, negotiate the range of agendas and conceptions of museum space which comprise any museum build. However, approaching the architecture of the museum as suggested here also highlights the inevitability and necessity of such changes if museums are to play an active part in society. Such an approach highlights the social significance of the architectural and spatial rearrangement of museums and galleries, increasing, rather than diminishing, the need for further research into the nature and production of a useful and relevant space for culture.

Acknowledgements

Thank you to Moira Lindsay, Alex Kidson and Adrian Forty for conversations over the last year and to Eilean Hooper-Greenhill who kindly read and commented on a draft of this chapter.

Notes

1 H. Pearman, 'No concessions', *The Sunday Times*. Available at: http://dspace.dial.pipex. com/town/park/di25/walsall.htm (accessed 19 July 2004).
2 J. Stewart-Young, 'Building barriers in Walsall?', *Museums Journal*, Vol. 100, No. 6, 2001: 30.

3 Jonathan Hill discusses the fallacy of a pure architectural space, highlighting the contingencies of architecture at every step of its production and use. See J. Hill (ed.), *Occupying
Architecture: Between the Architect and the User*, London and New York: Routledge,
1998.

4 The term 'community of practice' is drawn from E. Wenger, *Communities of Practice,
Meaning and Identity*, Cambridge: Cambridge University Press, 1998.

5 H. Lefebvre (trans. D. Nicholson-Smith), *The Production of Space*, Oxford: Blackwell,
1991.

6 Throughout this chapter, the terms architecture and space are used interchangeably to
refer to the physical structure and spatial layout and use of the museum. Although not
ideal, this terminology is a means of immediately expanding upon the existing limited
notion of architecture as the aesthetic outcome and activity of the architect.

7 I. Borden and J. Rendell (eds), *InterSections, Architectural Histories and Critical Theories*,
London: Routledge, 2000, p. 5.

8 In 1986 the Walker Art Gallery received national status. The gallery was renamed the
Walker, National Museums Liverpool, after its recent refurbishment.

9 *Liverpool Library, Museum, Art Gallery 49th Annual Report for the year ending 31st
December 1901*.

10 Quoted in S. Davies, 'Rethinking museum values and strategies', in G. Kavanagh (ed.),
Museum Provision and Professionalism, London and New York: Routledge, 1994, p. 35.

11 J. Till, 'Architecture of the impure community', in Hill, *Occupying Architecture*,
pp. 62–75.

12 For example, H. Searing, 'The development of a museum typology', in S. Stephens (ed.),
Building the New Museum, New York: Princeton Architectural Press, 1986, pp. 14–23.

13 See, for example, V. M. Lampugnani, 'The architecture of art: the museums of the 1990s',
in V. M. Lampugnani and A. Sachs (eds), *Museums for a New Millennium: Concepts,
Projects, Buildings*, Munich, London, New York: Prestel, 1999, pp. 11–14.

14 See, for example, Lampugnani, 'The architecture of art', and V. Newhouse, *Towards a
New Museum*, New York: The Monacelli Press, 1998.

15 A. D. King (ed.), *Buildings and Society: Essays on the Social Development of the Built
Environment*, London: Routledge and Kegan Paul, 1980.

16 Ibid., p. 1.

17 Ibid., p. 4.

18 See, for example, J. Wolff and J. Seed (eds), *The Culture of Capital: Art, Power and the
Nineteenth Century Middle Class*, Manchester: Manchester University Press, 1988.

19 D. Stevenson, *Cities and Urban Cultures*, Maidenhead, UK, Philadelphia: Open
University Press, 2003, p. 13.

20 D. Fraser, *Power and Authority in the Victorian City*, Oxford: Basil Blackwell, 1979,
p. 4.

21 On the changing role of culture and the increasing state involvement in the arts see
J. Minihan, *The Nationalisation of Culture: The Development of State Subsidies to the
Arts in Great Britain*, London: Hamish Hamilton, 1977.

22 Fraser, *Power and Authority*, pp. 28–31.

23 P. J. Waller, *Democracy and Sectarianism: A Political and Social History of Liverpool
1868–1939*, Liverpool: Liverpool University Press, 1981, p. 1.

24 Ibid., p. xvi.

25 Ibid., p. 23.

26 Ibid., p. 22.

27 Fraser, *Power and Authority*, p. 27.

28 Anon., *Walker's Warrington Ales Illustrated*, Manchester: Peter Walker and Sons,
c.1897.

29 E. Morris (ed.), *The Walker Art Gallery*, London: Scala Books/National Museums and
Galleries on Merseyside, 1994, p. 11.

30 On 12 September 1921 the Unemployed Workers' Movement occupied the Walker Art
Gallery before police forcibly evicted them. Fifty of the 156 protestors were arrested.
Waller, *Democracy and Sectarianism*, p. 290.

31 Ibid., p. 271.
32 Ibid., p. 277.
33 Ibid., p. 288.
34 S. Marriner, *The Economic and Social Development of Merseyside*, London: Croom Helm, 1982, p. 147.
35 In 1929, Liverpool council made an annual grant for the purchase of pictures for the first time.
36 Minihan, *Nationalisation of Culture*, p. 178.
37 Anon., 'The Walker Art Gallery', *Museums Journal*, Vol. 33, No. 7, 1933: 248.
38 Anon., 'The Director of the Walker Art Gallery', *Liverpolitan*, Vol. 3, No. 7, July 1934, p. 27.
39 F. Lambert, 'A new Walker Art Gallery', *Liverpool Daily Post* (Walker Art Gallery Supplement), 14 July 1951, p. 1.
40 C. Yanni, *Nature's Museums: Victorian Science and the Architecture of Display*, Baltimore, MD: Johns Hopkins University Press, 1999.
41 A. Forty, 'The modern hospital in England and France: the social and medical uses of architecture', in King, *Buildings and Society*, p. 61.
42 P. H. Rathbone, *The Political Value of Art to the Municipal Life of a Nation: A Lecture Delivered at the Free Library, Liverpool, 1875*, Liverpool: Lee and Nightingale, 1895, p. 40.
43 Waller, *Democracy and Sectarianism*, p. 160.
44 E. Morris, *Victorian and Edwardian Paintings in the Walker Art Gallery and at Sudley House*, London: HMSO, 1996, p. 6.
45 Rathbone, *The Political Value of Art*, p. 38.
46 Hill, *Occupying Architecture*, p. 6.
47 Ibid., p. 5.
48 Stevenson, *Cities and Urban Cultures*, p. 65.
49 Till, 'Architecture of the impure community', p. 73.
50 Ibid., p. 65.

References

Anon., *Walker's Warrington Ales Illustrated*, Manchester: Peter Walker and Sons, c.1897.
——, 'The Walker Art Gallery', *Museums Journal*, Vol. 33, No. 7, 1933: 248.
——, 'The Director of the Walker Art Gallery', *Liverpolitan*, Vol. 3, No. 7, July 1934, p. 27.
Borden, I. and Rendell, J. (eds), *InterSections, Architectural Histories and Critical Theories*, London: Routledge, 2000.
Davies, S., 'Rethinking museum values and strategies', in G. Kavanagh (ed.), *Museum Provision and Professionalism*, London and New York: Routledge, 1994, pp. 33–40.
Forty, A., 'The modern hospital in England and France: the social and medical uses of architecture', in A. D. King (ed.), *Buildings and Society: Essays on the Social Development of the Built Environment*, London: Routledge & Kegan Paul, 1980, pp. 61–93.
Fraser, D., *Power and Authority in the Victorian City*, Oxford: Basil Blackwell, 1979.
Hill, J. (ed.), *Occupying Architecture: Between the Architect and the User*, London and New York: Routledge, 1998.
King, A. D. (ed.), *Buildings and Society: Essays on the Social Development of the Built Environment*, London: Routledge & Kegan Paul, 1980.
Lambert, F., 'A new Walker Art Gallery', *Liverpool Daily Post* (Walker Art Gallery Supplement), 14 July 1951, p. 1.
Lampugnani, V. M., 'The architecture of art: the museums of the 1990s', in V. M. Lampugnani and A. Sachs (eds), *Museums for a New Millennium: Concepts, Projects, Buildings*, Munich, London, New York: Prestel, 1999, pp. 11–14.

Lefebvre, H. (trans. D. Nicholson-Smith), *The Production of Space*, Oxford: Blackwell, 1991.

Marriner, S., *The Economic and Social Development of Merseyside*, London: Croom Helm, 1982.

Minihan, J., *The Nationalisation of Culture: The Development of State Subsidies to the Arts in Great Britain*, London: Hamish Hamilton, 1977.

Morris, E. (ed.), *The Walker Art Gallery*, London: Scala Books/National Museums and Galleries on Merseyside, 1994.

——, *Victorian and Edwardian Paintings in the Walker Art Gallery and at Sudley House*, London: HMSO, 1996.

Newhouse, V., *Towards a New Museum*, New York: The Monacelli Press, 1998.

Pearman, H., 'No concessions', *The Sunday Times*. Available at: http://dspace.dial.pipex.com/town/park/di25/walsall.htm (accessed 19 July 2004).

Rathbone, P. H., *The Political Value of Art to the Municipal Life of a Nation: A Lecture Delivered at the Free Library, Liverpool, 1875*, Liverpool: Lee and Nightingale, 1895.

Searing, H., 'The development of a museum typology', in S. Stephens (ed.), *Building the New Museum*, New York: Princeton Architectural Press, 1986, pp. 14–23.

Stevenson, D., *Cities and Urban Cultures*, Maidenhead, UK, Philadelphia: Open University Press, 2003.

Stewart-Young, J., 'Building barriers in Walsall?', *Museums Journal*, Vol. 100, No. 6, 2001: 30.

Till, J., 'Architecture of the impure community', in J. Hill (ed.), *Occupying Architecture: Between the Architect and the User*, London and New York: Routledge, 1998, pp. 62–75.

Waller, P. J., *Democracy and Sectarianism: A Political and Social History of Liverpool 1868–1939*, Liverpool: Liverpool University Press, 1981.

Wenger, E., *Communities of Practice, Meaning and Identity*, Cambridge: Cambridge University Press, 1998.

Wolff, J. and Seed, J. (eds), *The Culture of Capital: Art, Power and the Nineteenth Century Middle Class*, Manchester: Manchester University Press, 1988.

Yanni, C., *Nature's Museums: Victorian Science and the Architecture of Display*, Baltimore, MD: Johns Hopkins University Press, 1999.

2

Black box science in black box science centres

Richard Toon

The modern science centre is a black box experience. The term black box refers both to the structures that house the experience of science, literally spaces without natural light, and the science content itself, which, following the usage of Bruno Latour, is usually based on black box or taken-for-granted scientific practice.[1] The ways in which these senses reinforce each other is described below as black box science in a black box science centre.

The main example discussed here is the Arizona Science Center (ASC), built in downtown Phoenix, Arizona (the sixth largest city in the United States).[2] It is not a unique story, but one applicable to other modern science and technology museums. The architect Antoine Predock designed the ASC. Predock is a major architect of the southwestern United States who has also designed buildings throughout the world, including several museums.[3]

ASC opened in 1997 and since then has received over three million visitors. Built as part of a redevelopment effort, it is close to many other new buildings and attractions, creating a 'destination' cluster.[4] Millions of visitors a year now regularly attend its cultural, sports and entertainment attractions. Other US cities similarly invested in downtown redevelopment projects in the 1980s and 1990s. Science and technology museums are featured in many of these efforts: Columbus and Cleveland, Ohio, and Kansas City, Missouri, are just a few recent examples.

The modern science centre as public monument

It is tempting to treat museum space as a vision formed by its architect alone, as if only he or she is provided the freedom of expression that subsequent users (museum professionals and visiting public) merely accept and occupy. Architectural books tend to reinforce such a view. For example, Justin Henderson's *Museum Architecture* (1998) and Victoria Newhouse's *Towards a New Museum* (1998) contain few photographs of gallery space in use. Similarly, in the Phoenix case, of the 22 photographs of the ASC in Predock's book, none shows exhibition gallery space and only four include people.[5] Such publications implicitly suggest that architecture is to be appreciated *sui generis* – expressions without the distraction of occupancy and use.

Figure 2.1 Arizona Science Center. Photograph ASC, with permission.

These books tend to feature building façades, entrances, stairways, lobbies, atriums and terraces as the main canvas for architectural expression. The reason for this is not merely display space subordinated to commercial space, although this certainly occurs, but also the notion that the content of gallery space should not have to compete with its setting. This leaves the exterior and the interstices as sites for architectural expression.

Museums are also public monuments, which through architectural expression make publicly funded statements about their communities, often becoming in the process 'economically viable as exhibits of themselves'.[6] Such situations have recently been labelled the 'Bilbao effect', after Frank Gehry's Guggenheim Museum in Spain,[7] but the phenomenon previously drew comment whenever buildings raised an institution's status, upstaged its content and contributed to its local economy.[8] While the ASC building has not achieved this status, the local community did make a considerable investment in a striking public monument: a publicly voted bond provided $20 million for construction. Land value and parking added another $10 million. In 2001, another public vote raised $10 million for expansion. Henderson and Predock describe the original building as follows:

> The museum is a composition of abstracted natural forms drawn from the desert and built in an urban context. The monumental, aluminum-clad

wedge serves as the unifying element and as a backdrop for the other forms, including the octagonal planetarium. Myriad plazas, terraces, and staircases serve as gathering places around the building exterior.[9]

The Center has the feeling of a citadel, somewhat enigmatic in that the inner life of the building – the hidden inner world of science – is not revealed externally. Its enigmatic presence is in contrast to central Phoenix, from which the desert has been essentially erased. The building affirms the power of the desert on a downtown site.[10]

While it is unlikely that visitors and taxpayers are aware of this complex symbolism, they do know that the building is 'different' and meant to be so. A consequence is that, as modern museums of the Phoenix type become cultural destinations, they may also become disconnected from their localities and communities. Precisely because they are civic monuments, they run the risk of losing, or never having, a sense of *communal* place. John Brinckerhoff Jackson describes what is meant when he writes:

I'm inclined to believe that the average American still associates a sense of place not so much with architecture or a monument or a designed space as with some event, some daily or weekly or seasonal occurrence which we look forward to or remember and which we share with others, and as a result the event becomes more significant than the site itself.[11]

The challenge for the museum is to attach this sense of place to the modern monument. Predock's use of the term 'citadel' is instructive, for it has the double meaning of both protecting and keeping in subjection its surrounding community. Similarly, the modern museum equivalent can be a haven for some and intimidating to others. An important part of museum practice, consequently, involves making visitors feel welcome.[12]

If attendance is anything to go by, science and technology museums are extremely successful in making visitors welcome despite many being housed in civic monuments.[13] Unfortunately for interactive science centres, the very basis of their popularity – hands-on and interactive exhibits featuring basic science – reinforces a disconnection from place. Sharon MacDonald remarked on this, through a comparison, '[science museums] seek to present science entirely contextualized in a "slice of history" in a particular community, whereas science centres are more concerned with universal laws and principles which transcend particular times and places'.[14]

There are natural affinities, therefore, between the spatial and design features of many modern science centres and their content. One can call this a double disconnection – the disconnection of the museum from locality and the disconnection of its science content from time and place.

The disconnection from the local environment is manifest most concretely in the characteristic lack of natural light in many science centre buildings. Gallery spaces are literally black boxes. Justin Henderson refers to the ASC as 'The windowless science center' and its exhibition galleries as 'spacious caverns' and 'windowless volumes'.[15] Similarly for other centres, Luca Basso Peressut referred to the Exploratorium as a place where 'darkness reigns' and to the Ontario Science Center as having, 'closed spaces, with minimal interior decoration and no windows'.[16]

These descriptions apply to other building types of North America, including the big-box store, the shopping mall, the convention centre, the hotel and a variety of entertainment venues, including the theatre, cinema and casino.[17] What these places have in common is not simply environmental control, but also control of psychological and aesthetic effects. The situation for the science centre can be contrasted with the art museum, which must still seek to create or recreate natural light or its illusion, and, thus, the black box of the science centre moves beyond the viewing constraints of the art museum's white cube.[18]

Science centre space

There are a number of tendencies that produce the black box spaces of the modern science centre: architectural monuments that concentrate their expression externally; a resulting disconnection from, or replacement of, locality; and the design of completely controlled spaces abstracted from place and time. The resulting interior experience in centres such as the ASC derives from the interactive space of exhibit galleries and the immersion experiences found in planetariums and giant screen film theatres. Joseph Pine and James Gilmore offer a typology of 'experience realms' that is helpful.[19] They distinguish two axes of experience: one that indicates degree of participation (from passive to active) and one that indicates connection of the visitor to the experience (from absorption to immersion). The result is a fourfold model of entertainment, education, aesthetics and escapism.

A large part of science centres' success can be found in their ability to provide experiences in each realm – what for Pine and Gilmore is hitting the 'sweet spot'.[20] While science and technology museums are usually discussed exclusively in educational terms, here emphasis is given to other elements in the 'sweet spot', particularly the escapist. For example, approximately 42 per cent of visitors to the ASC buy tickets to planetarium shows. A text panel at its entrance provides a description:

> A state-of-the-art Digistar projector, moving video images, and more than 50 slide projectors turn the planetarium's 60-foot-diameter dome into an exciting virtual world. It can replicate the desert night sky, explore the interior of a living cell, travel across the solar system, and simulate whatever human imagination demands.

The immersive planetarium experience is the result of a series of technological advances that build on those developed for the first planetarium in 1923 by the Carl Zeiss optical company for the Deutsches Museum in Munich. Even

29

though the technology and range of subjects treated has changed significantly over time, key elements remain: optical images of celestial bodies are still projected on to hemispherical domes, reproducing changing views of artificial night skies.

New 'visualization' technologies now allow presentations from many branches of modern science, but planetariums are still directly connected to earlier representational techniques such as 'magic lantern' shows, panoramas, dioramas and other non-natural forms of visual display experienced at museums, expositions, world's fairs and, more recently, theme parks. Today, these techniques include giant-screen films, immersion virtual reality, 3-D holography and so on. All are technologies and techniques of simulation through which nature is represented to observers. An important common characteristic is that they use technologies of representation to stimulate contemplation of the sublime. Of course, the planets and stars of the night sky have been a source of awe and fascination for millennia and their simulation in a planetarium is just a modern site for their contemplation and that of humanity's place in the cosmos. But, by virtualizing the experience, the technology that stimulates a sense of awe and wonder simultaneously functions to provide a reassuring sense of what has been called 'cognitive mastery'.[21]

The black boxes of planetarium and giant-screen theatre space move beyond the presence of real phenomena to simulations that offer the virtual experiences of immersion and movement, that is, 'being there'. The resulting cognitive/ aesthetic dimension is captured by the phrase 'the technological sublime', in which experiences linked to technology have transcendent significance. David Nye describes the history of the social role of the sublime in the United States, which includes the grandeur of the natural sublime (Niagara Falls, Grand Canyon, for example) and the development of the technological sublime with growth of railroads, bridges, skyscrapers, factories, electrification, the atom bomb, Apollo XI and newer simulation technologies like giant-screen films.[22] Nye explains their social and political significance:

> There is an American penchant for thinking of the sublime as a consciousness that can stand apart from the world and project its will upon it. . . . Those operating within this logic embrace the reconstruction of the life-world by machinery, experience the dislocations and perceptual disorientations caused by this reconstruction in terms of awe and wonder, and, in their excitement, feel insulated from immediate danger. New technologies become self-justifying parts of a national destiny, just as the natural sublime once undergirded the rhetoric of manifest destiny.[23]

Nye examines the simulations and attractions of world's fairs (particularly the 1939 fair) and IMAX films (particularly the Arizona installation close to the entrance to the Grand Canyon) and describes them disparagingly as a new 'consumer sublime' where the visitor purchases 'new sensations of empowerment'.[24]

A sense of empowerment applies both to planetarium and giant-screen films, which through new technology simulate the experience and wonder of nature (terrestrial and extraterrestrial) and reinforce the power of humans *over* nature. It goes beyond the perception of a process in harmony with nature to one where, as Nye puts it, 'The assumption of human omnipotence has become so common that the natural world seems an extension of ourselves, rather than vice versa'.[25] The forms in which science is presented and the technologies that are used to do so carry in themselves a powerful argument about the ability of science to both reveal and control nature, quite apart from the actual scientific content they present.

The octagonal black box of the Phoenix planetarium is a central feature of the building and occupies some 6 per cent of its floor space. Predock has described it as an artificial sky that simultaneously forms the floor of the Sky Terrace above it from where the real sky can be viewed.[26] This interplay of the (exterior) real and the (interior) simulated is, thus, exploited in the building's structure, but is reconciled or merged in the planetarium when the audience reacts to the artificial sky *as if* it were real. Immersed in the experience beneath the 60-foot domed ceiling, in their upward-tilted seats, the trope works because the body accepts as real what the mind knows is only a projection. The sense of awe and fascination from contemplating the star field is enhanced as the body feels movement through space, particularly when the sky is rapidly rotated to a different viewing angle. The double sense of anxiety and mastery associated with the sublime comes to the fore with each special effect its technology produces.

The experience of the planetarium space has features that operate similarly in the giant-screen theatre. Giant-screen films[27] are viewed by 31 per cent of those visiting the centre. Giant-screen film theatres, like planetariums, require a considerable investment in equipment and space – in Phoenix the theatre is some six stories high and over 6,900 square feet or 641 square metres. The preannouncement at the ASC welcomes visitors to the theatre, 'Where the experience is second only to being there'. Like the planetarium, a sign in the waiting area explains not what is shown, but the technology that does so:

> Science and entertainment come together on a giant-screen. . . . The Iwerks Theater System puts viewers 'into the picture' with spectacular images and sound projected by a 7,000 watt Xenon gas projection lamp on a 50 foot-high by 67 foot-wide screen. The theater's audio system is a seven-channel, 16,000-watt digital audio system, capable of reproducing a full-range of audio sound with uncompromising clarity and tonal quality. The 285-seat theater is one of the Center's showcase attractions, featuring exclusive screening of large-format (70mm) films.

Like the planetarium, the body is tricked by the lack of a visual frame into believing the movement is real. The ubiquitous shot from a helicopter as the camera shoots over a cliff edge or mountain range, or along a river, is the standard form sensation of movement takes in large format films. But there is really no motion, just passive absorption into the screen's experience. This notion is taken up by Anne Friedberg in her examination of the history of the 'panoptic gaze' (the scrutiny of the observer) and the 'virtual gaze' (the scrutiny by the observed) in the development of modernity.[28] Absorption into the 'frameless frame' of these technologies might be considered an extension of the panoptic view of power relations developed by Foucault, but Friedberg reminds us that around the same time as the invention of the panoptican (1791) came the panorama (1792) and the diorama (1823). These are devices not of confinement but of transportation. She also points to a paradox of these early forms that also applies to the giant screen and planetarium:

> The panorama and its successor, the diorama, offered new forms of mobility to its viewer. But a paradox here must be emphasized: as the 'mobility' of the eyes became more 'virtual'. . . . the observer became ever more immobile, passive ready to receive the constructions of a virtual reality placed in front of his or her unmoving head.[29]

The result is that the virtual space of the giant-screen film and the planetarium offer new spectacles to audiences, but ones firmly in a museum tradition of virtual-reality technologies going back some hundreds of years, which are themselves implicated in the politics of social control and mobility, and the disciplining of the body and its fleeting escape. These new technologies raise important questions about how science and technology are represented simultaneously as sources of imposed authority/control and yet also give a sense of personal power/freedom, explicitly and implicitly, through the communicative technologies of museums.

If planetarium and giant-screen theatre spaces tend to occupy the intersection of the immersive and passive areas of Pine and Gilmore's map of experience (the aesthetic), then exhibit gallery space tends to occupy the intersection of the active and absorbing (the educational) and this is indeed how science centre interactive exhibits are normally viewed and analysed. The five galleries of the ASC occupy the bulk of its public space – 35,000 square feet (3,252 square metres) – and contain some 300 interactive and hands-on exhibits, filling open gallery spaces but without prescribed pathways. Frank Oppenheimer, the Exploratorium's founder, in a much-quoted phrase, described such gallery space as '[a] woods of natural phenomena through which to wander'.

Oppenheimer wrote in 1968 of his desire to fashion a new institution on the model of the laboratory[30]: it would be a museum where visitors could personally and directly experience the methods and activities of 'real' scientists. It is useful to compare and contrast this notion of laboratory practice with the supposed 'laboratory' of the science centre. The most obvious difference is that 'real' laboratories are involved in the production and creation of scientific knowledge within the scientific community, whereas science centres are involved in its presentation and interpretation to a non-scientifically professional public. As such they rarely deal with 'science in the making' (science practice), so much as 'ready made science' or, as one might say, the 'facts' so constructed. Bruno

Figure 2.2 Interactive exhibits in Arizona Science Center's *All About You* gallery. Photograph by the author.

Latour's work chronicles the process by which science-making work in labs, if successful, goes from a highly contested and, therefore, well-defended struggle and ends up as received fact parcelled into one or more ready-made 'black boxes'.[31]

A black box is not a contested scientific entity, but one so well known that it forms part of the world-taken-for-granted within continuing scientific practice. Many such black boxes form the operational basis – in theory, method and equipment – of new 'science in the making'. Latour describes the process that creates a very narrow social network of science practice, ultimately containing only those with the same intellectual and material resources as the writer who claims a new scientific fact. Of those left out, who must rely on 'popularized' sources, he comments, 'It is hard to popularize science because it is designed to force out most people in the first place. No wonder teachers, journalists and popularizers encounter difficulty when we wish to bring the excluded readership back in'.[32]

There are only two possibilities for the excluded: they can read ethnographies like Latour's or they can familiarize themselves with the content of black boxes through various forms of popularization. It is this second choice that science centres offer, for they focus almost exclusively on what John Durant called 'clear, elementary principles' contained in Latour's black boxes.[33] The exhibits do not involve the visitor in the actual activity of real scientific work, but rather offer models of an objectively pure empiricism. Once the focus is on scientific principle rather than scientific practice, the results may be highly interactive and hands on, yet far from the activities of 'laboratory life'.

This presentation of science is popular despite the modern crisis of epistemology. Its popularity may be related to the crisis. Roger Silverstone noted a parallel between the academic deconstruction of certainty and what he considered the public's 'retreat into fantasy'.[34] In the face of this, the science centre experience, in various and varied black box spaces, offers a comforting level of certainty and security. The world is understandable according to (black box) principles that can be experienced either virtually or actually in varied black box settings. Technologies of the sublime also re-establish certainty and a sense of mastery over the forces of nature. In an age of uncertainty, science centres neither doubt the truths they display nor embrace irrationality, but instead offer an optimistic faith in an understandable and controllable world that continues to have broad appeal.

Museum place and space

With a model of science divorced from its social construction in time and place and in a building separated from its locality both symbolically and physically (the 'citadel'), the Arizona Science Center, like many other science centres, provides its users with a creative series of new places, each offering the visitor a particular version of the trope of a journey: in the planetarium, the possibility of travel to the stars; in the giant-screen film, immersion in exotic natural places; or in the gallery space, nomadic exploration through the 'woods of natural wonder'.

A useful way to understand such environments is Michel de Certeau's distinction between the geographically given *place* and the socially constructed *space* (*espace*): 'In short, *space is a practiced place*. Thus the street geometrically defined by urban planning is transformed into a space by walkers.'[35] This has two implications for this account: first, visitors transform museum place by their use and, second, travel and movement is the most significant act and metaphor for doing so.

John Fiske has employed Certeau's ideas to stress the inherent political antagonisms involved in the places provided to those who occupy them:

> The 'powerful' construct places where they can exercise their power –
> cities, shopping malls, schools, workplaces and houses to name only some
> of the material ones. The weak make their own 'spaces' within those
> places; they make the places temporarily theirs as they move through them,
> occupying them for as long as they need or have to.[36]

We may add the temporary occupancy of museum space by visitors to this list, but Fiske's formulation requires a more diffused notion of power, one operating at all levels within the cultural system. So, taking a less dichotomous view of power, and armed with the notion of space as practised place, museum space can be seen as a series of practices working within one another, rather like Russian dolls. A given place is transformed into a practised space at various levels. Urban planners designate a place for a new museum in the geometry of downtown redevelopment. An architect takes the constraints of this assignment and designs a new space for a science museum. Museum staff (graphic designers, exhibit builders, curators, etc.) take the given place of the museum and designate (by signage, installations and other means) the varied museum spaces, (galleries, classrooms, theatres, shops, eating areas, etc.). Finally, the museum visitor transforms the given place they enter by how they use and travel through it. There is production and consumption at each level in the system described above and, thus, many opportunities for appropriation and creativity. This is true for the architect who designs the places and spaces of the modern science centre, the various professional museum mediators and the nomadic visitors that make these places their own spaces.

A final irony is that spaces created by such journeys, because of the inherent disconnections discussed above, run the risk of joining Marc Auge's list of non-places: 'a place which cannot be defined as relational, historical, and concerned with identity, will be a non-place.'[37] This is a challenge the modern science centre too often faces. In Certeau's terms, it can only become a socially meaningful space if its users are able, in their real and virtual journeys, to find connections to their own identities. Failing this, journeys in the black boxes of the science centre remain at best fleeting moments of pleasure disconnected from the meaning of real (practised) space.

Notes

1 B. Latour, *Science in Action: How to Follow Scientists and Engineers through Society*, Cambridge, MA: Harvard University Press, 1987.
2 Some of what follows is drawn from the author's PhD research. R. Toon, 'Science centres and legitimacy', unpublished thesis, University of Leicester, 2003.
3 See, for example, A. Predock, *Antoine Predock: Architect*, New York: Rizzoli, 1994. A. Predock, *Architectural Journeys*, New York: Rizzoli, 1995. A. Predock, *Antoine Predock 2: Architect*, New York: Rizzoli, 1999. A. Predock, *Antoine Predock 3: Houses*, New York: Rizzoli, 2000.
4 In 1988, Phoenix voters approved a City of Phoenix bond issue to support a range of city services including monies for capital projects for cultural institutions. This was part of a 'revitalization' effort, for the city lacked a vibrant downtown and even this declined further in the 1980s as business, entertainment and population moved from the urban core. G. Gammage Jr, *Phoenix in Perspective: Reflections on the Developing Desert*, Tempe, AZ: The Herberger Center for Design Excellence, College of Architecture and Environmental Design, Arizona State University, 1999, pp. 55–7. B. Luckingham, *Phoenix: The History of a Southwestern Metropolis*, Tucson, AZ: The University of Arizona Press, 1989, pp. 238–40.
5 Predock, *Antoine Predock 2: Architect*, frontispiece, pp. 118–36.
6 B. Kirshenblatt-Gimblett, *Destination Culture: Tourism, Museums, and Heritage*, Berkeley, CA: University of California Press, 1998, p. 151. The implications of this, particularly in the Australian context, are discussed in A. Whitcomb, *Re-imagining the Museum: Beyond the Mausoleum*, London: Routledge, 2003.

35

7 A. Wilson-Lloyd, 'If the museum itself is an artwork, what about the art inside?', *New York Times*, 25 January 2004, pp. 29, 32.

8 W. Rybczynski, *Looking Around: A Journey through Architecture*, New York: Penguin Books, 2000, pp. 187–92.

9 J. Henderson, *Museum Architecture*, Gloucester, MA: Rockport Publishers Inc., 1998, p. 135.

10 Predock, *Antoine Predock 2: Architect*, p. 119.

11 J. B. Jackson, *A Sense of Place, A Sense of Time*, New Haven, CT: Yale University Press, 1994, pp. 159–60.

12 See E. Hooper-Greenhill, *Museums and Their Visitors*, London: Routledge, 1994, pp. 84–99, and Getty Center for Education and the Arts, *Insights: Museums, Visitors, Attitudes, Expectations*, Los Angeles, CA: J. Paul Getty Museum, 1991.

13 The majority of the adult population of the United States over a 20-year period has reported visiting a science or technology museum at least once a year (National Science Board, *Science and Engineering Indicators 2002*, Washington, DC: US Government Printing Office, 2002, table 7-50). With an overall US population of about 275 million and assuming that children visit at the same rate as adults, approximately 181.5 million Americans visit at least once a year.

14 S. Macdonald (ed.), *The Politics of Display: Museums, Science, Culture*, New York: Routledge, 1998, p. 15.

15 Henderson, *Museum Architecture*, pp. 138–9.

16 L. B. Peressut, *Musei Per La Scienza (Science Museums): Spazi E Luoghi Dell'esporre Scientifico E Tecnico (Spaces of Scientific and Technical Exhibition)*, Milan: Editizoni Lybra Immagine, 1998, p. 104.

17 The symbolic significance of space, darkness and large volumes in these structures is discussed in R. Venturi, D. S. Brown and S. Izenour, *Learning from Las Vegas: The Forgotten Symbolism of Architectural Form*, Cambridge, MA: MIT Press, 1977.

18 See B. O'Doherty, *Inside the White Cube: The Ideology of the Gallery Space*, Berkeley, CA: University of California Press, 1986.

19 B. J. Pine II and J. H. Gilmore, *The Experience Economy: Work Is Theatre and Every Business a Stage*, Boston, MA: Harvard Business School Press, 1999.

20 Ibid., p. 43.

21 S. Bukatman, 'The artificial infinite: on special effects and the sublime', in L. Cooke and P. Wollen (eds), *Visual Display: Culture Beyond Appearance*, New York: The New Press, 1995, p. 255.

22 D. E. Nye, *American Technological Sublime*, Cambridge, MA: The MIT Press, 1994.

23 Ibid., p. 282.

24 Ibid., p. 287.

25 Ibid., p. 289.

26 G. H. Baker, *Antoine Predock*, Chichester: Academy Editions, 1997.

27 Giant-screen films are by-products of world exposition and theme park attractions. IMAX is the best known system (but not the only one) and was developed from the very popular multi-screen attractions created for EXPO '67 in Montreal, Canada. The IMAX system premiered at EXPO '70 in Osaka, Japan. The first permanent IMAX projection system was installed at Ontario Place's Cinesphere in Toronto, Canada, in 1971, and the first IMAX dome system (called OMNIMAX) debuted at the Reuben H. Fleet Science Center in San Diego, California, in 1973.

28 A. Friedberg, 'The mobilization and virtual gaze in modernity', in N. Mirzoeff (ed.), *The Visual Culture Reader*, London: Routledge, 1998, pp. 253–62.

29 Ibid., p. 261.

30 The notion of laboratory is so central that Hilde Hein's subtitle to her history of the Exploratorium is *The Museum as Laboratory*. H. Hein, *The Exploratorium: The Museum as Laboratory*, Washington, DC: Smithsonian Institute, 1990.

31 Latour, *Science in Action*. B. Latour and S. Woolgar, *Laboratory Life: The Social Construction of Scientific Facts*, Beverly Hills, CA: Sage, 1979.

32 Latour, *Science in Action*, p. 52.

33 J. Durant (ed.), *Museums and the Public Understanding of Science*, London: London Science Museum in association with the Committee on the Public Understanding of Science, 1992, p. 10.
34 R. Silverstone, 'Science and the media: the case of television', in S. J. Doorman (ed.), *Images of Science: Scientific Practice and the Public*, Aldershot: Gower Publishing Company, 1989, p. 187. Silverstone attributed this thought to Christine Brooke-Rose (C. Brooke-Rose, *A Rhetoric of the Unreal*, Cambridge: Cambridge University Press, 1981).
35 M. de Certeau, *The Practice of Everyday Life*, Berkeley, CA: University of California Press, 1984, p. 117.
36 J. Fiske, *Understanding Popular Culture*, London: Routledge, 1989, p. 32.
37 M. Auge, *Non-Places: Introduction to an Anthropology of Supermodernity*, London: Verso, 1995, pp. 77–8.

References

Auge, M., *Non-Places: Introduction to an Anthropology of Supermodernity*, London: Verso, 1995.
Baker, G. H., *Antoine Predock*, Chichester: Academy Editions, 1997.
Brooke-Rose, C., *A Rhetoric of the Unreal*, Cambridge: Cambridge University Press, 1981.
Bukatman, S., 'The artificial infinite: on special effects and the sublime', in L. Cooke and P. Wollen (eds), *Visual Display: Culture Beyond Appearance*, New York: The New Press, 1995, pp. 254–89.
de Certeau, M., *The Practice of Everyday Life*, Berkeley, CA: University of California Press, 1984.
Durant, J. (ed.), *Museums and the Public Understanding of Science*, London: London Science Museum in association with the Committee on the Public Understanding of Science, 1992.
Fiske, J., *Understanding Popular Culture*, London: Routledge, 1989.
Friedberg, A., 'The mobilization and virtual gaze in modernity', in N. Mirzoeff (ed.), *The Visual Culture Reader*, London: Routledge, 1998, pp. 253–62.
Gammage Jr, G., *Phoenix in Perspective: Reflections on the Developing Desert*, Tempe, AZ: The Herberger Center for Design Excellence, College of Architecture and Environmental Design, Arizona State University, 1999.
Getty Center for Education and the Arts, *Insights: Museums, Visitors, Attitudes, Expectations*, Los Angeles, CA: J. Paul Getty Museum, 1991.
Hein, H., *The Exploratorium: The Museum as Laboratory*, Washington, DC: Smithsonian Institute, 1990.
Henderson, J., *Museum Architecture*, Gloucester, MA: Rockport Publishers Inc., 1998.
Hooper-Greenhill, E., *Museums and Their Visitors*, London: Routledge, 1994.
Jackson, J. B., *A Sense of Place, A Sense of Time*, New Haven, CT: Yale University Press, 1994.
Kirshenblatt-Gimblett, B., *Destination Culture: Tourism, Museums, and Heritage*, Berkeley, CA: University of California Press, 1998.
Latour, B., *Science in Action: How to Follow Scientists and Engineers through Society*, Cambridge, MA: Harvard University Press, 1987.
—— and Woolgar, S., *Laboratory Life: The Social Construction of Scientific Facts*, Beverly Hills, CA: Sage, 1979.
Luckingham, B., *Phoenix: The History of a Southwestern Metropolis*, Tucson, AZ: The University of Arizona Press, 1989.
Macdonald, S. (ed.), *The Politics of Display: Museums, Science, Culture*, New York: Routledge, 1998.
National Science Board, *Science and Engineering Indicators 2002*, Washington, DC: US Government Printing Office, 2002.
Newhouse, V., *Towards a New Museum*, New York: The Montacelli Press Inc., 1998.

Nye, D. E., *American Technological Sublime*, Cambridge, MA: The MIT Press, 1994.

O'Doherty, B., *Inside the White Cube: The Ideology of the Gallery Space*, Berkeley, CA: University of California Press, 1986.

Peressut, L. B., *Musei Per La Scienza (Science Museums): Spazi E Luoghi Dell'esporre Scientifico E Tecnico (Spaces of Scientific and Technical Exhibition)*, Milan: Editizoni Lybra Immagine, 1998.

Pine II, B. J. and Gilmore, J. H., *The Experience Economy: Work Is Theatre and Every Business a Stage*, Boston, MA: Harvard Business School Press, 1999.

Predock, A., *Antoine Predock: Architect*, New York: Rizzoli, 1994.

—— *Architectural Journeys*, New York: Rizzoli, 1995.

—— *Antoine Predock 2: Architect*, New York: Rizzoli, 1999.

—— *Antoine Predock 3: Houses*, New York: Rizzoli, 2000.

Rybczynski, W., *Looking Around: A Journey through Architecture*, New York: Penguin Books, 2000.

Silverstone, R., 'Science and the media: the case of television', in S. J. Doorman (ed.), *Images of Science: Scientific Practice and the Public*, Aldershot: Gower Publishing Company, 1989, pp. 187–211.

Toon, R., 'Science centres and legitimacy', unpublished thesis, University of Leicester, 2003.

Venturi, R., Brown, D. S. and Izenour, S., *Learning from Las Vegas: The Forgotten Symbolism of Architectural Form*, Cambridge, MA: MIT Press, 1977.

Whitcomb, A., *Re-imagining the Museum: Beyond the Mausoleum*, London: Routledge, 2003.

Wilson-Lloyd, A., 'If the museum itself is an artwork, what about the art inside?', *New York Times*, 25 January 2004, pp. 29, 32.

3

Space and the machine

Adaptive museums, pervasive technology and the new gallery environment

Ross Parry and Andrew Sawyer

Is ICT becoming integral to and innate within our notions of the modern museum? Here it is suggested that, first, the museum is an adaptive medium that has throughout its histories responded to change; second, that there is a long history of museums being shaped by information and communication technologies; and, third, that there is presently a complex and reciprocal relationship between digital media and building space. By charting the emergence of *digital* information communication systems, looking towards some recent high-profile examples within UK national museums, and drawing upon the portfolios of leading design houses, it is argued that digital interactives have, over the last three decades, permeated gallery spaces, and that these technologies are becoming ever more pervasive and embedded within the exhibition environment. Whereas before the application of digital media may have been rationalized by viewing it as 'merely a tool' and only 'a means to an end', we will contend, instead, that today this technology – where it is appropriate – carries a much more complex set of meanings and significances for the modern museum.

Museums as an adaptive medium

From temples of sacred objects,[1] to repositories of colonial trophies, and from monuments of civility, to spaces for self-expression and empowerment, the shape, the function and the appeal of the museum through history and across cultures has been fashioned by the preoccupations and expectations of each society that has chosen to construct them. Critics have noted the importance for the museum of this 'adaptation to changing circumstance and to the requirements of the time'.[2] In a European context, at least, this is seen in the manuscripts in the medieval library, the curios within the cabinets of the Renaissance, the paintings within the picture galleries of the Baroque, the specimens within the cases of the Enlightenment and the intangibles and e-tangibles in the databases of modernity. However, equally significant within this process have been the changes in ways of seeing and ways of knowing that each society has built for itself. As disciplines, discourses and taxonomies change so do museums.

In each respect, museums carry on being reoriented by the historiographies, art connoisseurship and paradigms of science that our societies continue to re-articulate and re-code. This is where we find the differences between the history exhibit cast within a historiography that is teleological, narrative and Whiggish, and that which is somewhat more reflexive and poly-vocal; or the distinctions between the art exhibit that is chronological, canonical and bereft of interpretation, and that which is something more thematic, personal and participatory; or the contrasts between the exhibit that conceptualizes science as an incremental advancement of knowledge and accumulation of truth, and that which presents science as something rather more incomplete, contentious and political.

We might, therefore, choose to perceive a continuum (a project, a force, a social construct) that we recognize as *the museum*. And yet, it is undeniable that the qualities of this force remain both historically and culturally contingent. As both a concept and a practice, the museum has always been changing. And within this shifting environment, museums have always been influenced by the devices and strategies used to manage and display their understanding and their collections. These are devices that we might usefully call *information and communication technologies* – a phrase that ought not be the privilege of the digital age.

For, through history, the adaptive museum has been fashioned to hold particular collections of objects. We need only look to the imperial palace of Rudolf II, in Prague, to see a space significantly reworked to accommodate the shape of a magnificent collection.[3] Similarly, aristocratic spaces such as the 'Double Cube Room' at Wilton House remain a fine example of the extent to which collectors will go to contrive architectural conceits to frame particular collections; in that case Inigo Jones's design (realized by his nephew John Webb), which provided a geometrically perfect solution for the display of the Earl of Pembroke's collection of Van Dyck portraits. We might also remember that the condition set by Elias Ashmole on his death in 1677 was that his collection could pass to the University of Oxford as long as a special building (what became, in 1683, the Ashmolean Museum) was designed specifically to house it.[4] And to this list we might add (among many others) Peter the Great's Kuntskamera in St Petersburg, constructed in the first decades of the eighteenth century as a museum specifically to accommodate the Tsar's collection,[5] or Landgrave Friedrich II of Hesse-Kassel's Museum Fridericianum, purpose-built for its collections between 1769 and 1779 by Simon Louis du Ry.[6]

So (even allowing for many notable exceptions)[7] the size and shape of the collections themselves have directly determined the design of many museum spaces. However, just as rooms and buildings have been fashioned to hold particular collections of objects, so too have they been designed to accommodate particular display techniques appropriate (or, in some cases, *essential*) for a particular collection. Display technology can become a major lever (if not the principal lever) on the shape of a museum's space. If we consider, for instance, the dense and intensely personal[8] repository that is Francesco I de' Medici's famous *studiolo* (1570–5) in the Palazzo Vecchio (Florence), it is ostensibly a private exhibition of manuscript books, gems and precious objects formed as evidence to the patron-collector's acquired wealth and learning. But, in another sense, it also exists as a testimony to how display technologies (in that case cupboards fronted by an iconographical programme of painted panels) could shape and define a space.[9] The *studiolo* is as much about the Prince Regent Francesco's skill in engineering such an ingenious spatial and communications device, as it is about the valuable objects it contains – as much, we might say, about the art of display as it is the display of art.

Elsewhere across Europe, other technologies of display were influencing the design of the exhibition space. It was, for instance, the use of boxes, chests, drawers, trays, tables and shelves that characterized spaces such as Archduke Ferdinand II's Kunstkammer in Ambras,[10] or the Munich Kunstkammer (with its *Tischl* and *Tafeln*).[11] Soon, however, innovative display and communication techniques began also to influence the arrangement of these expository spaces. The eighteenth-century spaces of the Royal Society Repository, for instance, are known to have made use of more elevated display techniques, hanging beasts and birds from the ceilings of their exhibitions.[12] The nineteenth-century presses of the King's Library at the British Museum enjoyed new lock technology to protect the 304 presses that carried the 65,000 books of George III's collection. Writing in 1872, Robert Cowtan, an assistant in the library of the British Museum, explained how the locks of the cases were 'of a new and singular construction; the key that locks each case shoots, at the same time, bolts above and below the door.'[13] By the nineteenth century museums were also deploying more sophisticated visual effects and projections as part of their displays. In 1804, for instance, Charles Wilson Peale's recently opened collection of natural history, ethnographic and scientific objects displayed in the State House, Pennsylvania, contrived an exhibition space where a person 'with Hawkins' ingenious Physiognotrace, draws the Profiles of such as chuse to pay the cost of paper, free of other expense'.[14] The use of modelling and three-dimensional visual effects advanced with Carl Akeley's breakthroughs in the process and presentation of taxidermy, informed by sculpture practice. His new techniques, perfected during his time at the Field Columbian Museum in Chicago from 1895, produced habitat groups of fauna of unprecedented realism.[15] At around the same time, the Brooklyn Children's Museum (the first children's museum in the world) innovated in its gallery design by rescaling its cases and desks, and devising movable hinged labels on boards for its younger visitors.[16] And then, in the last half of the twentieth century, the new levels of interactivity invited by Frank Oppenheimer's Exploratorium in San Francisco, from its foundation in 1969, saw Bernard Ralph Maybeck's space, originally designed for the Panama-Pacific Exhibition of 1915, transformed by three hundred interactive 'experiments'.[17]

From the *studiolo* to the Exploratorium (from drawers to dioramas, hooks and wire to hands-on interactives) museum spaces have continued to be shaped by their display technologies. Moreover, it is these technologies of display that have provided solutions to exhibiting large numbers of objects within limited space, that have heightened the sense of the museum as an immersive experience, that have brought precious collections (literally) closer to the public, that have aligned the museum to discourses of theatricality and visual spectacle, that have allowed museum spaces to be active and participatory experiences, and that have helped establish the museum as a place that transplants the visitor to another time or space. And it is because of these innovations in communications technology, adopted by museums over the centuries, that the museum could become the enabling, immersive, multi-sensory, information-rich experience that we know it to be today.

Digital media and the museum environment

Museums, then, are an adaptive medium, and (within this state of adaptation) museums have, it seems, always been shaped by their information and communication technologies. And, arguably, today we see this dialectic at play yet again in the compelling relationship that exists between digital information communication technologies and modern gallery space. It is a relationship that appears to work on several levels. At one level it is to do with design practice: a headline-grabbing design such as Norman Foster's, shaping the nature of our interaction with the Reading Room and the Great Court at the British Museum, is an obvious example – as a review in the *Daily Telegraph* gushed:

> new computer software . . . has given the practice hitherto undreamt of power to calculate complex shapes, particularly curves, and then have them cut to order. . . . Forms that would have been almost impossible before are now simple. . . . the boundaries suddenly melted away.[18]

Other enthusiasts claim that engineering approaches enabled by ICT mean 'we can have structures of 99 percent inspiration and only 1 percent perspiration, spaces as intricate and lucid as computer-graphic representations'.[19] Indeed, the first visualization of a new museum or exhibition may well be delivered as a digital representation or digitally prepared drawings. Less obviously, 'broadband access', 'cat 5 cabling', 'network points', 'intranets' and 'projection points' all affect the shaping of space to allow the exploitation of digital media, while ICT will enable the Project Manager's Gantt charts, and will have been used in the design of smaller, routine components in construction.

But, furthermore, there is also a subtle interaction taking place between the language and metaphors of digital media and physical space, specifically architectural space. Despite some literary and topographical terms – 'browse', 'read', site 'map' and 'navigate' for example – it is words from our relationship with buildings, such as 'home' page, 'portal', 'enter' and 'chat room', which are ubiquitous, while the concept of the 'visit' resonates especially with the sector.[20] It is spatial and architectural concepts that free us from the limitations of the web 'page' – by 1998, the appearance of the word 'Architecture' in the title of L. Rosenfeld and P. Morville's *Information Architecture for the World Wide Web* was beginning to make sense to most practitioners. Indeed, 'IT architecture' is now fundamental to the delivery of digital media – when building a significant digital product today, the role of the so-called 'IT architect' is now recognized, and architectural and building techniques are mirrored. 'Templates' and 'cascading style sheets' are digital manifestations of the standard cast parts, rigid portal frame connections and tension tie rods found in buildings such as Velázques Bosco's Palacio de Crystal in Madrid.[21] Just as new physical materials and techniques allowed a new 'aesthetics of the open span' in Madrid, new IT techniques paralleling the physical shaping of space – information architecture, programming, marketing, copyrighting, project managing, editing, asset resourcing, collections and content management and so forth – enable digital construction and maintenance. So, just as standards apply to building materials and constructions, so the web has generated its own forms of compliance – in semantic structure (XML, XHTML), in style language (CSS) and in code (ECMAScript, JavaScript).[22] These allow maximum interoperability across platforms and web-enabled devices, contributing towards accessibility standards (WAI), reusable components and reconfigurable digital spaces.

The imperative underlying information technology systems – whether they be physical or digital – is imposing itself on big digital resources as managers face up to 'lifespans', 'reusability', the 'recycling' of components and the maintenance (or 'sustainability') of programmes. The 'redecorations', 'alterations' and 'extensions' already familiar to managers of physical galleries and their structures may well become familiar issues for custodians of digital space, as the shaping and integration of the on-line resources of major institutions become a strategic issue.[23]

Moreover, the relationship between museum space and digital media has another (our third) dimension that helps explain the emergence of integral and innate technologies within gallery space – and it is a dimension related to the cultural value of digital media itself. For, from the 1980s onwards, the 'new media' transfixed not only museum professionals but the world.[24] Despite the drawbacks of the new technologies – excessive hype and the dotcom bust, serious concerns about excluded groups and societies, pornography, crime and viruses (it is claimed that the MyDoom virus of February 2004 cost around 22.6 *billion* dollars, for example)[25] – the impetus for ICT appears unstoppable. Our use of mobile phones, PDAs and PCs particularly is a tendency that is becoming instinctive, 'second nature' to many. Its significance is reflected at a political level, with national and EU policy initiatives for an 'eEurope'.[26] ICT now plays a defining part in many modern societies.

Like everyone else, museums are still coming to terms with what such technology can do. The emergence of the web has created a 'new ballgame', and with network operators, hardware suppliers, content providers, digital publishers and software houses all jockeying for power, it is far from clear who will be the winners and losers.[27] (The bumpy ride enjoyed by the music industry, in failing to adapt to the web – the rise, fall, and reincarnation of Napster-type sites – is perhaps one example of the surprises in store.) But the museum has always been an information communication technology, and its curatorial

expertise, quality content and impeccable branding can be expressed and lever-
aged in the new media as they can with the old. If, as we argue, information
communication technology is what museums do, the adoption of digital media
should not require a conceptual leap.

An evolution of in-gallery digital interactivity

Indeed, if we were to chart the progress of the relationship between museums
and new media, we might identify a technology (in the 1960s) that initially had
somewhat limited and specialized use in a museum context. This was the
moment when we begin to detect museum professionals using computer technology in their work – but with an approach that was experimental, largely
connected to research practices and documentation systems, and frequently
dependent upon the specific interests of particular curators. This was a moment
far removed from the levels of international collaboration and co-ordination
we experience today. Likewise, at a time of stand-alone machines and databases of text, this nascent period was also distant *technologically* from today's
on-line networks of multi-media information. We might also argue that this
selective adoption of computing by the sector was followed in time, from the
1980s onwards, by a discourse that acknowledged new technologies as a
powerful tool across many aspects of museum work – if only as 'a means, not
an end'.[28] This was the rationalizing discourse that finally placated those who
saw new technology as some kind of threat to the authenticity and authority
upon which the institution was apparently built. New media could support
learning, disseminate information and provide new ways of seeing and experiencing objects as long as (so the reasoning went) it was not allowed to become
the main focus.

Nonetheless, no medium can *just* be 'a means to an end'. It is half a century
since McLuhan emphasized that *what* is said is deeply conditioned by the
medium through *which* it is said.[29] (And just as buildings and galleries shape
the message, so it is claimed that 'these new media have, without doubt, renewed
the attractive quality of cultural images and the potential for their use'.)[30] We
might say that a new discourse has been constructed around digital media inside
and outside the museum – it is a discourse that acknowledges the agency and
cultural resonance that this technology now carries, and it is a discourse that
even permits the use of digital media as an end in itself.

In terminology, twentieth-century terms such as a 'virtual museum' (IT as a
means to an end) are giving way before 'broadcast' and 'programme' (IT
enabling new destinations). In practice, digital models of physical exhibits – and
digital exhibits themselves – can now be reconfigured in new and different ways,
enhancing interpretation, and making explicit associations and linkages that can
only be implicit in the physical site. According to Jean Colson, the Senior Editor
of the London Science Museum's *Making the Modern World Online*, the curators 'wanted to do a new interpretation . . . of the relationships of technology
and society between 1750 and 2000'. The original gallery represents

a web of associations between the 'placements' of the objects . . . they [the Museum] want the visitors to see the associations. . . . The problem is very few people know enough about the objects and their contexts in the first place. So the associated linkages are almost invisible.

It is the on-line manifestation of the gallery that can enable these associations to become visible.[31] Similarly, in freeing text from the label, and projecting it, for example, on to the floor of the gallery, we find children

> get interested in the manner in which text is presented to them . . . they are intrigued by the text . . . it becomes a strong, immersive environment . . . it becomes fun, kids run around chasing it, and adults watch the way it explodes and comes together – it becomes a very dynamic medium.[32]

For better or for worse, we find new media is changing the message.

Thus, from rather humble beginnings as a specialist research tool used by an interested few, digital media will, over two generations, have developed to become one of the primary qualities (one might even say, *defining* qualities) of the modern museum. And as computer technology within the museum has moved from being the privilege of a few to the tool of many, and then (as we have tried to argue here) a culturally resonant property of wider society, so, likewise, the use of new media within exhibitions has mirrored this process of incorporation.

Perhaps this evolution can be traced (see Figure 3.1). For although there are detail differences (to take one obvious contrast – in the difference in multi-media development between the 'AV tradition'[33] of science centres and science

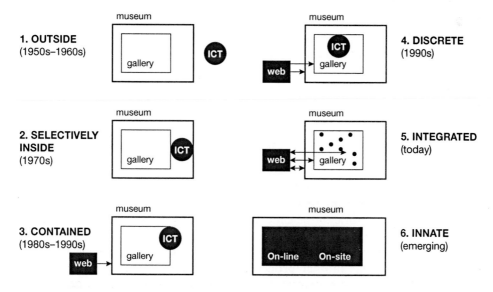

Figure 3.1 An evolution of in-gallery digital interactivity.

museums and what some professionals see as the 'traditional reticence'[34] of the art museum), it is clear that in the earliest phase, in about the middle of the twentieth century, ICT sits outside not only the space of the gallery, but also the museum. It is in the second phase that it enters the museum, but at first only in relation to certain practices such as collections management, documentation and research. Only in the third phase (in the last two decades of the century) does ICT begin to infiltrate the space of gallery on a large scale. But, significantly, this infiltration is only partial. In some cases it is only through so-called 'hived-off' galleries – separate spaces that keep the technology apart from the museum's collections. (The 'Micro Gallery' in the National Gallery, London – much reviewed, and enduring in the museum – was an early example that epitomized such approaches.) By the fourth phase, ICT has become something of a mainstay of exhibitions. But even though its presence is perhaps more familiar on the gallery floor, its integration with the rest of the exhibit is not always as close as it could be. As 'stand-alone' interactives, the 'kiosks' that characterized this phase of development could be both physically and conceptually disconnected from their surrounds. Notably, this fourth phase is also marked by the rapid development in on-line media. The advent of the web technology (growing exponentially from around 1993[35]) allowed both the museum (generally) and exhibitions (specifically) to have an extended digital presence.

In recent years, which we might call a fifth phase, the web presence has become more sophisticated and dialogic – with the on-line provision potentially feeding back to the on-site museum, to exhibitions, and even to specific interactives within those exhibitions. The fifth phase is also characterized by the extent to which the in-gallery digital media has become less discrete and more integrated into the content of the exhibition. A good example of this new dynamic can be found at the Victoria and Albert Museum, London. With on-site visitors being able to email exhibition content to themselves, and with some 40 discrete and 'politely housed' LCD screens thoughtfully and sensitively blended into the exhibition, the V&A's British Galleries (developed with Casson Mann) exemplify not only this level of on-site/off-site dialogue, but also these new levels of integration that are today being reached within gallery design. The next phase of the digital-supported gallery is that in which ICT becomes *innate* within the exhibition space. It is here that digital ICT is less an afterthought, or something adjunct to the exhibition, but is instead conceived as another quality of the gallery. In this phase digital ICT is (when applicable) integrated so deeply into the practices of curators and designers, harmonized so thoughtfully and appropriately into the interpretive strategy of the exhibit, and embedded so seamlessly into the fabric of the gallery, that it becomes an integral and ambient component of the exhibition. In this praxis digital ICT is no longer something to be conceived separately but rather (like object, text panel, display case) is assimilated as simply another property of what an exhibition is. Or, to put it another way, in this instantiation of the exhibition (*the exhibition of the informational age*) digital ICT acquires metonymic value.

Innate in-gallery ICT: immersive, intuitive, seamless

There are several traits that seem to accompany this integral approach. The first relates to immersion. When digital media becomes integral to an exhibition the potential for immersive experiences would appear to increase. This is the effect seen, for instance, at the Sellafield Visitors Centre (Seascale, UK). Engaging the controversies and questions surrounding nuclear energy, the designers placed visitors within 'a strong immersive environment' of animated texts projected to a high quality ('edge-to-edge') on to the surfaces of the gallery space.[36] In much the same way as the projectors of Imperial War Museum North's 'Big Picture' (Manchester) place the visitor effectively inside a three-dimensional film, so the visitor at Sellafield is utterly immersed within the active and changing debates of the exhibit. This is also the characteristic we see at play in the 'Crimes Against Humanity' exhibit at the Imperial War Museum (London) – a powerful, rolling six-chapter film confronting the causes of genocide. Despite the challenges posed by the attic space with which they were presented (a lattice vault of steel with a large window at the either end), the designers – again, Casson Mann – wanted visitors to be immersed in the film; to be engaged with it as much as possible. Their response, therefore, placed the media itself (rather than the architecture) at its centre. Roger Mann explains:

> We took the rectangle of the screen, and came backwards with structures, so we took a ceiling back from the top of the screen and brought it back and took a floor from the bottom exactly the same width as the screen. . . . The screen fills your vision, and goes floor to ceiling, so at times it is almost seamless, the space you exist in the real world appears almost seamless with the space within the film, and the people on the screen are almost the same size as you, and you begin almost to share the same space as them.[37]

Rather than placing digital media *into* a gallery environment, the solution was, in a sense, to place the gallery within a digital media environment. The exhibit was shaped literally as a digital medium.

A more extreme example is found in the design of Imperial War Museum North, where effectively ICT was a condition on the shape of the entire build. Daniel Libeskind's concept for the building took the idea of a war-rocked world being shattered into pieces, with the resulting shards (representing conflict on land, in air and on water) combined dramatically to form the building's distinctive ensemble of smooth curves and acute jutting angles. Significantly, however, part of the building – the air shard that raises skywards – is cut so that the massive curvature of its external façade is set to take an image from a specific projection point. Libeskind's building has been shaped by the ICT that was anticipated to be used within it – in this instance, its exterior walls doubling as a projection screen. ICT has, in other words, become an essential quality of its space. Such influences align the museum, therefore, to our long history of museums shaped by information and communications technologies. We might say, for example, that just as Alfred Waterhouse's nineteenth-century design for the

Natural History Museum in South Kensington (London) assumed the presence of Victorian information management and display technologies in its spatial solution for ordering and exhibiting the natural world, so Libeskind's Imperial War Museum North – 150 years later – makes the statement in its design that a museum is a space partly conditioned by the audio-visual technologies of its post-industrial era.

Interestingly, the further we enter this condition (of integrated and integral digital media) the more the join between ICT and the rest of the museum and the gallery can become more difficult to identify. We may be only in the early days of 'stripping away the hardware', but examples of this approach are emerging. The 200 digital terminals wired into the Wellcome Wing of the Science Museum (London), for instance, help generate an environment where new technology is close to being pervasive. In its Digitopolis exhibit (appropriately, an exhibition about digital media) the technology is 'hidden', and – to quote the museum's interactives engineer – 'the computers disappear'.[38] In the space of Digitopolis (and exhibits like it) the computer hardware becomes ambient – it blends with its surrounds and becomes an integral element of the gallery environment. And as it disappears so it becomes more intuitive – with the barriers sometimes associated with the human–computer interface (including small screens and the need to know the conventions of various input devices) being reduced. It is this sort of intuitive design that can make a nautical exhibit (as in the National Maritime Museum Cornwall) replace a keyboard with a winch. This approach is writ large in the Cabinet War Rooms' Churchill Museum (2005), where as well as physical exhibits there is an archive, or dataset full of documents. As the Project Manager noted:

> our biggest problem and our biggest solution was this huge collection of documents, a public archive that very few people actually get to see . . . yet it is full of fascinating information about Churchill . . . our challenge was how to entice people to look at something they wouldn't normally look at.[39]

The solution was to turn the exhibit into the more familiar form of a desk covered in papers – a physical table, stretching across the diagonal of the gallery, edged by a strip which enables users to search, select and arrange the exhibits that are projected upon it, 'changing people's attitudes to "boring archival documents"'.[40] A radical, effective use of ICT, but at the same time, 'it's a table, a big table, it's not a screen . . . I'd like to think that the hardware has disappeared'.[41]

By looking towards some recent projects within UK museums, and drawing upon the portfolios of some leading design houses we have tried to chart the emergence of digital media technologies within gallery space, and comment on the extent to which these technologies are becoming ever more pervasive and integrated within the exhibition environment. Our suggestion here is that ICT is becoming integral to and innate within our notions of both the modern museum and the modern gallery. We are not claiming that all museum exhibitions will be built this way, or that ICT will be innate all the time in all exhibitions. There will always be exhibitions that choose not to use (or are not in a position to choose) digital ICT. But when ICT is deployed successfully, its function will more likely be as an innate quality of the exhibition, rather than a special feature, interloper or 'add-on'. Our suggestion (from the current evidence) is that when it is used it will be used in more familiar and congruous ways, ambient within its surrounds, and concordant with our practices – because we are learning how to design more imaginatively with it, because museums are becoming more comfortable with it, and because visitors in their everyday lives are developing habits and behaviours around it. Digital ICT will be used more and more in the space of the museum, but we will just notice it less and less.

Notes

1 D. Murray, *Museums: Their History and Their Use. With a bibliography and list of museums in the United Kingdom*, 3 vols, Glasgow: James MacLehose and Sons, 1904, I, pp. 7–12.
2 Ibid., I, p. 284.
3 See T. daCosta Kaufman, *The School of Prague: Painting at the Court of Rudolf II*, Chicago, IL: University of Chicago Press, 1988, p. 17; and A. MacGregor, 'The cabinet of curiosities in seventeenth-century Britain', in O. Impey and A. MacGregor (eds), *The Origins of Museums: The Cabinet of Curiosities in Sixteenth- and Seventeenth-century Europe*, Oxford: Clarendon Press, 1985, p. 152.
4 E. Miller, *That Noble Cabinet: A History of the British Museum*, London: Andre Deutsch, 1973, p. 24.
5 D. J. Meijers, 'The Kuntskamera of Tsar Peter the Great (St Petersburg 1718–34): King Solomon's house or repository of the four continents?', in M. Giebelhausen (ed.), *The Architecture of the Museum: Symbolic Structures, Urban Contexts*, Manchester and New York: University of Manchester Press, 2003, p. 18.
6 F. A. Dreier, 'The *Kunstkammer* of the Hessian Landgraves in Kassel', in Impey and MacGregor, *Origins of Museums*, p. 108.
7 For instance, referring to Paris (1867 and 1878) and Philadelphia (1876), Ian Ritchie explains that the world exhibitions illustrated very clearly through their pavilion buildings 'an architectural taste for style, often quite independent of the *contents* on display'. I. Ritchie, 'An architect's view of recent developments in European museums', in R. Miles and L. Zavala (eds), *Towards the Museum of the Future*, London and New York: Routledge, 1994, p. 10.
8 G. Olmi, 'Science-honour-metaphor: Italian cabinets of the sixteenth and seventeenth centuries', in Impey and MacGregor, *Origins of Museums*, p. 7.
9 L. Jardine, *Worldly Goods: A New History of the Renaissance*, London and Basingstoke: Papermac, 1997, p. 183.
10 E. Scheicher, 'The collection of Archduke Ferdinand II at Schloss Ambras: its purpose, composition and evolution', in Impey and MacGregor, *Origins of Museums*, pp. 29–30.
11 L. Seelig, 'The Munich Kunstkammer, 1565–1807', in Impey and MacGregor, *Origins of Museums*, p. 80.
12 J. Macky, *A Journey through England*, 2nd edn, London, 1722, p. 261, as quoted by Murray, *Museums*, I, p. 209.
13 Cowtan was less enthusiastic, however, in his description of the 'show-cases' of engraving and etchings that were in the middle of the room, which

> though perhaps the best that could be devised for the purpose, are very ugly, and are a great disfigurement to this beautiful room. When the curtains are drawn around

them . . . they present very much the appearance of huge coffins lying in state, and entirely destroy the perspective of this otherwise splendid gallery.

R. Cowtan, *Memories of the British Museum*, London: Richard Bentley and Son, 1872, pp. 40–4.

14 *Guide to the Philadelphia Museum*, Philadelphia, PA, 1804, 8 vols, as quoted by Murray, *Museums*, I, p. 179.

15 E. P. Alexander, *The Museum in America: Innovators and Pioneers*, Walnut Creek, CA, and London: AltaMira Press, 1997, pp. 34–5.

16 Ibid., p. 135.

17 Ibid., p. 128. Also see H. Hein, *The Exploratorium: The Museum as Laboratory*, Washington, DC: Smithsonian Institute Press, 1990.

18 G. Worsley, 'The future for Foster', *Daily Telegraph*, 3 June 2000, p. A1.

19 T. Robbin, *Engineering a New Architecture*, New Haven, CT, and London: Yale University Press, 1996, p. 118.

20 We use information *architecture* to *build* web *sites*, using *templates* to shape information that, as *visitors*, we *enter*, usually at the *home* page, *touring* them or *exploring* them using *site maps* to find chat *rooms*. We use *portals*, we need to *maintain* our on-line resources, and then we *exit*.

21 Robbin, *Engineering a New Architecture*, facing page 20.

22 Brooke Elgie and Ed Walker (Web Developers, mwr, Winchester UK), personal communication with authors, 20 January 2004.

23 [*Making the Modern World Online*] . . . is a separate space altogether to that of *Ingenious*, structured very differently. But there are authored links in *Making the Modern World*, at a granular level, taking you to *Ingenious* . . . like going from a classroom to a library.

Martyn Farrows (Chief Publications Officer, mwr), personal communication with authors, 27 March 2004, of two related web sites by The Science Museum, London.

24 The later twentieth century saw 'the introduction of new technologies that transfixed not only the museum profession, but the world'. B. L. Rottenberg, 'Museums, information and the public sphere', *Museum International*, 216, 2002: 21.

25 J. Perrone, 'Microsoft offers reward for MyDoom author', *Guardian Unlimited* online. Available at: http://www.guardian.co.uk/online/security/story/0,14230,1144145,00.html (accessed 19 July 2004).

26 'eEurope is part of the Lisbon strategy to make the European Union the most competitive and dynamic knowledge-based economy . . . by 2010'. European Commission, *eEurope 2005: An Information Society for All*, Brussels: Commission of the European Communities, 2002, p. 2.

27 G. Nairn, 'The picture gets brighter', *Financial Times, FT-IT Review*, 26 November 2003, p. 5.

28 A. Mintz, 'Media and museums: a museum perspective', in S. Thomas and A. Mintz (eds), *The Virtual and the Real: Media in the Museum*, Washington, DC: American Association of Museums, 1998, p. 34.

29 M. McLuhan, *Understanding Media: The Extensions of Man*, London: Routledge, Keegan and Paul, 1964, especially chapter 1.

30 I. Vinson, 'Editorial', *Museum International*, 215 (1), 2002: 4.

31 Jean Colson (Editor, mwr), personal communication with authors, 27 March 2004.

32 Roger Mann (Designer, Casson Man Ltd, London), interview with authors, 3 February 2004.

33 Joe Cutting (Interactive Media Engineer, The Science Museum, London), interview with authors, 3 February 2003.

34 'It is arguably a reticence informed by the associations carried by "sanctified" art space, the auratic art object, the practices of art history, and the expectations of the art establishment.' Jemima Rellie (Head of Digital Programmes, Tate Britain, London), interview with authors, 3 February 2003, contrasting the London Science Museum's long association with interpretive media, and the shorter history of the Tate's use of such media.

35 D. Bearman and J. Trant, 'Interactivity comes of age: museums and the World Wide Web', *Museum International*, 204 (4), October–December 1999: 20–4.
36 Roger Mann (interview).
37 Roger Mann (interview).
38 Joe Cutting (interview).
39 Ann Carter (Project Manager, Churchill Museum at the Cabinet War Rooms, London), interview with authors, 3 February 2004.
40 Roger Mann (interview).
41 Roger Mann (interview).

References

Alexander, E. P., *The Museum in America: Innovators and Pioneers*, Walnut Creek, CA, and London: AltaMira Press, 1997.

Bearman, D. and Trant, J., 'Interactivity comes of age: museums and the World Wide Web', *Museum International*, 204 (4), October–December 1999: 20–4.

Cowtan, R., *Memories of the British Museum*, London: Richard Bentley & Son, 1872.

daCosta Kaufman, T., *The School of Prague: Painting at the Court of Rudolf II*, Chicago, IL: University of Chicago Press, 1988.

Dreier, F. A., 'The *Kunstkammer* of the Hessian Landgraves in Kassel', in O. Impey and A. MacGregor (eds), *The Origins of Museums: The Cabinet of Curiosities in Sixteenth- and Seventeenth-century Europe*, Oxford: Clarendon Press, 1985, pp. 102–9.

European Commission, *eEurope 2005: An Information Society for All*, Brussels: Commission of the European Communities, 2002.

Hein, H., *The Exploratorium: The Museum as Laboratory*, Washington, DC: Smithsonian Institute Press, 1990.

Jardine, L., *Worldly Goods: A New History of the Renaissance*, London and Basingstoke: Papermac, 1997.

MacGregor, A., 'The cabinet of curiosities in seventeenth-century Britain', in O. Impey and A. MacGregor (eds), *The Origins of Museums: The Cabinet of Curiosities in Sixteenth- and Seventeenth-century Europe*, Oxford: Clarendon Press, 1985, pp. 147–58.

McLuhan, M., *Understanding Media: The Extensions of Man*, London: Routledge, Kegan & Paul, 1964.

Meijers, D. J., 'The Kuntskamera of Tsar Peter the Great (St Petersburg 1718–34): King Solomon's house or repository of the four continents?', in M. Giebelhausen (ed.), *The Architecture of the Museum: Symbolic Structures, Urban Contexts*, Manchester and New York: University of Manchester Press, 2003, pp. 17–31.

Miller, E., *That Noble Cabinet: A History of the British Museum*, London: André Deutsch, 1973.

Mintz, A., 'Media and museums: a museum perspective', in S. Thomas and A. Mintz (eds), *The Virtual and the Real: Media in the Museum*, Washington, DC: American Association of Museums, 1998, pp. 19–34.

Murray, D., *Museums: Their History and Their Use. With a bibliography and list of museums in the United Kingdom*, 3 vols, Glasgow: James MacLehose & Sons, 1904.

Nairn, G., 'The picture gets brighter', *Financial Times, FT-IT Review*, 26 November 2003, p. 5.

Olmi, G., 'Science-honour-metaphor: Italian cabinets of the sixteenth and seventeenth centuries', in O. Impey and A. MacGregor (eds), *The Origins of Museums: The Cabinet of Curiosities in Sixteenth- and Seventeenth-century Europe*, Oxford: Clarendon Press, 1985, pp. 5–16.

Perrone, J., 'Microsoft offers reward for MyDoom author', *Guardian Unlimited* online. Available at: http://www.guardian.co.uk/online/security/story/0,14230,1144145,00.html (accessed 19 July 2004).

Ritchie, I., 'An architect's view of recent developments in European museums', in R. Miles and L. Zavala (eds), *Towards the Museum of the Future*, London and New York: Routledge, 1994, pp. 7–30.

Robbin, T., *Engineering a New Architecture*, New Haven, CT, and London: Yale University Press, 1996.

Rottenberg, B. L., 'Museums, information and the public sphere', *Museum International*, 216, 2002: 21–7.

Scheicher, E., 'The collection of Archduke Ferdinand II at Schloss Ambras: its purpose, composition and evolution', in O. Impey and A. MacGregor (eds), *The Origins of Museums: The Cabinet of Curiosities in Sixteenth- and Seventeenth-century Europe*, Oxford: Clarendon Press, 1985, pp. 29–38.

Seelig, L., 'The Munich Kunstkammer, 1565–1807', in O. Impey and A. MacGregor (eds), *The Origins of Museums: The Cabinet of Curiosities in Sixteenth- and Seventeenth-century Europe*, Oxford: Clarendon Press, 1985, pp. 76–89.

Vinson, I., 'Editorial', *Museum International*, 215 (1), 2002: 4.

Worsley, G., 'The future for Foster', *Daily Telegraph*, 3 June 2000, p. A1.

4

Creative space

David Fleming

In a paper entitled 'Positioning the museum for social inclusion', which arose out of a conference on Social Inclusion held in March 2000 at the University of Leicester, I made reference to the role of architecture in excluding people from museums:

> Many museums were designed to overwhelm visitors. The classical columns and pediments, the banks of steps, the ornate iron gates – these are devices that convey numerous messages, all quite conscious, about what an entry to this grand edifice will lead to. Museum architecture has always been, and still is, an area where pomposity and vainglory can run riot. Museum architects do seem to think that the building is more important than what's in it, and we have a number of recent examples of how wrong this can be. It is the cavernous interior that often reduces people to hushed whispers and an impression that, somehow, they oughtn't to be there.[1]

In the context of the paper, this was a point made almost in passing, but it touches upon the nature of museum spaces, and the ways in which architecture helps, hinders, or perhaps just bypasses, the essential role of the museum in creating experiences and stimulating impressions that lead to learning, and to a new understanding of identity.

My views on the architecture of museums have been formed over a period of 23 years, during which time I have been involved in the building of five new museums (in York, Hull, Preston and Wallsend), the major refurbishment of two more (in Newcastle and Sunderland) and a couple of dozen more modest refurbishments in other museums (in Hull, South Shields, Gateshead and Newcastle). Each of these schemes involved working with a different architect, and I have worked with a number of museum designers on a variety of displays and exhibitions, on subjects ranging from council housing to pterosaurs. I have been a client across the whole gamut of museum space – new entrances, shops, cafes, stairways, exhibition galleries for collections of fine and decorative art, social and industrial history, military and maritime history, land transport and archaeology, Egyptology and geology; temporary exhibition spaces, education facilities, community spaces, darkrooms, lecture theatres, audio-visual theatres, cloakrooms and toilets, as well as workshops, conservation facilities, security control rooms, stores and offices; and half a Roman villa, a Roman barracks and a working Roman bath house, a Winter Gardens and a pig sty. I have in all this had responsibility for Grade II, Grade II* and Grade I listed buildings, and three Scheduled Ancient Monuments, and I have been involved in the conversion to museum space of a social club, a staff canteen, a small ship, a Tudor school and a bacon store. My conclusion? There is nothing simple about creating museum space! How museums work, how their buildings work, and how people interact with buildings and displays is an exceedingly complex matter, and we should beware cute generalizations.

The fact is that museum architecture is capable of achieving all sorts of impacts. It can inspire or confuse; dominate or complement; welcome or forbid; include or exclude. It can assist day-to-day running operations, or hinder them in an exceedingly frustrating fashion. It can look like an organic part of a cityscape, or like it has landed from another planet.

I do not consider myself particularly 'spatially aware'. In museums I respond primarily to content, not context, and message, not medium. When I am told that the building itself contains the message – as in the Jewish Museum, Berlin, where, for example, empty spaces 'invite visitors to contemplate the destruction of Jewish life in Germany by National Socialism, and to visualise their loss' and where lines of windows refer to the impact of Jews on Berlin's culture – then I am afraid I am all at sea; this is too abstract for me as a visitor, and I am more likely to respond to something more tangible, such as a concentration camp site.[2] Of course I understand that museum objects in a dramatic space, such as the Anzac Hall in the Australian War Memorial, may have a greater impact than if displayed in serried ranks at ground level, but not on everyone. One question I want to ask, therefore, is am I alone in resisting the seduction of museum spaces with little in them, or by pretentious architecture, and in being more interested in, and affected by, close encounters with museum content?

This is, of course, a gross oversimplification of how museum spaces work, so let us ask a more fundamental question: what do we mean by 'museum space'? In essence, the answer is it is the sequence of rooms, voids and bits in between that a visitor encounters having entered the museum. But museum space is also the physical environs of the building – the exterior of the building itself, and its immediate surroundings, whether this be a street, square, park or other public area, or even countryside. The nature of these surroundings can have a great impact on visitors, and may deter, rather than attract, trade. Some museums, through their physical design, can deter people, especially those who have to screw up their courage to attempt a visit in the first place. Not everyone is comfortable with grand entrances, but then sometimes it is hard to find the entrance at all – recent examples I have visited include Urbis in Manchester and the Imperial War Museum North in Trafford. I have to say, nothing annoys me more than being unable to find the entrance to a museum. Unless, that is, it's not being able to find my way out again. . . . We are beginning to touch upon the relationship a museum has with its city, if that is its context, and I shall return to this.

I want to ask another basic question here, though. At what point does museum space begin? As the museum hoves into physical view? I suggest not. Leaving aside the issue of the virtual space of the internet, and other than in those circumstances when one encounters a museum by accident, the visitor enters the 'psychological space' of the museum perhaps long before actually visiting. And it is a space shared with people who have no intention of visiting the museum. The whole point of marketing and publicity, and image-building and branding, is to prepare people to make contact with a museum. I had heard, for example, all sorts about Te Papa, the National Museum of New Zealand, long before I ever made a visit. Moreover, we all glean different messages from the psychological contact. In my case I had developed an idea of Te Papa as a museum I had to visit if I wanted to see an especially intelligent approach to diversity. I am sure that plenty of New Zealand families head for Te Papa just because they've heard it's fun.

I have often been asked the key to building new, diverse audiences for museums in Hull, Tyne & Wear and, latterly, in Liverpool. My stock answer is 'pro-gramme', allied with popular media coverage. In other words, it doesn't matter what you do in the museum if no one knows about it, and if you want to diversify traditional museum audiences then you must penetrate the popular media. In Hull this meant primarily the *Hull Daily Mail*; in Newcastle it was the *Evening Chronicle*; in Liverpool it's the *Liverpool Echo* – and local radio and television. I don't mean sporadic coverage, but relentless interest in what the museum is up to, so that regular readers of those newspapers, each of which has a massive C2DE readership, are fed a constant diet of museum, alongside news about crime, health, the soaps, the stars and all other preoccupations of normal people. So, newspaper readers actually enter the psychological space of the museum perhaps a long time before they make a decision to visit. What we have to do then to turn them into regular visitors and advocates is not to disappoint them when they first come. Of course, many people visit a museum, often as children, don't like it, then carry around with them for years, maybe decades, a negative image of the museum that prevents them from ever visiting again, until or unless a new trigger motivates them to return. The concept of the psychological space of the museum needs to be understood by the modern museum.

Let us return to the museum in its physical setting, and in particular to consider the relationship a museum has with its city. Often the ambitions of a museum's creator and designers, as realized in the building they produce, as well as in its contents, encompass the museum as an instrument of urban understanding and urban change. There can be no denying the importance of museum archi-tecture in the urban environment, in terms of regeneration, cultural tourism, memorialization, symbolism, metropolitanization and so on. Moreover, it is only because society at large has been persuaded that museums are agents of change – social and economic – that we have seen the unprecedented period of radical reshaping, building and rebuilding in which we find ourselves. We cannot disassociate museum design, the creation of museum space, from the prevailing climate which is characterized worldwide by a drive for inclusiveness, accessibility and diversity. It would be a peculiar new museum indeed that did not reflect these preoccupations. Not solely because it is in the museum's best interests to do so, but because museums are now fast becoming radical, reformist constructs in a world driven by the need to address anew concepts of diversity, equality and human rights; increasingly in the control of people who are committed to these concepts.

Compare this with previous eras of UK museum expansion. For example, the Victorian era was characterized by a desire to inform, instruct, improve and, to a degree, control, but hardly by democratic appropriation. The independent museum boom of the 1970s and 1980s owed more to a desperate drive to rescue the material detritus of a lost industrial age than to a need for social engineering. Museum space is now recognized for its latent power, its capacity to transform and its role in our modern lifelong learning and social inclusion agendas, seen by many as the saviours of our increasingly diverse society, and especially of our urban communities. I say 'now recognized', because this has been a while coming. I wish, for example, that the work done by the brilliant young team at Hull Museums in the mid to late 1980s had been built upon, rather than largely neglected and forgotten.

To return to the issue of interior spaces and the way they work: the fact is that most museum spaces were designed long ago, and their basic configuration owes little to modern notions of accessibility or democracy. Indeed many were never intended to house museums at all and were designed for quite different purposes. For every Bregenz Kunsthaus there is a score of Walker Art Galleries, and a fair number of Musée d'Orsays. The Victorians had quite basic requirements of their museum architecture, as we can see from the following extract from G. Brown Goode's address to the 1895 Museums Association Conference:

> The museum building should be absolutely fire proof and substantially constructed; the architecture simple, dignified and appropriate – a structure worthy of the treasures to be placed within. Above all things the interior should be well lighted and ventilated, dry and protected from dust. The halls should be well-proportioned, the decoration simple and restful to the eye. No decorative features should be permitted which tend to draw attention from the collections or reduce the floor or wall spaces. Museum architecture affords no exception to the principle that an edifice should be perfectly adapted to the purpose for which it is designed. No architectural effect which lessens the usefulness of the building can be pleasing to an intelligent public.[3]

Imagine Brown Goode's reaction to the following observations on modern museums by *Financial Times* columnist Richard Tomkins:

> a clue to their destiny came in 1976 when France housed its national museum of modern art in the Pompidou Centre in Paris, an extraordinary new building with all its utilities on the outside. Tourists came in their

millions to gawp – not at the paintings but at the pipes. An even bigger clue came in 1997 when the Guggenheim Museum opened in Bilbao, a depressed industrial city in northern Spain. Probably, nobody would ever have visited the museum were it not for the fact that the building itself, Frank Gehry's curvaceous, free-form, sculptural fantasy became one of the most talked-about pieces of architecture in years. Suddenly, Bilbao – Bilbao! – was on the cultural map. Cultural tourism had been around for years, of course, but had never been properly recognised or harnessed. Bilbao opened the world's eyes to the potential. Nobody enjoyed visiting fusty museums full of flint arrowheads, broken pots, primitive spoons and old bones. What they wanted was glamour, excitement, spectacle and pizzazz – and the museum industry, or at least the more clued-up bits of it, was ready to give it to them. Now we have museums in which the contents, while necessary to give the building authenticity, are almost irrelevant to the visitor's experience.[4]

More than a touch of journalistic hype there, but you may see what he's getting at in identifying some of the risks involved when statement architecture threatens to overpower the museum's contents and, perhaps, the museum's inclusive narratives and dialogues. So, the act of uplifting certain aspects of the museum's role relegates another. Probably the clearest recent example of this tension can be seen in the remarkable Jewish Museum Berlin where, as if to mock the shade of G. Brown Goode, Daniel Libeskind's museum was designed and built with no reference whatsoever to the museum collections it was intended to house. In valiantly attempting to explain the outcome of this, Ken Gorbey wrote:

> The Jewish Museum was not designed as a traditional series of neutral and malleable gallery spaces. Rather, the building offers a unique opportunity to create a museum in which architectural philosophy and exhibition concept arise out of the same approach to the same subject.[5]

The degree to which curators succeeded in introducing displays and narratives into this powerful building is at least open to question, and I am sure that those curators would have preferred to have had a hand in the design of the museum's interior spaces, given the opportunity. Then they might have avoided this stinging criticism from *Blueprint*: 'In Berlin, Daniel Libeskind's brilliantly disorientating Jewish Museum has been saddled by an exhibition that is pedestrian at best.'[6]

There are other examples of architecture dominating and overwhelming the museum. As Victoria Newhouse writes of Richard Meier's Barcelona Museum of Contemporary Art: 'architecture, not art, is what his museum is about.'[7] On the other hand, much early twentieth-century architecture has been criticized for being too conformist, too neutral, suitable possibly for twentieth-century art but not for other genres. For example, the San Francisco Museum of Modern Art is condemned by Newhouse in these terms:

There is a formulaic impersonability to galleries that ... seem to have been designed to accommodate anything that might go on their walls – a one-size-fits-all approach ... the galleries relate neither to the art they exhibit nor to the city.[8]

This kind of criticism arises when spaces are perceived as being devoid of identity, with no prospect of a relationship with the art they contain. Museums that are often cited as enabling a positive interaction between architecture and content include the Bilbao Guggenheim and the Groninger Museum.

Indeed, it is all too easy to incur the wrath of artists and critics by, in their perception, exhibiting art badly, and altering its intended meaning through context. I have made a number of references to art galleries, or museums of art. This is because there is a much greater literature on the architecture of art museums, and therefore more controversy, than there is concerning other types of museums. On reading much of this literature you might be forgiven for thinking that there *are* only art museums. Victoria Newhouse's book *Towards a New Museum* is only about art museums, and the book's preoccupation is whether the architecture suits the art. Furthermore, the 'New Museum' Newhouse sees us heading towards is one that is as important architecturally as it is for the art it contains.[9] For those of us who are not architects, nor architectural critics, nor art historians, nor art curators, this is all very interesting, but it misses out an awful lot about museums, the great majority of which are not art museums. The relationship of architectural space with collections of social history, or the natural sciences, can be utterly different from its relationship with art. Untroubled by the need to please or placate artists, or by fears of confusing the message passing from artist to viewer, the designer of social history museum spaces is able to concentrate on, for example, creating narratives, setting up dialogues or creating personal spaces, or spaces where different kinds of intervention can be made, such as performances, demonstrations or community activities, or spaces in which to promote emotional learning, or self respect or tolerance.

My point here is that we must resist falling into the trap of discussing only art museums simply because of the close relationship between architecture and art, and because of the celebrity of a number of recent museum projects. We must consider the whole range of types of museum, each of which has its own special characteristics, problems and possibilities. For instance, by definition, museums that attempt to address immensely complex issues – such as the history of the Australian people – risk appearing confused and confusing in their layout. And this is exactly what has been said of the new National Museum of Australia.[10] Similar comments have been made of the Imperial War Museum North.[11] So, perhaps it is particularly difficult for a history museum to appeal to those looking for architectural harmony, which may explain the *Blueprint* negativity about the displays in the Jewish Museum Berlin.

I want to say a little more about the museum as a civic and secular forum, and the importance of the type of spaces it contains. Museums are 'somewhere', not 'anywhere'. Each is unique and the most successful are of their place, of their setting. Each has a specific context. They are similar in some ways to churches, or to shopping centres and other gathering places, but they have a function quite different from these places: they contain things of power; they deal in the tangible, as well as in ideas; and they require no belief, just enquiry. Moreover, museums are places where people go and, in an ideal world, mix with others unlike themselves. If they are to have a broad appeal museums must be multi-layered, and have to please a great variety of people. This, to me, is the fundamental challenge for museum space.

What our diverse audiences need is a diversity of spaces, spaces that excite and thrill, spaces that calm and provoke intense reflection, and spaces that stimulate thinking and learning. Nothing could be worse than museums all looking and feeling the same, based on a misconceived notion that there is a perfect model for which to strive. There is no right way to design an entrance hall, or a community space or an exhibition hall: there is a multitude of ways, with different solutions for different types of collection, different aims and different motivations. And it's not all about subject matter or message. Richard Tomkins wrote witheringly:

> The buildings themselves are often the main attraction, closely followed by the amenities within. Tate Modern is more mall than gallery: by far its most crowded parts are its shops, cafés and restaurants. The British Museum, thanks to its newly refurbished Great Court, is a spectacular, destination café with some antiquities in the basement.[12]

Similar comments have been made about the new entrance at the Louvre.[13] Such po-faced criticism springs from the view that bemoans the 'decline' of the museum into a place of entertainment, where facilities such as shops and restaurants have too much prominence. They interfere with the purity of the cultural experience. And yet, in most museums such facilities are key virtues in the eyes of the public, and are just as central to the operation of the museum as any space containing collections. I have to say, not many museum shops and cafés, at least not in the UK, make any money to speak of anyway – they are there to enhance a visit rather than to honour some Faustian commercial pact made by the museum director.

This exemplifies a simple fact about museums and the design of their spaces: there is no consensus about anything. Some people love Bilbao's Guggenheim, some hate it. Some people can find their way around inside, some can't (some people can't even find their way in . . .). Some people think Te Papa is an ugly building. I think the interior works as well as any museum I have visited. The point is that museum space has endless possibilities for use, especially when we escape the straitjacket of conforming to a 'giving' role and move into a 'sharing' mode. Our greatest challenge remains that of finding ways of breaking down the widespread resistance to visiting museums in the first place.

At the time of writing I am involved in a new museum scheme, the Museum of Liverpool, wherein National Museums Liverpool are hoping to create a

10,000 square metre city history museum, bang in the middle of what is now a World Heritage Site. This is still early days, though we hope to be able to open the museum in 2008, the year that Liverpool is to become the European Capital of Culture. The site of the museum is on the banks of the River Mersey, adjacent to the 'Three Graces', a group of beautiful early twentieth-century buildings – the Royal Liver Building, the Cunard Building and the Port of Liverpool Building. These three comprise the most familiar view of Liverpool, and together they render the site one of the most impressive waterfronts in the world.

In the current 'pre-development' stage we are spending a great deal of time not just getting right the detailed technical specification for the museum, but trying to define the larger questions about space and adjacencies. We want to create a 'nobility' about the spaces, but we must also resolve orientation, interpretive sequences, lighting, air handling and a host of other issues, at the same time as ensuring we offer challenge, variety and surprise. The principles of space design and utilization are exactly the same as in any museum.

Where we begin to generate uniqueness is in the narratives – the stories about Liverpool, with its exhilarating, roller-coaster history. The degree to which we are able to blend these narratives with the architectural spaces will define the success of the museum.

Notes

1 D. Fleming, 'Positioning the museum for social inclusion', in R. Sandell (ed.), *Museums, Society, Inequality*, London: Routledge, 2002, pp. 213–14.
2 Stiftung Judisches Museum Berlin, *Discovering the Jewish Museum Berlin*, Berlin: Stiftung Judisches Museum, 2001, p. 4.
3 G. Brown Goode, 'Principles of museum administration', in *Museums Association Report of Proceedings, Sixth Annual General Meeting, Newcastle upon Tyne*, 1895, pp. 69–141.
4 R. Tomkins, 'Museums make a sorry exhibition of themselves', *Financial Times*, 30 May 2003, p. 12.
5 K. Gorbey, 'The exhibitions', in Stiftung Judisches Museum Berlin, *Discovering the Jewish Museum Berlin*, Berlin: Stiftung Judisches Museum, 2001, p. 3.
6 G. Gibson, 'Editorial', *Blueprint*, No. 210, August 2003: 11.
7 V. Newhouse, *Towards a New Museum*, New York: Monacelli Press, 1998, p. 71.
8 Ibid., p. 65.
9 Ibid., *passim*.
10 See, for example, J. Eccles, 'The history wars', *Museum Journal*, December 2003: 30–3.
11 For example, H.-C. Andersen, 'War and order', *Museums Journal*, August 2002: 34.
12 Tomkins, 'Museums make a sorry exhibition of themselves'.
13 See, for example, Newhouse, *Towards a New Museum*, pp. 171–6.

References

Andersen, H.-C., 'War and order', *Museums Journal*, August 2002: 34.
Brown Goode, G., 'Principles of museum administration', in *Museums Association Report of Proceedings, Sixth Annual General Meeting, Newcastle upon Tyne*, 1895, pp. 69–141.
Eccles, J., 'The history wars', *Museum Journal*, December 2003: 30–3.

Fleming, D., 'Positioning the museum for social inclusion', in R. Sandell (ed.), *Museums, Society, Inequality*, London: Routledge, 2002, pp. 213–14.

Gibson, G., 'Editorial', *Blueprint*, No. 210, August 2003: 11.

Gorbey, K., 'The exhibitions', in Stiftung Judisches Museum Berlin, *Discovering the Jewish Museum Berlin*, Berlin: Stiftung Judisches Museum, 2001, p. 3.

Newhouse, V., *Towards a New Museum*, New York: Monacelli Press, 1998.

Stiftung Judisches Museum Berlin, *Discovering the Jewish Museum Berlin*, Berlin: Stiftung Judisches Museum, 2001.

Tomkins, R., 'Museums make a sorry exhibition of themselves', *Financial Times*, 30 May 2003, p. 12.

Part II

Architectural reshaping

5

From cultural institution to cultural consumer experience

Manchester Art Gallery Expansion Project

Moira Stevenson

Historical context

Manchester Art Gallery had its origins in the Royal Manchester Institution, a Society for the Promotion of Literature, Science and the Arts founded in 1823. The Institution building was designed by Charles Barry in the Ionic Greek Revival style.[1] Greek Ionic was the order adopted for the British Museum, designed by Robert Smirke and begun in 1823.[2] Greek Revival was the style favoured for many public buildings commissioned in the post-Waterloo building boom promoted by George IV. He became the Royal Patron of the Manchester Institution and gave casts of the Elgin Marbles to adorn the entrance hall.[3] The building served the Royal Manchester Institution until, in 1880, unable to pay off their overdraft on the revenue accounts, they asked Manchester Corporation to take over the building and its collections.[4] The Corporation agreed to the transfer and from January 1883 took occupation of the building, when it became known as the Art Gallery. The need to adapt and extend the accommodation to display the expanding fine art collection was acknowledged in the 1880s and alterations were carried out to provide a suite of galleries at first-floor level. In 1898 land and buildings adjacent to the Institution were purchased by the Corporation and the adjacent Athenaeum Club, also designed by Barry, was acquired in 1938.[5] The Athenaeum was subsequently used for exhibitions and displays of the City's collections. Schemes for a new building or extension to the existing one had been developed on at least four occasions during the twentieth century but all failed due to lack of funding. By the 1990s major refurbishment of the historic buildings and space to display the City's major fine and decorative arts collections were urgently needed.

Developing the building project

In 1994, with the prospect of funding from the national lottery on the horizon, Manchester City Council commissioned an RIBA architectural competition for the site that comprised the Royal Manchester Institution building, the Athenaeum and the adjacent vacant land. The winning scheme, by Michael Hopkins and Partners, formed the basis for the application to the Heritage Lottery Fund (HLF) in 1995. The HLF awarded £15 million towards the Project in 1997. The building design team was led by Michael Hopkins and Partners with Ove Arup as structural and M&E engineers, Arup Facade and Arup Lighting for specialist design and Inskip and Jenkins Architects as historic building consultants. The cost consultants were Gardiner & Theobold and MPM Capita provided project management support to Manchester City Council's Special Projects Team, which was responsible for the many major capital projects undertaken in the City during the 1990s and leading up to the Commonwealth Games in 2002.

Planning Permission for the Manchester City Art Gallery Expansion Project was submitted and outline permission was achieved early in 1998 very shortly after the appointment of the new Director in January and the Assistant Director (Project Management) in March. The latter was appointed to be the Gallery's main point of contact for the building design team and to manage the fit-out of the Gallery. In February 1998 the City Council, on cost grounds, decided that the Gallery was to be constructed in a single phase, not in the two-phase programme originally conceived. In retrospect it would have been impossible to sustain a satisfactory service to visitors and ensure the safety of collections given the scale of the building works. The consequence of the decision was a total relocation of staff, collections, furniture and fittings. This was a period of massive change for the organization as, throughout this process of relocation, the implementation of the new staff restructure was proceeding and a new Departmental Management Team and additional marketing and education staff were appointed. The need for team building and staff development was identified in order to galvanize the new staff structure into effective teams to deliver the redevelopment of the Gallery. It was essential that everyone could share the vision for the new Gallery if we were to gain the level of commitment necessary to deliver the project.

Defining the mission, objectives and purpose of the new Gallery

During 1998 the curatorial, education, marketing and support staff took part in a series of workshops to establish what the Project should achieve. This involved the review of our current situation in terms of collections management and the market research study undertaken by Arts About Manchester 1997/8.[6] All staff received copies of the executive summary and had access to the full report. The study reported that visitor figures for September 1995 to August 1996 were for the Art Gallery site 159,116 and for the Athenaeum site 65,411, giving a total of 224,527 visitors. Visitors attending both sites on the same visit were calculated at 96,322 and therefore 128,205 for the site as a whole. Following an analysis of the frequency of visits being undertaken the study went on to establish that 224,527 visits were made by a loyal core of

23,310 visitors, making an average of eight visits each year. This equated to only a 5 per cent penetration into the gallery-going market and offered plenty of opportunity for growth. In terms of the qualitative research, while some visitors appreciated the historic building and its ambience others wanted a more lively and welcoming atmosphere. Speaking about the entrance hall one respondent described it thus: 'it is almost like going into a prison at present', and about the reception another commented: 'once I get in I feel fine but they could do with someone there with a cheery smile.' In terms of the capacity of the Gallery to accommodate major exhibitions another states 'this is a major city and we should be able to have major exhibitions'.

The implications of the quantitative and qualitative research outlined in the report were that:

> A visitor focused approach is crucial to increase significantly the number of visitors at Manchester City Art Galleries. The organisation has to consider all aspects of the visitor experience: the welcome given by staff, the orientation possible once inside the building, the variety of interpretation and the range of choice of services and facilities.

> Visitors are coming for a combination of reasons of which seeing temporary exhibitions is one but not the sole, or most significant, reason. Promotion has to reflect the diversity of attractions that Manchester City Art Gallery offers the visitor.[7]

The key concerns could be broadly grouped under three headings: collections care and asset management, image of the Gallery held by the public, the council and staff, and the visitor experience including access in its widest sense. Through a process of sharing aspirations and visions for the Project the staff eventually arrived at the following mission statement that the majority felt able to support and commit to:

> We will become central to the creative and cultural life of Manchester by the engagement with people through art. We will:
>
> - Champion creativity and enhance the national and international reputation of Manchester as a centre for cultural activity.
> - Use our collections and exhibitions to enrich the lives of people in Manchester.
> - Increase attendances by ensuring that our service is appropriate to the needs of our current and potential users.
> - Offer visitors enjoyable, inspirational and educational experiences.
> - Encourage and enable staff to achieve our mission.
> - Ensure that the City's galleries and collections are cared for and added to for future generations.

The task was then to establish the objectives for the Expansion Project. In physical terms this was identified as:

To plan, design, build and fit out a gallery that will:

- Provide a landmark building which makes a significant contribution to the whole environment.
- Provide appropriate environmental conditions to ensure the preservation of the collections.
- Increase the size of the Gallery to display a significant percentage of the collections.
- Provide better visitor facilities – larger café, retail and information facilities.
- Improve education facilities.
- Improve storage.
- Provide facilities for major exhibitions.

The purpose of the Project was to address the concerns that initiated the Project, deliver the City Council's objectives and create an institution that would be a flagship for Manchester and the region.

The management of the Gallery Project

Having defined the mission, objectives and purpose for the Expansion Project we then had to develop a project management structure to enable the staff to deliver the redisplay and interpretation of the collections and the repositioning of the Gallery in the perception of stakeholders, funders and past and future visitors. The development and delivery of the concept and content for the Gallery ran in parallel to the management of the building project and was essentially managed within the Gallery staff with MPM Capita providing procurement and project management support. A project management structure was established that gave responsibility for different elements of the Project to individual members of the Departmental Management Team (DMT).

The first level in the hierarchy of responsibility was defined as: to plan, build and equip the building and provide staff to reopen Manchester Art Gallery by November 2001 (later revised to May 2002 following delays in the building programme). This top-level objective was further divided into seven task areas. These seven tasks were further subdivided into smaller sub-projects, which were led by members of the DMT or Principal Officers. Individuals took on the responsibilities for specific galleries or the delivery of specific elements within the overall development. The co-ordination and monitoring of progress was carried out at regular Expansion Project Review Meetings chaired by the Assistant Director, who was responsible for the overall co-ordination and delivery of the fit-out. The seven tasks and how they were achieved are outlined below:

Task 1: To provide the Building Design Team with information necessary to enable the building to meet the service delivery objectives

The Assistant Director was the Gallery's main link with the Building Design Team and provided the conduit for information between the architect and end user. The basic allocation of spaces in the scheme was planned in advance of the HLF application. The building had already reached RIBA Stage D and had planning permission early in 1998 when the Gallery staff started to look in detail at the development of the Gallery and its services. There was therefore only a limited opportunity for major changes in the design to be implemented. It was clear from the architectural plans that orientation and navigation through the complex of three buildings brought together in Hopkins' design scheme would be a challenge for visitors. A study of the existing layout and the proposed building extension was commissioned from consultants at the Welsh School of Architecture.[8] The study comprised:

- Computer modelling and analysis of the greater urban layout.
- Computer modelling and analysis of the building layout including the existing buildings and proposed extension.
- Computer simulations of design alternatives proposed by the research team in the light of findings of the study in order to improve the performance in the pattern of movement and use.

The Grade One and Two Star listed nature of the two historic buildings prevented the implementation of a number of the recommendations in the report. However, the study did confirm the use of the Portico on Mosley Street as the primary entrance and influenced the positioning of new interpretative displays from the collections, called the Destination Galleries (one on each floor and one in each of the three buildings). In the light of this research it was also decided to reposition the shop with the aim of drawing visitors through the building.

Task 2: To research and deliver a strategy for the interpretation and redisplay of the collections to meet departmental objectives

Planning the strategy for the relocation, redisplay and interpretation of the collection engaged the majority of curatorial, education and marketing staff in developing the proposals. It was clear that the display strategy outlined in the HLF application would not deliver the audience development objectives outlined in the business plan. A strategy to develop galleries that would appeal to specific target audiences was essential and a higher level of interpretation and design would be required to deliver the necessary audience appeal. This resulted in proposals for three Destination Galleries:

- The Manchester Gallery relating the collections and the building to the City and targeted at local residents and tourists.
- The Children's/Interactive Gallery based on works from the collections and targeted at families with young children.
- The Gallery of Craft and Design that would showcase the important collections of decorative arts and appeal to a general audience interested in craft and design, collectors and students of design.

These three galleries had the highest level of investment. Based on industry norms this was between £2,500 and £3,500 per square metre. Sponsorship for the Manchester Gallery was attracted from CIS, and the Clore Duffield Foundation supported the Interactive Gallery. Multidisciplinary teams were allocated for each gallery and external designers recruited – Casson Mann for the Gallery of Craft and Design and the CIS Manchester Gallery and Event Communications for the Clore Interactive Gallery.

The remaining general galleries were organized around the concept of *Vista* galleries and *Close Up* or *In Focus* galleries. The galleries were organized in a predominantly chronological order but with a thematic approach playing to the strengths of the collections. The Vista galleries would house the key works for which the Gallery is known and displays would be staged for five to ten years. Displays in the Close Up or In Focus galleries would last for eighteen months to two years.

There were also four temporary exhibition spaces. The largest of 421 square metres provides a large clean space, top lit, with natural and artificial light controlled by photocell-operated louvre blinds, which are capable of reducing lighting levels to 50 lux for most of the year. A second adjacent space of 173 square metres with a concrete coffered ceiling is dependent on artificial lighting, enabling total blackout that facilitates the display of contemporary new media works. These two primary temporary exhibition galleries are located on the second floor within the new building. Two smaller spaces were provided, one on the first floor of the Athenaeum for the display of works on paper and the MEN Gallery, adjacent to the CIS Manchester Gallery on the ground floor of the Institution building, which is used for a wide range of temporary exhibitions and installations.

Technical advice was procured for lighting, nailable walls and display case design to assist with the development and fit-out of the general galleries. The colour scheme for individual galleries was the result of protracted discussions between the curators and the architects until consensus was reached.

Task 3: To research, plan and deliver programmes for exhibitions and interpretation, publication and education to meet the department's objectives

The development and delivery of exhibitions, interpretation, publications and education involved cross-divisional working between curatorial, education and marketing teams. Interpretation for the Gallery as a whole was led by the Head of Education. A strategy for the interpretation of the permanent collections in the general galleries was developed. This involved a hierarchy of information in a range of media. Introductory panels and individual labels for each thematic gallery were developed in Ekarv[9] text at 14pt Humanist to a maximum length of 52 characters per line, 8 lines per paragraph, 15 lines for labels and 22 lines for panels including spaces. The introductory panels were translated into Hindi, Urdu, Cantonese and Bengali, representing the languages of the four largest population groups in the City, and into four tourist languages (German, Spanish, French and Japanese). These were made available as laminated sheets. Three audioguides were developed and targeted at general, family and visually impaired audiences. A touch trail was also linked to the visually impaired audio-guide. Additional laminated sheets were also produced with more detailed narratives related to the theme of each gallery.

Humour was also introduced in the audio guides and in a series of 20 cartoons by the children's book illustrator, Tony Ross. These provided 'visual labels' related to key works selected by the illustrator. A number of interactive ex-hibits were introduced within the general galleries to complement the Clore Interactive Gallery and appeal to young children. The Clore Drawing Space, adjacent to Gallery 11, where works on paper are displayed, is the most significant of these and the most popular with visitors.

In relation to publications, *Up Close*, a full-colour introduction to the Gallery highlighting key works from the fine and decorative art collections, was produced jointly with the specialist art publisher Scala. Other printed material includes the floor plan guide, introductions to the audioguide and the quarterly events and exhibitions programme. Tactile plans and Braille guides are also available.

Events for different audiences are planned in relation to each major exhibition in addition to general gallery tours and signed tours for the hearing impaired. Artists are engaged to work with the gallery on specific installations in the permanent collection and for events. The outreach programme engages with local communities and often works with artists. Works produced by outreach projects are frequently included in the permanent collection displays, the CIS Manchester Gallery and the MEN Gallery.

The exhibition programme across the four temporary spaces was developed to address the artistic aspirations and audience development targets and to achieve a range of changing exhibitions with links to the City's collections. The programme aimed to have a broad appeal but also introduce challenging work.

Task 4: To agree the use of non-gallery spaces in the new City Art Gallery and deliver a strategy to occupy the building to agreed deadlines

The reoccupation of the building and the fit-out of office and non-gallery spaces fell within more than one area of the DMT. Staff facilities and IT provision were led by Support Services. Co-ordination of the public areas involved the Marketing and Business Development team and the Assistant Director in the procurement of the physical infrastructure for the retail, catering and visitor facilities. Detailed co-ordination between the building team and the contractors for the retail and catering and the service providers was necessary to ensure the fit-out met with service delivery needs.

Task 5: To define the changes needed to improve service delivery and implement procedures and staff development training to deliver these changes

Identifying the changes required to bring about improvements in service delivery came out of the market research undertaken in 1997/8, the focus group work that took place (during the planning of the Gallery) with target audiences of older people, children and families and the accepted standards required for collection care. Some of these changes rested with the provision of facilities while others were dependent on staff development to meet the changing needs of the organization. These needs were addressed by both recruitment and training. Training in team building, staff management and leadership and project management was introduced for specific staff. Self-help workshops and buddy systems were adopted to develop writing skills for the Ekarv texts. A specific two-week induction programme was introduced for newly recruited Visitor Services staff. A significant proportion of the Visitor Services staff appointed had a specific interest in working in the arts and had a younger profile than the existing team. Interpersonal skills were high on the selection criteria for the new staff in order to address the visitor-friendly approach and image we aimed to create. During the Expansion Project it was necessary to support the capacity of individuals and the organizations to cope with stress and change and to develop strategies to manage this. Lunchtime yoga classes were introduced and initially funded from the training budget for those who expressed interest.

Task 6: To plan and implement a marketing and communication strategy to meet the organization's image and audience development objectives

The development of marketing and communication strategies ran in parallel to the changes in the redisplay and interpretation. The Head of Marketing and Business Development had commissioned the audience research in 1997/8. This provided the baseline for the profile of our visitors and the perception of the Gallery. Research was also undertaken on existing and potential target audiences through focus groups of older gallery goers and non-gallery goers and families with children. Play Train, a specialist consultancy, was recruited to work with an after-school club of 7–12-year-old children in Benchill in order to develop ideas for the Clore Interactive Gallery. The closure in June 1998 gave the Gallery the opportunity to carry out a complete rebranding exercise and reposition the image of the Gallery. Steers McGillan were appointed to develop a new corporate identity. This involved renaming the gallery as Manchester Art Gallery and the department as Manchester City Galleries. The corporate image/logo adopted was designed to be 'people focused' as were all the images in the promotional print. Staniforth Communications was recruited to undertake a media public relations campaign in the lead-up to the reopening in 2002. New members of staff were recruited to the Marketing and Business Development team, including a Press Officer and an Audience Development post.

Task 7: To plan and implement an income-generation and fund-raising strategy that is designed to meet the financial targets of the organization

The Departmental Management Team reviewed the capital budget and revenue projections in 1998. The Business Plan submitted to HLF in 1996[10] suggested an increase in visitor numbers of over 100 per cent; however, there was little change in the nature of the displays and exhibitions in order to produce that level of audience development. The realization of this initiated a review of both the capital and revenue budgets.

The cost plan submitted to HLF for the fit-out of the Gallery in 1996 was £1.9 million. This was based largely on provision of office, catering, retail and storage furniture in addition to exhibition cases and graphics. Only one gallery, 'Arts Alive', had a high level of design and interactive technology. A total review of the nature of the displays and level of interactives resulted in a revised budget of £5.7 million, which is closer to industry norms, and a second application to the Heritage Lottery Fund in 2001.

A fund-raising consultant was appointed to create a strategy for raising the match funding for the Heritage Lottery Fund application. This subsequently led to the establishment of an in-house development team to lead on capital fund-raising and sponsorship. A new post, Head of Development, was created at DMT level. The team went on to deliver the £1 million necessary to match the second HLF grant of £3.8m and deliver the successful relaunch of the Patrons Scheme.

A new three-year business plan was produced in 2000 and this ultimately resulted in the approval of an additional £1 million for the revenue budget to enable the Gallery to deliver the level of service to which the Council aspired. Consultants were also engaged to advise on the catering and retail operations. These operations were tendered to external companies. Additional staff members were recruited to develop the corporate hire and conference business, which has proved to be very successful. Income generation has become increasingly important to the budget as Manchester City Council is operating within tight financial constraints.

Review and evaluation of Manchester Art Gallery

It would have been comforting to think that we had a clear vision and a logical plan from the start of the Project. The nature of major capital projects, however, is that they evolve as your knowledge develops and as the context in which you are working unfolds and changes. The Art Gallery Project was delivered on site to the level required by the stakeholders in time for the Commonwealth Games in the summer of 2002. However, work has continued on the development and improvement of facilities behind the scenes for a further two years and we continue to reassess what we are doing and whether it meets the requirement and needs of our funders and audiences. We do not see the job as complete and we continue to evaluate and ask whether we have been successful in what we set out to achieve. Have we really delivered the outputs and outcomes required by the stakeholders, whom we identified as the City Council, the Heritage Lottery Fund, sponsors and audiences?

In terms of the City Council's expectations, we achieved a landmark building with a high profile in time for the 2002 Commonwealth Games. The new Art Gallery has gone on to achieve regional and national recognition from various awarding bodies. The press coverage for the exhibition and education programme has been overwhelmingly positive and has contributed to the positive cultural image of the City.

In terms of the Heritage Lottery Fund we have achieved the successful delivery of a major capital project that has exceeded its visitor numbers and revised business plan projections. Collections care conditions have greatly improved. We now have a gallery that has doubled in size and provides a series of varied architectural spaces suitable for the display of a range of work differing in size, style and date. The environmental conditions are controlled and managed by a sophisticated building management system. There is an integrated security system of sensors and CCTV cameras. Photocells control artificial lighting, which is linked to louvre blinds to control daylight levels. Art handling is greatly improved with an enclosed loading bay and a goods lift to serve four floors of the new building.

For our sponsors we have created a prestigious gallery with a high profile and a positive media image with which they want to be associated. The corporate hire business continues to expand and make a significant contribution to the income targets and the positive image of the organization in the business community.

An audience research study undertaken by Morris Hargreaves McIntyre in the year following the reopening established that we had both increased and broadened our audience.[11] It established that, in addition to the 16,000 visitors returning, the reopening has been a catalyst to attract approximately 38,000 irregular and lapsed visitors to return and 62,000 brand new visitors to attend for the first time. In fact, 55 per cent of all visitors are now new to the Gallery. In terms of visitor experience, image and perception of the gallery, the survey has asked a sample of visitors to respond to a series of statements stating whether they agreed or disagreed or strongly agreed or disagreed:

- Was it friendly and welcoming? 98 per cent agreed, 77 per cent agreed strongly.
- Was it comfortable and attractive? 88 per cent agreed, 79 per cent agreed strongly.
- Was there something for everyone? 95 per cent agreed, 81 per cent agreed strongly.
- Did it make art accessible? 77 per cent agreed, 66 per cent agreed strongly.
- Is it prestigious and important? 86 per cent agreed, 57 per cent agreed strongly.
- Is it a gallery to be proud of? 91 per cent agreed, 79 per cent agreed strongly.

It is interesting that the lowest score is for the question 'Does the Gallery make art accessible?'. Further research has been undertaken in this area of intellectual access and learning. Helen Rees Leahy, Director of the Centre for Museology at the University of Manchester, was commissioned to undertake a study funded by Resource.[12] The aims of this research project were: to investigate and identify the ways in which a visitor uses and experiences the Art Gallery and its collections and displays, and the factors that influence both the nature of their engagement and the role of informal learning within their overall experience. The objectives of this research were:

- To describe and interpret the diverse ways in which visitors use the interpretation provided by Manchester Art Gallery and its effects on their experience and their perception of their visit.
- To contribute to the body of evidence-based research into the experience of visitors to art galleries in general and the process and effects of their learning at Manchester Art Gallery in particular.
- To enable Manchester Art Gallery to understand both the ways in which the visitor uses interpretation and also the learning benefits derived from different kinds of resources.

The analysis of this research suggests that the majority of independent visitors did not come to Manchester Art Gallery with the explicit desire or intention to learn. With the exception of the Clore Interactive Gallery and the CIS Manchester Gallery, visitors tended to move through the galleries fairly quickly, engaging with relatively few works of art and failing to engage with the curatorial rationale for the galleries' organization and presentation of work. There was also a low uptake of interpretative media, particularly audioguides. This can be partially attributed to visitors' lack of awareness of its availability and also to some resistance to overt didacticism. The visitors did not use the vocabulary of education and learning to describe their experience. Instead they talked about enjoyment, relaxation, enrichment and taking time out of the daily round. The exception was the CIS Manchester Gallery, which suggests that many visitors are interested in art as history, as opposed to art history; they respond positively to the integration of art and artefacts, with narratives of social and individual history. This was also demonstrated in the observation of visitors in the Gallery of Craft and Design.

In terms of peer review Maurice Davies in a recent edition of *Museum Practice* wrote:

> Manchester Art Gallery is now the most ambitious major gallery in the UK in terms of its interpretation and approach to display. In comparison, the National Gallery, the National Portrait Gallery, Tate Britain and Tate Modern are conservative. The only art display at a national museum to come close is the British Galleries at the V & A. Among the non-nationals, even the new Art Gallery Walsall and the Wolverhampton Art Gallery fall short of Manchester's interpretation.[13]

Despite this professional view, in our public's perception 23 per cent of our visitors do not agree with the statement that the new Gallery 'makes art accessible'.

Building on success: the new challenges

Since the Manchester Art Gallery reopened in May 2002 it has exceeded visitor targets by over 30 per cent and generated positive media and professional review. However, the qualitative and observational research suggests that there is still significant room for improvement in assisting visitors to orientate themselves in the building complex. There is also further work to be done to improve intellectual access to the collections and related narratives. How we set out to do this will be influenced by the development in central and local government policies and the Renaissance in the Regions agenda. There is now a far greater awareness of the role that museums and galleries can play in delivering on the government's agenda. Based on the research and within the context of the national and local government priorities the challenges for the Gallery are how do we:

- encourage visitors to slow down and look more closely at possibly fewer works of art and to be more active in their visual enquiry?
- make it easier for visitors, especially those visiting for the first time, to move through the building with confidence and a clearer sense of direction?
- make the visitor experience more welcoming for all visitors, not just those who are already confident in visiting Manchester Art Gallery and other galleries?
- increase the take-up of interpretative media?
- develop the range of interpretative media in response to visitor needs and not staff interest?
- further improve the asset management of the buildings and collections for public benefit?
- exploit IT to ensure we make collection and related information available to new audiences?
- contribute to the delivery of national and local government policies for educational attainment, social inclusion, e-government and asset management?

The three key objectives for the Gallery over the next five years are:

- To build on our past success to improve the quality and effectiveness of our collections care, displays and visitor facilities.
- To develop the use of new media and information technology to improve asset management and access in its widest sense.
- To exploit virtual space and the architecture of the web to take our collections and related narratives to new audiences.

Our aim is to exploit creatively both actual and virtual space, to maximize the use and value of the collections to meet the corporate objectives of the City Council and for the inspiration of our actual and virtual visitors.

Notes

1 C. Hartwell, *Manchester: Pevsner Architecture Guides*, London: Penguin, 2001, pp. 89–91, 165.
2 J. Summerson, *Architecture in Britain 1530–1830*, London: Penguin, 1969, pp. 305–6.
3 J. H. G. Archer (ed.), *Art & Architecture in Victorian Manchester*, Manchester: Manchester University Press, 1985, pp. 28–45.
4 T. Clifford, *A Century of Collecting 1882–1982, Manchester City Art Galleries*, Manchester: City of Manchester Cultural Services, 1983, pp. 11–14.
5 Ibid.
6 Arts About Manchester, 'Manchester City Art Galleries Market Study, February 1998', unpublished research, Arts About Manchester for Manchester City Art Galleries, 1998.
7 Ibid., p. 7.
8 T. Grajewski and S. Psarra, 'Manchester City Art Gallery: a study of the existing layout and of proposed building extension', unpublished research, Welsh School of Architecture, University of Cardiff for Manchester City Art Galleries, 1999.
9 M. Ekarv, 'Combating redundancy: writing texts for exhibitions', in E. Hooper-Greenhill, *The Educational Role of the Museum*, London: Routledge, 1994, pp. 140–3.
10 Manchester City Council, 'Manchester City Art Gallery: Proposal Document to the Heritage Lottery Fund', Vol. 2, unpublished, 1996.
11 Morris Hargreaves McIntyre, 'A successful start: findings of visitor research at Manchester Art Gallery, December 2002–January 2003', unpublished research, Morris Hargreaves McIntyre for Manchester City Galleries, 2003.
12 H. Rees Leahy, 'Research learning at Manchester Art Gallery', unpublished research, Centre for Museology, University of Manchester for Manchester City Galleries, 2003.
13 M. Davis, 'Greater Manchester', *Museum Practice*, 21, Vol. 7, No. 3, 2002: 18.

References

Archer, J. H. G. (ed.), *Art & Architecture in Victorian Manchester*, Manchester: Manchester University Press, 1985, pp. 28–45.

Arts About Manchester, 'Manchester City Art Galleries Market Study, February 1998', unpublished research, Arts About Manchester for Manchester City Art Galleries, 1998.

Clifford, T., *A Century of Collecting 1882–1982, Manchester City Art Galleries*, Manchester: City of Manchester Cultural Services, 1983, pp. 11–14.

Davis, M., 'Greater Manchester', *Museum Practice*, 21, Vol. 7, No. 3, 2002: 18–23.

Ekarv, M., 'Combating redundancy: writing texts for exhibitions', in E. Hooper-Greenhill, *The Educational Role of the Museum*, London: Routledge, 1994, pp. 140–3.

Grajewski, T. and Psarra, S., 'Manchester City Art Gallery: a study of the existing layout and of proposed building extension', unpublished research, Welsh School of Architecture, University of Cardiff for Manchester City Art Galleries, 1999.

Hartwell, C., *Manchester: Pevsner Architecture Guides*, London: Penguin, 2001, pp. 89–91, 165.

Manchester City Council, 'Manchester City Art Gallery: Proposal Document to the Heritage Lottery Fund', Vol. 2, unpublished, 1996.

Morris Hargreaves McIntyre, 'A successful start: findings of visitor research at Manchester Art Gallery, December 2002–January 2003', unpublished research, Morris Hargreaves McIntyre for Manchester City Galleries, 2003.

Rees Leahy, H., 'Research learning at Manchester Art Gallery', unpublished research, Centre for Museology, University of Manchester for Manchester City Galleries, 2003.

Summerson, J., *Architecture in Britain 1530–1830*, London: Penguin, 1969, pp. 305–6.

6

Spatial culture, way-finding and the educational message

The impact of layout on the spatial, social and educational experiences of visitors to museums and galleries

Sophia Psarra

The success of museums and galleries is measured by the numbers of visitors they attract. This depends on the collections as much as on the quality of the building itself. But while the iconic role of architecture in attracting a large audience is effectively understood, there is little acknowledgement of the impact of the layout on the character of the visit. This chapter addresses the ways in which the spatial characteristics affect the patterns of movement and the transmission of the educational message. It presents four museum studies undertaken as part of research and consultancy work. Using computer modelling techniques and detailed observation surveys of visitors' flows these studies analyse and predict the use patterns of existing spaces and new development plans. The aim is to provide design solutions that can assist museum managers and designers in improving the spatial, social and economic sustainability of museums and galleries.

Introduction

The power of space to influence the visitors' experience in museums and galleries is the main focus of this chapter. Its purpose is to draw attention to the relationship between the architecture and the ways in which visitors circulate, locate the collections and grasp the exhibition content. Apart from the strength of individual displays in influencing the pattern of the visit, spatial organization has a strong role to play. Using computer-generated analysis of the layout and observations of the patterns of movement and use this chapter traces the impact of architecture on two contemporary and two historical museums in Britain: the Art Gallery and Museum, Kelvingrove (Glasgow), the Natural History Museum (London), the Burrell Museum (Glasgow) and the Museum of Scotland (Edinburgh).

The main objective of these studies was to help to improve the functioning of these buildings in terms of legibility of the layout and the distribution of visitors through their spaces.[1] The outcome was design guidelines to enable museum managers, curators, architects and exhibition designers to meet criteria for performance. However, the analysis of different museum cultures, the use patterns of their audiences and the interaction with those involved in their management has enabled a study of these buildings that takes into account the educational message and the cultural values that are accommodated and projected into their architecture and their spaces.

Museums have repeatedly redefined their image. They have expanded their audiences, and have helped to unlock the memories of people and to redefine and frame the identity of cities and places. Their iconic, cultural and political strength has continuously attracted critical attention and scholarship. However, the contribution of architectural space in shaping the viewers' experience and legitimizing cultural perspectives through its logic of spatial connections has remained largely invisible. Strengthening the contribution of space to the museum debate is the second objective of this chapter: how does the spatial configuration of the four buildings relate to changing ideologies about knowledge, the shaping of cultural identities and the shifting frameworks in their social and cultural significance?

The two lines of inquiry are examined separately, starting from the ways in which the buildings perform, guide and direct the visitors through their spaces. The discussion then moves to the spatial characteristics and their capacity to accommodate theories of knowledge, culture and identity.

The four museums: from knowledge to identities

The four buildings fall into two main categories, one contemporary and one historic. The Museum of Scotland and the Burrell Museum, built at the end of the twentieth century, have not yet needed to respond to changing demands over time. In contrast, dating from the turn of the nineteenth century, the Natural History Museum and the Kelvingrove Museum have long since experienced the tension between a monumental historical fabric, the expansion of the collections and changes in curatorial and social perspectives.

The Museum of Scotland has its origin in the Williams report and its proposal for a building to rehouse the old Museum of Antiquities and present the history of the land and its people. The Burrell, on the other hand, houses the diverse art collection of William Burrell, a wealthy Glasgow ship-owner. The former is situated in a historical area in Edinburgh. In contrast, the latter is located close to dense woodland in Pollock Park, making the natural setting an integral part of the display. The Museum of Scotland consists of a set of volumes separated from each other through top-lit voids and shafts crossed by balconies and bridges. The inner volume contains the core galleries and is crowned by a roof terrace offering views to the city and its monuments. The collection is organized chronologically from the prehistoric period in the basement, to the twentieth century on the top level. The Burrell Museum was designed as a perimeter route, starting along a glazed boundary at the north of the layout.[2] The display moves from ancient Egypt at the northwest side, to Oriental and Medieval European art at the central north section of the building. Islamic art and stained glass are at the eastern end of the layout, while a collection of paintings is located at the mezzanine level. The museum contains reproductions of three rooms from Burrell's residence, Hutton Castle near Berwick-on-Tweed, recalling the context from which the collection originated. These are located around a sky-lit courtyard that receives the visitors soon after they enter the building.

The two buildings and their collections have little in common. However, they both bring diverse displays under a single roof and give them a concrete physical presence. Within the museums' walls Burrell the man, his generosity, taste and wealth on the one hand, and the artefacts encompassing the memories of the people of Scotland on the other, acquire an identity mediated through architectural space and architectural expression.

By comparison with the two contemporary buildings, the Natural History Museum and the Kelvingrove are examples of late Victorian architecture and two of the most visited museums in Britain. They are associated with Alfred Waterhouse, who produced the final design for the former, and was involved in the selection of a winning scheme for the latter. In spite of being historic contemporaries, the museums were examples of different approaches to collecting and displaying. The Natural History Museum housed an encyclopaedic collection of natural history after its removal from the British Museum. In contrast, the Kelvingrove has a wider content from natural history to archaeology, and from science and technology to fine and decorative arts. The former was shaped by the vision of Sir Richard Owen, its superintendent, for a taxonomic museum that would contain the imperial collection and show the diversity of nature. The Kelvingrove was part of an educational schema in Victorian Scotland that saw the study of nature as connected to other areas of knowledge.

Although different from each other, the two museums used the architecture to organize their content. Waterhouse's building retained most of the characteristics of Owen's schematic plan, including a distinction between living and extinct species along the west and east sides of the building, and a central space that would function as an index for the collection. Similarly to Waterhouse's Museum, the Kelvingrove used the symmetry between the east and west wings to distinguish natural history from technology and archaeology on the ground floor. The fine arts were placed on the first floor with the exception of sculpture and music events, which occupied the entrance hall.

Victorian museums produced knowledge, but also formed spectacles in their own right. Scientists and experts were already debating whether museums should be accessible to a large public, or to a small audience.[3] In spite of these debates, the production and exhibition of knowledge was their main objective. Today museums have a different role, which in the case of the two contemporary buildings extends from the organization of knowledge to the expression of identity, and from the principles of classification to those of interpretation. The themes of classification on the one hand, and personal or national identity on the other, mark the transformation of museums from universally accepted facts to socially constructed themes and contents, from displaying certainties to shaping individual meanings and contexts, from science to narrative, and finally from social reform and cultural improvement to the complexity of the visitor's experience.[4] Parallel to these changes there has been an astonishing growth of museums and heritage industry, supported by new technologies, and diverse ways of defining and communicating a cultural message.[5] The trajectory of museum architecture in this transformation has moved from public monument to spatial experience, from scientific centre to popular destination and landmark, and from forming a social event to shaping national and cultural aspirations. The two groups of museums we are looking at here demonstrate these shifts and serve as examples to explore how spatial configuration relates to these transformations.

Structuring the spatial experience

Route structure and axiality

In terms of operational requirements museum design has two fundamental problems to solve: a route structure that facilitates the encounter between the displays and visitors, and spatial mechanisms that aid orientation and enable the building and the exhibitions to be seen as one whole. In terms of their expressive and cultural potential, museums have to combine the value invested in objects with the value invested in architecture through an imaginative approach that uses the one to strengthen the other. It is essential to discuss how the four buildings respond to these requirements before presenting the results of the spatial analysis. We can then compare the architectural intentions and the ways they actually work with the structure of spaces and the actual routes of their users.

With the exception of the Natural History Museum all the buildings have a large circulation loop that covers the periphery of the layout. In the Museum of Scotland this route is structured horizontally as well as vertically, culminating in the roof terrace. The perimeter route might favour seeing the displays in sequence. However, this is not the only way to move in these buildings, as smaller circulation circuits intersect with the peripheral path. The Natural History Museum moves in the opposite direction. Its plan, with galleries arrayed like the spine and teeth of a comb, does not enable linear procession or alternative pathways. It requires retracing one's steps to move to the next gallery space, channelling movement through its Main Hall and corridor spaces.

With regard to axiality, the two contemporary museums and the original plans of the historic buildings are traversed by long axes that stretch from side to side, establishing large-scale connections. Axiality in the Kelvingrove and the Natural History Museum was a device useful in aiding orientation and a characteristic of an architectural language that was once based on shared values of order. In the Museum of Scotland and the Burrell Museum the axes are punctuated by balconies, bridges and stairs, openings and slits, top-lit shafts and architectural historical fragments that are inserted in their physical fabric. The intention is to make the layout legible as well as to provide an architectural experience that is diverse, memorable and well structured. Axiality in this case is not seen as a universal ordering principle, but as one that defines the architect's idiom and structures the visitor's perception.

In relation to changes in the historic buildings, the Natural History Museum has grown into a large complex that has affected the original symmetry of the building. The Kelvingrove has undergone no transformation in size and has remained largely symmetrical along two principal axes. Changes in the exhibition design in both buildings have created complex arrangements inside gallery rooms that have affected the overall symmetry of the axial structure. The length of some vistas that previously stretched from side to side has been reduced, consequently decreasing the number of intersections among axes. The impact of axiality and route structure on the spatial configuration of the four buildings will be addressed in the section that follows.

Integration and accessibility

To find out how the buildings perform and what influences their performance we carried out a computer analysis using 'space syntax', a theory and method that studies spatial characteristics and relates them to the patterns of movement, use and cultural meaning originally developed by Hillier *et al.* at UCL.[6] The fundamental consideration is that layouts have 'natural use patterns' and, 'other things being equal', the ways people move inside them is an outcome of the logic of spatial connections.[7] Extensive application of this method indicates that good levels of spatial accessibility maintain good levels of movement and interaction among different types of users.

A representation of the layout is produced first, capturing the linear extension of spaces through axes of sight and movement (axial lines), and local properties of space in two dimensions as in the case of gallery rooms (convex spaces). The measure of 'integration' is calculated next, accounting for how far each element is from all other elements in the building. Integrated elements are close to other spaces and are easily accessible from every part of the layout. In contrast, segregated elements are distanced from everywhere else and become accessible through complex routes. Previous studies have shown that integrated areas attract movement, while segregated ones are poorly used. Integration thus captures the extent to which galleries and displays are accessible and the likely use rates in the various parts of a building.

The most integrated elements in all museums are the atrium/main hall and the axes that link this space with the main entrance and galleries (see Figure 6.1). The spatial structure implements the architectural intention in terms of providing an orientation space that receives visitors, guides their exploration and

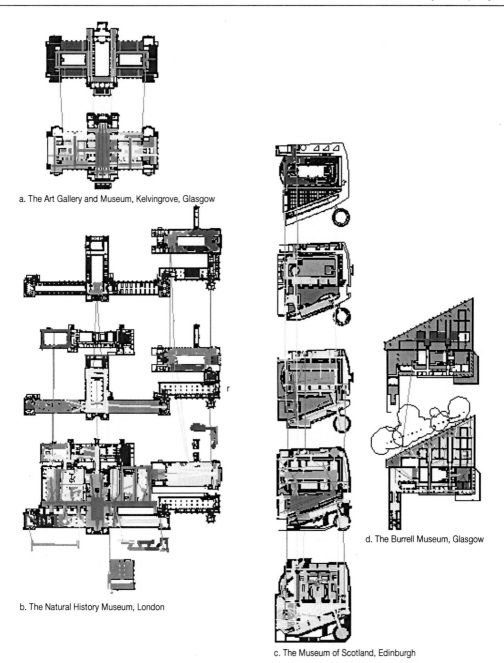

a. The Art Gallery and Museum, Kelvingrove, Glasgow

b. The Natural History Museum, London

c. The Museum of Scotland, Edinburgh

d. The Burrell Museum, Glasgow

Figure 6.1 Levels of integration at (a) the Art Gallery and Museum, Kelvingrove, Glasgow, (b) the Natural History Museum, London, (c) the Museum of Scotland, Edinburgh, and (d) the Burrell Museum, Glasgow. Light tones show high levels of integration. Dark tones show progressive segregation.

83

organizes large-scale movement. The long axial lines penetrating the atria and linking with the galleries are responsible for these properties. However, the top floors in all buildings are generally segregated. The structure of routes appears clear on the ground floor, but navigation becomes increasingly complex on the upper levels.

This characteristic is accentuated in the Museum of Scotland where the central spaces on the basement, the top floors, the mezzanine levels and the peripheral staircases show progressive degrees of segregation (Figure 6.1c). The stairs and lifts in the atrium are well integrated, delivering movement higher in the building, but the spatial structure is difficult to negotiate as visitors begin their exploration at the top floors, especially from the south and west sides of the layout. In the Burrell Museum segregation affects mainly the mezzanine level (Figure 6.1d). The galleries on the ground floor are segregated also but are located close to axes that are well integrated, reducing the impact of segregation. In the Kelvingrove clusters of segregated spaces are situated inside gallery rooms, affecting access to the two staircases at the end of the east and west courts and to the first floor (Figure 6.1a). The Natural History Museum suffers from a poor integration between the Life and Earth Galleries. The most popular exhibitions like 'Dinosaurs', 'Human Biology' and 'Blue Whale', are easy to find, as integrated axes reach their entrances (Figure 6.1b). However, their interior is segregated, working as a separate sub-complex without reference to the structure of circulation and the rest of the building.

The Museum of Scotland is a unique case in the sample in terms of rich visual links that create horizontal and vertical connections across atria and voids. When these links are included in the analysis the top levels become more integrated. Integration concentrates in the atrium and the lofty gallery space at the centre of the main galleries, creating a visually unified core at the heart of the building. The difference between strong visual integration and spatial segregation might create confusion. Seeing spaces across levels the visitors are prompted to continue their journey. However, the deeper they progress in the layout the more difficult it becomes to reach the global distributors of movement.

Why are some areas segregated, and what explains the differences in the four buildings? In the Museum of Scotland the shafts between the core galleries and the peripheral spaces prevent some axes from reaching the extremities of the layout and connecting with the staircases located at these positions (Figure 6.1c). In the Burrell Museum the Hutton rooms, the lecture theatre and the temporary exhibition form a divide affecting the axial connections of the north galleries with the south part of the layout (Figure 6.1d). In the Kelvingrove tall cabinets and objects block the axes running along the length of the plan, subdivide rooms into smaller areas and hide the staircases at the east and west courts (Figure 6.1a). Finally, in the Natural History Museum the axes linking the galleries with the circulation system rarely extend throughout a space or connect two or more rooms (Figure 6.1b). The same characteristic is responsible for the poor connection between the Life and Earth Galleries, as the global structure of each section does not penetrate inside the other. In addition to axial fragmentation, the exhibitions are designed as 'containers' separated from other architectural qualities of the building, including natural light and the material and decorative treatment of the original surfaces. In the Kelvingrove the axes were broken not to create separate exhibition containers, but to reduce the effect of symmetry in the building and enable orientation. However, they have the opposite effect, severing access to the top level.

In the contemporary buildings segregation results from an architectural device based on layered stratification that mediates the relationship between different parts of the layout. In the other two museums it is the outcome of the exhibition design. In the former architecture establishes a sense of transition and discovery from one area to the other. In the historical buildings it forms a background to a complex exhibition arrangement inside gallery spaces. In the Burrell Museum and the Museum of Scotland architecture establishes its expressive potential and authority as the cultural agent that stands between the viewer and the displays. From the Index Museum to the contemporary buildings it shifts from 'knowing' to 'showing' and 'telling', and from a container of knowledge to an active participant in the viewer's experience.

How visitors experience the museums

Circuits and sequences: three styles of moving and viewing

Studying the viewer's experience we mapped the visitors' routes, counted movement flows across thresholds, and recorded activities in spaces and exhibition rooms. In the Museum of Scotland we conducted a different study, looking at how a moving observer sees the building based on serial vision. The computer analysis and the observation techniques enabled a picture of the total pattern of aggregate movement. The study of visual experience in the Museum of Scotland, on the other hand, showed how spaces are sequentially perceived along a path and through time.

On entering the Burrell Museum people have a choice to continue to the north galleries, or turn right and walk along the south part of the building (Figure 6.2c). However, the majority of visitors observed (65 per cent) are drawn to the north boundary by the top-lit court and the castle portal, an architectural fragment incorporated on the sandstone wall at the end of the axis of entry. Before accessing the courtyard the first Hutton room on the south side attracts their attention. Reaching the first gallery they stop to look at another Hutton room before they continue their exploration.

As there is no strict viewing sequence, people disperse inside the galleries, browsing the collections through circuits of movement. However, the majority leave the museum from the southeast boundary (60 per cent). The small circulation loops intersecting the large circuit of movement and the two other circuits created by the lateral axes take them deeper into the layout, and bring them back again in a clockwise fashion. The design establishes the priority of the courtyard and the Hutton rooms over the rest of the building. It allows a relaxed exploration during the middle stages of the visit, but the starting and finishing point are predetermined by the large sequence.

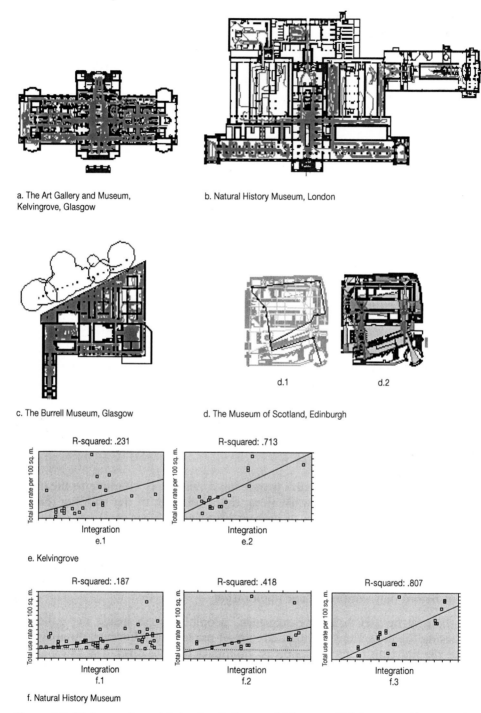

a. The Art Gallery and Museum, Kelvingrove, Glasgow

b. Natural History Museum, London

c. The Burrell Museum, Glasgow

d. The Museum of Scotland, Edinburgh

d.1   d.2

R-squared: .231

Total use rate per 100 sq. m.

Integration
e.1

R-squared: .713

Total use rate per 100 sq. m.

Integration
e.2

e. Kelvingrove

R-squared: .187

Total use rate per 100 sq. m.

Integration
f.1

R-squared: .418

Total use rate per 100 sq. m.

Integration
f.2

R-squared: .807

Total use rate per 100 sq. m.

Integration
f.3

f. Natural History Museum

Figure 6.2 Visitor paths at (a) the Art Gallery and Museum, Kelvingrove, Glasgow, (b) the Natural History Museum, London, (c) the Burrell Museum, Glasgow, and (d) the Museum of Scotland, Edinburgh.

In the Kelvingrove, people move freely, using the rings of circulation instead of following a prescribed path (Figure 6.2a). There is a tendency to move towards the east and west courts and the temporary exhibition, but the other four galleries flanking the main hall attract a share of the flow, which they also distribute to their adjoining spaces. In contrast, on entering the Natural History Museum the visitors immediately target destinations like the 'Dinosaurs', 'Ecology' and 'Creepy Crawlies', which attract 75 per cent of the total number of people (Figure 6.2b).

Recording visual experience in the Museum of Scotland we drew visual fields[8] along a peripheral route defined by the intersections of the longest axes,[9] as these expose maximum information along two or more directions (Figure 6.2d.1). All visual fields produced in this way link with the atrium (Figure 6.2d.2). On the contrary, those drawn from the rest of the exhibition rooms are strictly limited to gallery spaces. Superimposing all visual fields to derive the sum of a person's experience, we notice that the entire ground floor can be seen through a peripheral path, with the atrium as a constant point of orientation. It is also possible to perceive the layers surrounding the central gallery volume and grasp the volumetric articulation.[10]

Three kinds of experience are structured inside the four buildings: at the large scale the Natural History Museum has retained the comb-like structure that sends people to predetermined locations. At the small scale it creates rigid sequences inside gallery spaces. The Kelvingrove creates a relaxed and informal experience based on many rings of circulation. The Burrell Museum combines free browsing in the gallery rooms deviating from and returning to a large viewing route. In the Museum of Scotland the circulation loops connect the central gallery spaces with those at the periphery of the layout. However, it is possible to skip these galleries and move along a peripheral route that rises to the roof terrace. As the study of visual fields showed, this path reveals the three-dimensional sculpturing of the building.

Is space responsible for the pattern of use?

We will now compare the movement of visitors and their occupancy rates with the spatial characteristics. The question we are trying to answer is: what is the impact of the spatial configuration on the use pattern? To answer this question we correlate the integration value of spaces with the average number of people observed in each space (Figure 6.2e.1). If in the Kelvingrove and the Burrell Museum we exclude strong attractors, such as the temporary exhibitions, the restaurant and the shop, we have a significant result. Seventy per cent of the variance in the rates of people is determined by the structure of the layout (Figure 6.2e.2).

In the Natural History Museum there is a poor correlation, showing that the spatial characteristics alone cannot determine how people use the layout (Figure 6.2f.1). However, when spaces are grouped into broad categories of neighbouring rooms and correlated with the average integration value for each category, the correlation improves (Figure 6.2f.2). The space located above the regression line is the 'Dinosaurs' gallery, which is populated by a far greater number of visitors than its position in the spatial pattern suggests. If this space is excluded a strong correlation arises between the integration values and occupancy rates (0.80) (Figure 6.2f.3). Therefore, spatial characteristics determine the distribution of people to the broad sections of spaces branching off the areas of circulation.

These findings are consistent with the visiting pattern in the two buildings as expressed by the visitors' routes. The layout of the Kelvingrove and the Burrell Museum guides people through an informal and relaxed exploration through galleries, whereas the Natural History Museum guides them in their navigation through the major circulation areas as they target popular exhibitions.

Today's museums and galleries put an increasing emphasis on constructing experiences and diverse interpretations. The results of our study suggest that acknowledging the power of space is essential in enabling them to meet their spatial, social and aesthetic objectives. Having examined the operational role of the layout in terms of the ways people circulate and occupy these buildings, we now move to how architecture relates to the exhibition arrangement and the educational message.

Structuring the educational experience

Nature as creation and as resource

A computer analysis of the historic buildings in their original state without the displays shows that they were more integrated than in their current arrangement. It also shows that different gallery rooms had similar integration values. Based on the principles of classification, these spaces were like square units in a chequerboard pattern, simple and equally accessible for the purposes of taxonomic scholarship and comparison. Studying the impact of theories of knowledge on the Natural History Museum, Peponis and Hedin suggested that the design of exhibitions like 'Human Biology' moved away from simple arrangements, such as that of the former 'Birds' Gallery', to accommodate exhibition approaches depending on intricate patterns of space.[11]

However, it is important at this stage to clarify a strong difference between the layout of the Natural History Museum and that of the Kelvingrove. The comb-like structure in the former is strongly contrasted to the circuits of movement in the latter.[12] The differences between the two buildings can be explained by differences in the approach to the study of nature in Victorian England and Scotland. In the former natural history was separated from the man-made world. In the latter it had a pragmatic dimension. Scotland saw nature as a resource associated with science and technology. Seeking to preserve national identity it promoted education and cultural activities for the practical ends of industry and trade. The Museum of Science and Art in Edinburgh grew out of these principles, combining natural history, industrial and decorative arts for the edification of the middle classes and the promotion of commerce.[13] The diverse collection of the Kelvingrove and its hybrid programme as art gallery and museum shows that it was part of a similar scheme. The architecture of the building came to the support of fluid categories of knowledge through its interconnected spaces, which encouraged multiple ways of seeing and enabled associations among different rooms. In contrast to Owen's static vision of nature as Divine creation, the Kelvingrove was secular, pragmatic and dynamic. The Natural History Museum was considered obsolete, by a scientific audience at the time it was completed,[14] and by its curators at later stages who altered its spatial logic to suit their intentions. The Kelvingrove, built along a fluid conception of knowledge, remained informal and relaxed until recently,[15] the outcome of the cultural ideology of a nation with international links based on industry, culture and trade.

The strong differentiation in terms of the distribution of integration introduced by the contemporary exhibition design in the Natural History Museum, or by spatial layers in the contemporary buildings, goes hand in hand with the transformation in museums from knowledge to interpretation. Roberts writes that 'the view that knowledge is objective and verifiable has been widely challenged by the notion that knowledge is socially constructed and shaped by individuals' particular interests and values'. So a shift has occurred from scientific thought to social thought based on the creation of narratives. Narratives are not acceptable for their ability to structure verifiable truths or facts, but one version of the truth, 'forming vehicles for ideas and experiences'.[16]

However, the two historical buildings show that knowledge was not a fixed and verifiable body in Victorian times either, but 'guided by human action and locally suited practices'.[17] So, although it is legitimate to accept that a shift from knowledge to narrative has occurred, it is important to establish that, while engaging with knowledge and scientific paradigms, Victorian museums were also preoccupied with the construction of cultural meaning. Their difference from contemporary museums is that they were not shaped by today's advanced social and cultural self-consciousness and did not overlay a layer of discourse or a narrative on their contents.

Nature as art – history as progress

Like other forms of cultural expression narratives are characterized by movement from a beginning to a finishing point, enacting a relation to space and time.[18] Narrative can be strongly or weakly structured. When strongly structured, it has orientation based on sequence and causality, establishing a hierarchy among its elements in terms of their position in the expression. A weak narrative structure uses interconnections to enable its narrative units to equally structure its meaning. The narrative message becomes, thus, 'integrated', including new latent messages arising from a number of connections. In the first case narrative favours temporal progression over space, and is grasped through time. In the second case it emphasizes relations that defy time, collapsing into an integrating frame of space.

The viewing sequence in the 'Ecology' exhibition in the Natural History Museum, for example, implies a narrative based on temporal progression. While in the past the Index Hall stood between the visitor and the displays as short-hand for the entire collection, today the 'Rain Forest' stands between the hall and the ecological message. The need to preserve the natural environment is communicated through nature interposed between humans and their inter-pretations. Holding the first position in the sequence it defines the general orien-tation of the sequence, and its distinction from the rest of the spaces in the exhibition. The viewing circuits in the Kelvingrove Museum, on the other hand, connect contents from different areas of knowledge, creating a message based on spatial integration. Finally, using both a perimeter route and circuits of move-ment the Burrell Museum and the Museum of Scotland are based on both temporal progression and spatial integration.

Narrative as temporal progression
Starting from the perimeter route in the Burrell Museum, we saw that the Hutton rooms and the courtyard are accessed first, and the south sequence of spaces last, bringing visitors back to the departure point and staging the visit. In this way, Burrell the man mediates the relationship between entering and leaving, the viewer and the displays. The message the building conveys is that it is the donor who enabled this journey through art to become possible. As Thomas Marcus has written, the museum becomes a modern reproduction of Burrell's house and celebrates him as a person.[19]

But it is not only the three rooms that carry this message. Starting from the northwest side of the museum the viewing sequence links displays of diverse contexts and unifies them visually through a long vista punctuated by columns and objects. Arranged next to the trees on the north side of the park this route was conceived as a 'walk in the woods'. The pleasures of nature are, in this way, overlaid on the enjoyment of culture. At the same time the viewer is surrounded by echoes of castles, from the Hutton rooms and the curved stones embedded into the walls, to the tapestry exhibition at the centre of the layout arranged like a Medieval hall with armour and weapons. The architecture and the exhibition design call attention to moving and viewing as ordering experience and balance associations of order over the wilderness of nature. The perimeter sequence gives Burrell and his collection a context through move-ment and the complementary signs of woodland and stone, forest and castle, and culture and nature.

In the Museum of Scotland the peripheral spaces expose the central gallery volume, surrounded by layers as one moves gradually along the perimeter. Visitors do not begin their itinerary from that area, but they are drawn to it intrigued by the top-lit shafts, and the bridges and balconies hovering over the narrow voids. Architecturally and visually revealing but spatially segregated the perimeter sequence communicates the idea of history as a multi-layered inte-rior. Peeling the layers of history requires one to make an effort and negotiate the building through physical movement.

Starting from prehistory and geological beginnings in the basement, the exhibition progresses to the upper levels in chronological order. On the ground floor it begins from the Renaissance and the Old Kingdom of Scotland at the central galleries, and is followed by the role of the Church and the Reformation in the periphery. The distribution of the exhibitions on the other floors is based on the same principle. It advances from the lofty space at the centre of the core galleries to the twentieth century at the top floor and to the roof terrace, which offers panoramic views to the city and other monuments. So, the spatial sequence implies chronological sequence; history becomes a progression routed into the past and marching forwards into the future. At the same time, the architecture makes allusions to Scotland's medieval traditions. The circular tower at the northwest corner echoes the form of Edinburgh Castle's half-moon battery, and the main core galleries the tower or keep. The walls that define the gallery spaces on the ground floor are visibly thick, while the central gallery is like a castle hall, expressed by the oak carvings and a painted ceiling.[20] The castle metaphor gives the building the patina of time. Contemporary achievement, which forms a part of the new museum, needs historical depth to stabilize its identity. From the 'labyrinth' of the streets to the 'labyrinth' of the exhibitions, and from the 'labyrinths' of time to the privilege of the panorama over the city, Scotland celebrates its past to strengthen its present and future.

Narrative as spatial integration

Coming to the choice of movement offered to visitors, the multiple spatial links in the contemporary buildings bring objects from different sections and areas of knowledge together. Although artistic or historical periods are in different locations, it is not their separate historical or artistic circumstances that are privileged, but the interaction of their contents as though they are compatible and continuous. In this way, the spatial structure establishes a thematic coherence. In the Burrell Museum, where the exhibition context clearly lacks thematic consistency, vistas and rings of circulation add relations to the objects that 'are both intentional and a surprise'.[21] For the architects this reinforces the idea of the museum being a home for a private collection as well as an exhibition.

In the Museum of Scotland the spatial integration of contents and their thematic coherence implies the message of history as a flow between periods, events and achievements, but takes different manifestations in different gallery sections. On the ground floor, it is marked by relations between the Renaissance and the Reformation. On the levels above it is shaped by domestic, social, scientific and engineering displays, characteristics of later centuries. The fluid network of movement is reinforced by strong visual links connecting a cascade of terraces overlooking the lofty space that carries the roof terrace and is illuminated by clerestory windows. An eighteenth-century stone building of a beam engine, steam boilers, railway engines and a catwalk made of steel are spatially unified and thematically integrated, expressing Scotland's industrial tradition.

The spatial sequence from the bottom to the top of the building on the one hand, and the permeability and inter-visibility creating links across different periods on the other, articulate two different views of history: a diachronic view based on chronological progression and a synchronic view that cuts a cross section through its ages to reveal the core of the matter – from the old kingdom to the Enlightenment, and from the historical depths of the castle to the freedom of the machine. Rising to the roof terrace the identity of Scotland is fortified by its past and carried forward by its historical commitment to technology and progress.

Knowledge, narrative and the future of museum architecture

The route sequence and the circuits of movement in the two contemporary museums create the illusion of a continuous thread and a unified message. It is generally accepted that knowledge is a social construction, but we should not confuse it with the message it is made to represent. Knowledge is obtained through facts that are constantly rearranged and reinterpreted. Certain material is explained while some remains unclear, leading to discontinuities and inconsistencies. Scientific thought as based on paradigms aims at establishing verifiable descriptions of the world. Social thought as based on narratives deals not with truths, but with the creation of story and meaning.

The history of Scotland is neither coherent nor complete; nor is the Burrell collection. The two museums do not represent culture as it actually is, but substitute our infinite and incomplete knowledge with a finite image. Actively engaging with the exhibition design and content they bring architecture to the support of cultural artifice and fiction. With fictional universes we can suspend disbelief because we engage with a world that has its own ontological structure.[22] Unlike the actual universe, where no single pathway to knowledge exists, with architecture and narrative we can engage with a world that is made coherent through a set of intelligible routes and reading instructions.

Our study of the four buildings traced the role of architecture in the construction of the spatial and educational experience, and in the change of museums from knowledge to narrative. Whether narratives are legitimate diagrams of the world, or whether the public should read them critically, is a subject of a different study. It is not the content of narrative that we choose to focus on; it is the shadow that its increasing importance and appropriation in the construction of experiences may cast on architecture. It can divorce the building from its contents, as in the Natural History Museum, or make it obsolete and replace it with big sheds.

In spite of the differences from the historic examples, the two contemporary buildings are rooted to a traditional vision of architecture as were their Victorian predecessors. In contrast with contemporary demands for flexibility that reduce architecture to empty containers for the distribution of services, commodities and the consumption of experiences, these buildings bring their architectural language to the support of the museum collection, the city and culture. They are part of the same need that created and sustained the institution of the museum: to preserve authentic artefacts and show what influenced our relationship with nature and the man-made world; but, most importantly, to provide a place for the displays so that they can remain in our memory. In order to make them stay there as securely as possible we must associate them with buildings that are as interesting as the objects themselves.

The power of architecture to structure the visitors' experience and cultural meaning shaped our study. Its power to inform and influence the museum debate lies not only in study and research, but also in good architectural practice. In terms of its capacity to shape our collective memory, architecture has a more difficult task to fulfil: to give objects a context that is so well structured and so remarkable that we cannot help but remember them.

Notes

1 These studies were commissioned by the National Museums of Scotland, the Glasgow Museums and the Natural History Museum, and conducted in collaboration with the late Dr Tadeusz Grajewski.
2 B. Gasson, *Notes on the Building*, Glasgow: Harper Collins Publisher in association with Glagow Museums, 2001, pp. 15–18.
3 C. Yanni, *Nature's Museums*, London: The Athlone Press, 1999, pp. 1–13, 111–46.
4 L. Roberts, *From Knowledge to Narrative*, Washington, DC: Smithsonian Institution Press, 1997, pp. 131–52.
5 S. Pearce, 'Collecting as medium and message', in E. Hooper-Greenhill (ed.), *Museum, Media, Message*, London and New York: Routledge, 1999, pp. 15–23.
6 B. Hillier and J. Hanson, *The Social Logic of Space*, Cambridge: Cambridge University Press, 1984, pp. 82–142.
7 B. Hillier, *Space is the Machine*, Cambridge: Cambridge University Press, 1996, pp. 149–81.
8 Known as 'isovists', these fields are visual polygons linking a vantage point with the edges of visible surfaces. Invented by Michael Benedict, this tool is extensively used by space syntax research in the analysis of buildings and urban layouts.
9 M. Benedict, 'To take hold of space: isovists and isovist fields', *Environment and Planning b*, 6, 1979: 47–65.
10 S. Psarra and T. Grajewski, 'Architecture, narrative and promenade in Benson and Forsyth's Museum of Scotland', *Architectural Research Quarterly*, 4 (2), 2000: 122–36.
11 J. Peponis and J. Hedin, 'The layout of theories in the Natural History Museum', *9H*, 3, 1982: 21–5.
12 S. Psarra and T. Grajewski, 'Track record', *Museum Practice*, 7 (19), 2002: 36–42.
13 Yanni, *Nature's Museums*, pp. 91–110.
14 Ibid.
15 The Museum is currently undergoing a major restructuring funded by the Millennium Commission. The study undertaken by the author and Dr T. Grajewski provided guidelines that were incorporated into the new master plan.
16 L. Roberts, *From Knowledge to Narrative*, p. 117.
17 Yanni, *Nature's Museums*, pp. 1–13.
18 P. Cobley, *Narrative*, London and New York: Routledge, 2001, pp. 7–21.
19 T. Marcus, *Buildings and Power*, London and New York: Routledge, 1993, pp. 211–12.
20 D. MacMillan, 'Museum of Scotland', in Benson+Forsyth in association with August Media (eds), *Museum of Scotland*, London: August Media in association with Benson+Forsyth, 1999, pp. 110–19.
21 Gasson, *Notes on the Building*, pp. 15–18.
22 U. Eco, *Six Walks in the Fictional Woods*, Cambridge, MA: Harvard University Press, 1995, pp. 97–116.

References

Benedict, M., 'To take hold of space: isovists and isovist fields', *Environment and Planning b*, 6, 1979: 47–65.

Cobley, P., *Narrative*, London and New York: Routledge, 2001, pp. 7–21.

Eco, U., *Six Walks in the Fictional Woods*, Cambridge, MA: Harvard University Press, 1995, pp. 97–116.

Gasson, B., *Notes on the Building*, Glasgow: HarperCollins Publisher in association with Glagow Museums, 2001, pp. 15–18.

Hillier, B., *Space is the Machine*, Cambridge: Cambridge University Press, 1996, pp. 149–81.

—— and Hanson, J., *The Social Logic of Space*, Cambridge: Cambridge University Press, 1984, pp. 82–142.

MacMillan, D., 'Museum of Scotland', in Benson+Forsyth in association with August Media (eds), *Museum of Scotland*, London: August Media in association with Benson+Forsyth, 1999, pp. 110–19.

Marcus, T., *Buildings and Power*, London and New York: Routledge, 1993, pp. 211–12.

Pearce, S., 'Collecting as medium and message', in E. Hooper-Greenhill (ed.), *Museum, Media, Message*, London and New York: Routledge, 1999, pp. 15–23.

Peponis, J. and Hedin, J., 'The layout of theories in the Natural History Museum', *9H*, 3, 1982: 21–5.

Psarra, S. and Grajewski, T., 'Architecture, narrative and promenade in Benson and Forsyth's Museum of Scotland', *Architectural Research Quarterly*, 4 (2), 2000: 122–36.

—— and ——, 'Track record', *Museum Practice*, 7 (19), 2002: 36–42.

Roberts, L., *From Knowledge to Narrative*, Washington, DC: Smithsonian Institution Press, 1997, pp. 131–52.

Yanni, C., *Nature's Museums*, London: The Athlone Press, 1999, pp. 1–13, 111–46.

7

The Grande Galerie de l'Evolution

An alternative cognitive experience

Fabienne Galangau-Quérat

Some ten years ago the Grande Galerie de l'Evolution (GGE) of the National Museum of Natural History opened in Paris following extensive renovation. The story of this renovation is part of a 250-year-old scientific project. Although it has been the subject of much criticism because of the museographical choices, the GGE represents a decisive advance in the thinking upon museum space. In this chapter, I will look back to the history of a building and the history of a collection, to present the choices which triggered off the renovation of a gallery that had been closed for over 25 years, in order to see to what extent the modern features of this updated space can exemplify new museological and museographical tendencies. I will try to understand whether the interpretation of what this space is offers an opportunity of casting a new outlook on understanding the living world and setting up science exhibitions.

From the Cabinet of Natural History to the Gallery of Zoology

The origin of the GGE dates back to a decision taken in 1626 by Louis XIII towards the modernization of the teaching of medicine and medical botany through the creation of a Royal Garden of herbs, together with the transformation of an existing building into a Cabinet of Drugs. In the seventeenth century, the Garden gradually lost some of its strictly medical orientation, and the Cabinet, in which the many variegated curiosities produced by nature were crammed together, was given the name of 'Cabinet of Natural History'. Between the Renaissance and the eighteenth century, the realm of sciences was confronted by major transformations. In the late seventeenth century, a new approach on taxonomy appeared, based upon ideas of objective observation and science order. During the first half of the eighteenth century, the main worry of naturalists was to describe and to classify. In the cabinets of natural history, the need for classification became increasingly important.

Buffon, one of the major French naturalists, had been in charge of the Garden since 1739 and he was to play an important part, influencing the scientific policy of the establishment and making it better known. This philosopher, whose many volumes of writing on natural history were considered as standard reference books for over a century, was particularly keen on reorganizing the Cabinet and increasing the number of new specimens.[1] The Cabinet partially escaped a harsh scientific presentation of the items as Buffon favoured an aesthetic presentation.[2] This museological choice probably met the expectations of the visitors, who were first admitted in 1750; in the eighteenth century, presenting science was not a job, but a way for an enlightened audience to discover how useful, spectacular and beautiful nature was.

The Cabinet was a small building, ill fitted to the presentation of the collections. In 1779, the architect attached to the Garden, Charles-François Viel, planned the construction of a new magnificent Cabinet, consisting of three galleries, one for each realm of nature, specially arranged in the shape of a T:

> We would like the majesty of the building to correspond to the importance of the productions it holds. . . . Deeply convinced by the idea and certain that – just like our churches must inspire reverence and awe through their structure – likewise such a monument must arouse a feeling of surprise thanks to its inner and outer architecture, in a word, it must herald the Temple of Nature of which it must be the sanctuary.[3]

This disposition, very similar to what would be done later, was influenced by the grand medieval hall where the first nineteenth-century museums had been arranged.[4] However, Buffon eventually favoured a more economical solution, having the existing building enlarged several times.[5]

It was in the days of the Revolution that the Garden became the National Museum of Natural History (MNHN). Research in natural history became an academic realm of the institution, with zoology having the lead over the other academic fields of natural history.[6] The Cabinet was then renamed the Galleries of Natural History and reorganized according to scientific – rather than aesthetic – criteria. The aim was to put together analogous specimens in accordance with the rules of classification and to reassemble as many samples as possible in order to determine the limits of a species. For the scientists of the Museum, the Galleries were above all open storage space meant to shelter the collections.

Because of the lack of storage spaces, the collections were gradually moved to new buildings. For example, the collections of mineralogy, geology and botany settled in a brand new gallery, typical of neo-classical architecture, built during the period of extensive architectural embellishments performed throughout Paris in the 1800s. This event offered the opportunity for renewed debate about the validity of presenting all the collections in the same place. Indeed, the scattering of the storage places was contrary to the presentation aimed at showing side by side the great realms of nature. It was also an opportunity for heated debate concerning how the older building could be used, and how the collections could be presented.[7] Very soon only the collections of zoology were left. But the lack of adequate housing for the ever increasing zoological collections led to a continuing conflict between the need for storage spaces and the need for research space. As the professors complained, there was a lack of space to open the crates, to study the overflowing samples and to exhibit them.

Confronted by this dramatic situation, the Museum's newly appointed architect, Jules André, resumed the studies made by the former architect Charles Rohault de Fleury. He suggested that a new Gallery of Zoology should be erected – a large oblong building inserted in front of the former galleries. However, in the end, the decision was taken to build a new museum. This decision, which could be read as a break from the past, actually conveyed the determination of the institution to modernize. The former galleries, bearing witness to past days, were to be abandoned then totally demolished in the 1960s.

The opening of the new Gallery of Zoology in 1889 was an expression of a special context: museums became one of the major symbols of national modernity (see Figure 7.1).[8] The popularization of science and the rise of the Third Republic, with its efforts at reforming the educational system, coincided with a fast increase in the number of museums – 82 museums, including presentations of natural history, were opened over the course of the nineteenth century.[9]

In the late nineteenth century, the design of the most newly erected museums were centred around a grand glass-walled hall, where a sense of space was rediscovered. Builders had access to new building materials. In place of the round central space, a reminder of the past, were substituted the naves, similar

Figure 7.1 The centre of the courtyard of the Gallery of Zoology provided a spectacular view. A group of giraffes stood in the centre alongside other big mammals. Next to them hung six whale skeletons. With permission of the National Museum of Natural History, Paris.

97

to a cathedral but showing iron and glass structures, symbols of the values of progress and the industrial societies of the time.[10] The front of the Gallery of Zoology looks very academic: both because of its ornamentation consisting in Corinthian columns and in allegorical figures of the sciences of nature, and because of its similarity with the style then favoured in railway stations. The tone was set: the premises were to form a stately temple for sciences.

The inner space of the building was centred around a nave, surrounded by side galleries on three levels:

> The key point was that all of the exhibits had to be viewed by natural light. . . . The exhibit halls had no gas lighting, to compensate for this, the planners erected a stone-faced shell, surrounding rectangular galleries cantilevered out over an enormous courtyard (55 metres long and 26 metres wide). . . . The raw material was cast iron, permitting a sculptured pattern in which (three) galleries were supported by fluted and headed columns and fringed by crenelated railings. The central court was roofed with an enormous array of windows supported by an iron framework.[11]

It exemplified the technique of cast iron, which peaked in the Eiffel Tower built at the same time. For five years, the fitting of this magnificent space was the grounds for clashes among the professors of the Museum. That same space was to play an important part in the renovation to take place over a century later.

However, let's stay in the nineteenth century for a while. Some suggested that the story and the life of living and fossil cetaceae should be exhibited in the new Gallery, while others asserted that the most precious exhibits among all the collections of the Museum should be gathered there, somewhat like the cabinets of curiosities. Finally, the exhibition became an aesthetic and scientific presentation of ungulates and skeletons of cetaceae, among which visitors could stroll.[12] On the opening day, the enthusiastic press articles praised the union of science and the sense of theatre. But the design of the Gallery held the seeds of difficulties yet to come: a lack of storerooms and the numerous specimens presented already filled up all the available space. Everything was exhibited, with no space for development: the space of the gallery was at the same time storing space and displaying space for the living world. This contradiction prevented the Gallery from playing a part in the museological revolution, starting in the 1930s with the development of dioramas.[13]

After the Second World War, budgetary constraints would not allow both the financing of research and the updating of the Gallery of Zoology and, in 1965, the Gallery closed down for security reasons. The collections were kept in the premises until the 1980s, when underground storerooms were built next to the Gallery, thus enabling the collections to be sheltered in secure and controlled conditions. But that was not sufficient to save the Gallery. A series of artists did their utmost to rescue the shipwrecked state-forsaken ark. For example, the painter Jürg Kreienbülh devoted eight years of his life to produce a stunning series of paintings celebrating the nave and the spectacular items it contained, and a popular French singer organized a *son et lumière* show in the courtyard. These public efforts supported those from scientists of the Museum who, for over 20 years, had kept fighting to save the Gallery. In fact, this long pending period turned out to be an unexpected stroke of luck as it enabled the premises to escape the dark destructive wave of modernization of the 1970s.

The Grande Galerie de l'Evolution (GGE): the discovery of the space

A museum for evolution: the idea is not recent, it had already been suggested in the eighteenth century. After a long period of uncertainty the choice of transforming the Gallery of Zoology into a Grande Galerie de l'Evolution was finally accepted by the scientific community.[14] Funds were earmarked towards the renovation within President Mitterand's programme of 'Grands Travaux de l'Etat' (The State's leading public works). No other museum had yet attempted to show the living world in such a way; so far the living world had been cut up according to the various disciplines.

In the museological recommendations for the international competition of architecture organized in 1987,[15] it was specified that the architectural quality of the building mainly depended on how the inner space was to be dealt with. Inspired by the ideas of the architect Auguste Perret in the 1930s, according to whom the quality of the lighting improved the museum, light was considered as an essential element in structuring space and creating and heightening the magic of the place. The presence of huge animals would be, as it was in the nineteenth century, a major element of stage-organization. What was really important was to make a museum in which, beyond the visual perception of items, visitors should be offered the opportunity of taking part in a new type of museal experiment, thanks to their perceiving spaces, lights and sounds. This renovation was an interesting challenge for the designers, dealing with the relationships between the inner space, the collections and the underlying scientific discourse.

The choice of the jury was nearly unanimously in favour of Paul Chemetov and Borja Huidobro, who advocated basic but strong ideas. The entrance was to be at the end of the building length-wise and lifts placed against the blank front of the building would turn it into an active inner wall. The central hall was to consist of two levels of boarding, similar to a stage. This would be adjustable and multi-purpose, although this flexibility would later be given up for security reasons. The ceiling was to be turned into an active sky through the use of pictures projected on to the occulted glass roof.[16]

Paul Chemetov is a well-known architect who has worked on major public projects, created social housing units and written a book about nineteenth-century metal architecture, which he considers as a form of experimentation towards Modern Art.[17] For the renovation, the architects refused to copy and to imitate the style, to produce false ancient design – everything which, in conservation architecture, can present too many ambiguities and may freeze the memory. The architects wanted every step of the transformation of the building, its history of change, to be recorded in the structure. The major point raised by Chemetov was the need to focus on the relationships between the older architectural elements and more recent ones, so that they could be both opposed and reconciled. 'It is not possible to renew a work in its original form, the ageing cannot be avoided, . . . it must be turned into something different, . . .

Figure 7.2 The inner space of the Grande Galerie de l'Evolution, National Museum of Natural History, Paris. With permission of the National Museum of Natural History, Paris.

we must create, graft something new, . . . take risks in creative processes.'[18] How could they transform and keep at the same time, be faithful and forgetful at the same time? They had to stage a space, a Gallery and a scientific theory, the Evolution of species. That was the task given to René Allio (1924–95), a painter, a set designer and a film director – the difficult task of staging a space that had been asleep for over 25 years.

The narrative framework

The narrative framework of the Grande Galerie de l'Evolution, developed by a team of museology specialists led by Professor Michel Van Praët, is staged in three parts that are meant to illustrate and explain the evolutionary processes. Part 1 covers 'the diversity of the natural world today' and takes place under the nave and in the nave. Praët and his colleagues wanted to awaken awareness about the unity and diversity of Life and to question visitors about the origin of such diversity. Here, land and marine ecosystems – tropical forest, savannah, coral reefs – are widely illustrated by the wealthy collections of the MNHN through a spectacular scenographic design. Part 2 is concerned with 'the evolution of living organisms'. This part aims at telling a renewed vision of the History of Life and explaining theories and mechanisms of Evolution, including the very latest discoveries, and is situated on the top level balcony. Finally, Part 3 is concerned with 'the relations between Man and the natural environment', focusing on the impact humans have had on evolution over the past 10,000 years, and is situated on the first-floor balcony.

After five years of works on the building and the contents, the Grande Galerie de l'Evolution was opened in June 1994. The open displays of sea-life form the first space of exhibition the visitors are confronted with. They are set in a space dug out under the nave and only lit by fibre-optic lights. The nave itself is an open stage with a surface area of 650 square metres structured by a central museographical element (the African caravan), which occupies one quarter of the surface, and around which are scattered three other units corresponding to three different environments (tropical forest, desert and polar). The staging of this space is based on a visual symphony meant to organize as pictures the various ecosystems. The aim is not to recreate nature but to trigger off the imagination, which can call on far more memories and more images than any diorama will ever be able to.[19] More traditional displays are lined up around the U-shaped upper balconies.

Through the narrative use of the light, the stage-designer aims at calling upon the imagination. He creates a *son et lumière* show centred on the nave and on the specimens of natural history. A new atmosphere livens up the inner space of the Gallery. Against the words of the museum attendant of the old Zoological Gallery 'This gallery is dead, I am off', we shall oppose what the stage-designer was saying: 'Not too many things, but not too much space left empty, the need to show everything, but not at the same time, to look for a dynamic space, to dissociate items on the move to items lying still.'[20]

Here, the inner space has been thoroughly reshaped thanks to the work with light. Lighting expresses numerous messages that can direct, inform, part or gather, conceal or reveal, enlarge or limit. The stage-designers organized and used the space of the Gallery, shaping the volumes through light and sound, and setting items along determined routes in order to give sense and create an evocative environment where what is to be seen is alluded to, rather than conjured up.[21] These allusive spatial organizations offer up scientific information as much as any traditional panel. Not much is written; lights, sounds, colours and distribution of specimens are the main museographic tools used by the designers to translate the characteristics of each natural ecosystem.

The space created in Part 1 is closely related to those made in art galleries, where artefacts and design are sustained by light.[22] This original and refined combination of art and science aims to offer a source of wonder, of knowledge, of reflections and questions, enabling the visitor to open up to the understanding of the world.

The space of the Grande Galerie de l'Evolution through the eyes of visitors

The experience of the visitors has always been a major concern for the institution, reflected in its choice of opening days, the facilities offered in the gardens, the guides and so on. In the nineteenth century, the Museum was a favourite place attended by all the social classes towards the same purpose: to learn, to enjoy themselves and to see the wonders of nature.[23] The collections presented held the visitors in their spell, as the painter Eugène Delacroix wrote in his diary: 'I have been filled with a feeling of happiness.'[24]

When the Gallery of Zoology opened in 1889, it was a success, even if some, as others would do a century later, regretted that popular appeal had been put before science. But during the twentieth century, as it was not possible to modernize the displays, visitors began to forsake the gallery until it finally closed in the 1960s. Since the opening in 1994, the GGE is one the most visited sites within the National Museum of Natural History, and, five years after it had opened, loyal visitors were secured. These visitors, however, consist of regular visitors of science, art and history museums and do not reflect a broad social demographic. This is far from the democratic process envisaged by the designers of the gallery. For existing audiences, if the discovery of the 'monument-Museum' triggers off the first visit, the purpose of further visits is mainly learning. The general level of satisfaction has remained more or less the same since the opening – about 95 per cent.[25]

In a very interesting article Peignoux *et al.*[26] describe the visitor experience in the GGE. Above all, they highlight that various ways of moving around have been detected.

The research showed that, in the submarine space under the nave, visitors simply reshape space by strolling along the display cases or by being guided by attractive items: they unanimously appreciate the stage-design, the choice of the samples, the light and sound effects and the feeling of being immersed in an undersea world full of mysteries.

On the level of the nave, the volumes of the architecture and the materials utilized in the renovation create a positive first impression with visitors. Visitors first marvel at the overall view and the combination of lights and sounds, before being irresistibly carried around the caravan showing animals from the savannah. The three remaining ecological systems – tropical forests of the Americas, Sahara and Arctic and Antarctic – are only perceived by visitors walking around the nave a second time. Contrary to the visit to the undersea environments, interspersed with other display spaces, the visit to the nave never takes long.

The scientific questionings generally concern the undersea environments, less familiar to the visitors, whereas the African caravan arouses responses in the visitors' memories, and is dealt with in a descriptive mode. The notion of biodiversity always occurs in what the visitors say when they have visited the whole of Part 1, but, contrary to what the designers and museologists had expected, in that study they never ask themselves questions about the origin of such a biological diversity.

On the upper balconies (Parts 2 and 3), the museological discourse is shaped by the presence of screening panels and does not sit comfortably within the U-shaped space structure. The contrast between the showy stage-design of Part 1 and the balconies' more forbidding and intimate design is often resented as disconcerting. Especially in Part 2, the space is not utilized by the museographical language and the exhibition looks more classical. This leads to a change in the behaviour of the visitors, who interpret any clue offered by the Museum design according to their own search for what evolution can be, even if it induces some misunderstanding. Visitors are four times more likely to use the interactive computers here than in the first part of the GGE, where they are secondary tools for understanding.

Finally, commenting on the overall visit, the satisfaction ratings concerning the aesthetic quality and the collections come before those concerning the scientific contents.[27]

While the memory of the gallery kept after the visit is mostly dominated by the space of the nave and the beauty of the presentation there, the detailed thematic divisions of the whole gallery do not seem to be clearly understood by the visitors. Besides words and pictures associated with classical learning experiences, the visitor experience in the GGE is also described through a large range of positive emotions.[28]

The research has led some to question the effects produced by the GGE design, although unanimously praised, which could be considered as an obstacle to the understanding of the scientific contents. But the experience of a visit is something global, resting on numerous parameters; it cannot be approached only in a unique cognitive way.[29] During a museum visit, all the senses are involved – the body, the emotions, the knowledge and the social background.[30] On the other hand, it is difficult to get a complete picture of the visitor experience because we lack the comprehensive model with which we could study it.[31]

In any case, compared with the former Gallery of Zoology, the GGE has been transformed by a renewed shaping of space, with a new use of inner space modelled by lights and sounds. This original arrangement favours a new type of polysemous visitor experience.[32] Each visit is potentially a new one, with new, unpredictable routes of understanding, new discoveries of spaces and different approaches or strategies of learning. It appears also that those who are the most satisfied with a visit in the GGE are the regular visitors, familiar to the very innovative language of this exhibition.[33] Eventually, one of the possible explanations of the regular visits could be that the specific structuring of space determines an always renewed interpretation of its magical universe.

Conclusions

Nowadays, we can outline the society as divided into two kinds of people: the scientists who hold the scientific knowledge, and the anonymous crowd who do not necessarily hold educated opinions about science.[34] One of the key challenges for museology is to explore new ways of filling that gap. The analysis of the renovation of the GGE enables us to understand more about the learning experience in science museums. The visitors are encouraged to experiment with a new way of discovering and understanding the living world, through an original structuring of space. This museal experience is based on a multi-layered cognitive experience. It means that the visit calls upon the simultaneous use of many senses. In particular, the planning of space can be considered as the fundamental element for a creative experience – at the same time architectural and cognitive. At this point, it is possible to identify some characteristic traits of creative space. Space can become creative when it expands the potential of the visitor's cognitive freedom. Here, space is no longer an apathetic element – a shapeless vehicle for the museum contents once and for all, forever forced on the visitors. On the contrary, space can be creative when it enables the visitor to get a dynamic and new understanding of the exhibits and contents, or when it becomes a part or a formal meaningful element which can integrate exhibits, giving them sense. In other words, space can be creative when there is an holistic integration between the space, exhibits and visitors, so that none of these elements can play an autonomous part without the help of the others. More clearly, in such a spatial context, the elements can no longer exist separately. In this sense, the exhibition scene as a whole is more than the sum of the elements composing it – the cognitive experience of the scene emerges as an unpredictable novelty involving semantic, emotional, sensory and symbolic dimensions.

Acknowledgements

I am grateful to M. Van Praët, J. Maigret and J. Le Marec for interesting discussions on museological issues. I am also thankful to F. Ailhaud for her revision of the manuscript.

Notes

1 J. Roger, *Buffon, un philosophe au Jardin du Roi*, Paris: Fayard, 1989, pp. 73–96.

2 Y. Laissus, 'Adieu à la galerie de Zoologie', in P. Bérenger and M. Butor (eds), *Naufragés de l'Arche*, Paris: La Différence, 1981, pp. 164–88.

3 C.-F. Viel, 'Projet d'un monument consacré à l'histoire naturelle. Dédié à Monsieur le Comte de Buffon, intendant du Jardin du Roi (1776)', in D. Bezombes (ed.), *La Grande Galerie du Museum national d'Histoire naturelle. Conserver, c'est transformer*, Paris: Le Moniteur, 1994, pp. 22–4.

4 L. Hautecoeur, *Architecture et aménagement des musées*, Paris: RMN, 1934 (2nd edn, 1993), pp. 17–27.

5 F. Bourdier, 'Origines et transformations du cabinet du Jardin Royal des Plantes', *Revue française des sciences et des techniques*, 18, 1962: 39–49.

6 E. C. Spary, 'Le scalpel et l'Etat. Le Museum de Paris', *La Recherche*, 300, 1997: 50–3.

7 C. Roux, 'Un exemple d'architecture publique muséale des années 1830. La galerie de Minéralogie et de Géologie au Jardin des plantes à Paris', unpublished master's thesis, Paris: Université Paris IV, 1991, pp. 25–37.

8 D. Poulot, *Patrimoine et musées: l'institution de la culture*, Paris: Hachette, 2001, pp. 99–104.

9 M. Van Praët and C. Fromont, 'Eléments pour une histoire des musées d'histoire naturelle en France', *Musées et recherche*, Dijon: OCIM, 1995, pp. 55–70.

10 L. Basso Peressut, *Musées. Architectures 1990–2000*, Milan, Arles: Motta, Actes Sud, 1999, pp. 9–18.

11 C. Ganz, 'The once and future Museum', *Natural History*, 7, 1989: 48–55.

12 H. Demaret, 'Systématique et muséologie: le cas de l'ancienne galerie de Zoologie du Muséum national d'Histoire naturelle', unpublished master's thesis, Paris: MNHN, 1996.

13 M. Van Praët, H. Demaret and J.-M. Drouin, 'L'esprit du lieu, un concept muséologique', in J. Eidelman and M. van Praët (eds), *La muséologie des sciences et ses publics*, Paris: PUF, 2000, pp. 15–29.

14 P. Blandin and F. Galangau-Quérat, 'Des "Relations Homme-Nature" à "L'Homme, facteur d'évolution": genèse d'un propos muséal', in J. Eidelman and M. van Praët (eds), *La muséologie des sciences et ses publics*, Paris: PUF, 2000, pp. 31–51.

15 Document for the competition: 'Galerie de l'Evolution/Concours de concepteurs, Juillet 1987/Ministère de l'Education Nationale.' These documents can be found in the Departement des galeries-MNHN/Paris.

16 D. Bezombes, *La Grande Galerie du Museum national d'Histoire naturelle. Conserver, c'est transformer*, Paris: Le Moniteur, 1994.

17 P. Chemetov and B. Marrey, *Architectures à Paris 1848–1914*, Paris: Dunod, 1980.

18 P. Chemetov, 'La mémoire et l'oubli', in D. Bezombes (ed.), *La Grande Galerie du Muséum national d'Histoire naturelle*, Paris: Le Moniteur, 1994, pp. 92–5.

19 Ibid.

20 R. Allio, *Charte scénographique*, Grande Galerie de l'Evolution, Paris: MNHN, 1991.

21 Chemetov, 'La mémoire et l'oubli', pp. 92–4.

22 L. Allégret, *Musées*, Paris: Le Moniteur, 1987, Vol. 1, pp. 4–5.

23 T. Efrat, 'L'objet naturalisé et la nature objectivée: curiosités urbaines et collections d'histoire naturelle en France (1830–1930)', unpublished doctoral thesis, Paris: EHESS, 2002, pp. 356–83.

24 P. Taquet, 'De l'évolution de ses galeries à la galerie de l'évolution, genèse d'un projet', in Mission Musées, DAGIC, MNHN (eds), *La Galerie de l'Evolution: concepts et evaluation*, Paris: MNHN, 1990, pp. 7–16.

25 J. Eidelman, F. Lafon and C. Fromont, 'Public en évolution', in J. Eidelman and M. van Praët (eds), *La muséologie des sciences et ses publics*, Paris: PUF, 2000, pp. 95–121.

26 J. Peignoux, F. Lafon and E. Vareille, 'L'expérience de visite', in J. Eidelman and M. van Praët (eds), *La muséologie des sciences et ses publics*, Paris: PUF, 2000, pp. 159–79.

27 Ibid.
28 E. Vareille and C. Fromont, 'Les mémoires de la visite', in J. Eidelman and M. van Praët (eds), *La muséologie des sciences et ses publics*, Paris: PUF, 2000, pp. 95–121.
29 D. Jacobi and J. Le Marec, 'Sur quelques figures de l'interprétation dans la culture', in P. de la Broise (ed.), *L'interprétation: objets et méthodes de recherche*, Lille: Université Charles-de-Gaulle, 2003, pp. 47–57.
30 F. Belaën, 'L'expérience de visite dans les expositions et techniques à scénographie d'immersion', unpublished doctoral thesis, Université de Bourgogne, 2002.
31 J. H. Falk and L. D. Dierking, *The Museum Experience*, Washington, DC: Whalesback Books, 1992, pp. 115–25.
32 H. S. Hein, *The Museum in Transition: A Philosophical Perspective*, Washington, DC: Smithonian Institution, 2000.
33 Eidelman *et al.*, 'Public en évolution', pp. 95–21.
34 B. Bensaude-Vincent, 'A genealogy of the increasing gap between science and the public', *Public Understanding of Science*, 10, 2001: 99–113.

References

Allégret, L., *Musées*, Paris: Le Moniteur, 1987, Vol. 1, pp. 4–5.
Allio, R., *Charte scénographique. Grande Galerie de l'Evolution*, Paris: MNHN, 1991.
Basso Peressut, L., *Musées. Architectures 1990–2000*, Milan, Arles: Motta, Actes Sud, 1999, pp. 9–18.
Belaën, F., 'L'expérience de visite dans les expositions et techniques à scénographie d'immersion', unpublished doctoral thesis, Université de Bourgogne, 2002.
Bensaude-Vincent, B., 'A genealogy of the increasing gap between science and the public', *Public Understanding of Science*, 10, 2001: 99–113.
Bezombes, D., *La Grande Galerie du Muséum national d'Histoire naturelle. Conserver, c'est transformer*, Paris: Le Moniteur, 1994.
Blandin, P. and Galangau-Quérat, F., 'Des "Relations Homme-Nature" à "L'Homme, facteur d'évolution": genèse d'un propos muséal', in J. Eidelman and M. van Praët (eds), *La muséologie des sciences et ses publics*, Paris: PUF, 2000, pp. 31–51.
Bourdier, F., 'Origines et transformations du cabinet du Jardin Royal des Plantes', *Revue française des sciences et des techniques*, 18, 1962: 39–49.
Chemetov, P., 'La mémoire et l'oubli', in D. Bezombes (ed.), *La Grande Galerie du Muséum national d'Histoire naturelle*, Paris: Le Moniteur, 1994, pp. 92–5.
—— and Marrey, B., *Architectures à Paris 1848–1914*, Paris: Dunod, 1980.
Demaret, H., 'Systématique et muséologie: le cas de l'ancienne galerie de Zoologie du Muséum national d'Histoire naturelle', unpublished master's thesis, Paris: MNHN, 1996.
Efrat, T., 'L'objet naturalisé et la nature objectivée: curiosités urbaines et collections d'histoire naturelle en France (1830–1930)', unpublished doctoral thesis, Paris: EHESS, 2002.
Eidelman, J., Lafon, F. and Fromont, C., 'Public en évolution', in J. Eidelman and M. van Praët (eds), *La muséologie des sciences et ses publics*, Paris: PUF, 2000, pp. 95–121.
Falk, J. H. and Dierking, L. D., *The Museum Experience*, Washington, DC: Whalesback Books, 1992, pp. 115–25.
Ganz, C., 'The once and future Museum', *Natural History*, 7, 1989: 48–55.
Hautecoeur, L., *Architecture et aménagement des musées*, Paris: RMN, 1934 (2nd edn, 1993), pp. 17–27.
Hein, H. S., *The Museum in Transition: A Philosophical Perspective*, Washington, DC: Smithsonian Institution, 2000.
Jacobi, D. and Le Marec, J., 'Sur quelques figures de l'interprétation dans la culture', in P. de la Broise (ed.), *L'interprétation: objets et méthodes de recherche*, Lille: Université Charles-de-Gaulle, 2003, pp. 47–57.
Laissus, Y., 'Adieu à la galerie de Zoologie', in P. Bérenger and M. Butor (eds), *Naufragés de l'Arche*, Paris: La Différence, 1981, pp. 164–88.

Peignoux, J., Lafon, F. and Vareille, E., 'L'expérience de visite', in J. Eidelman and M. van Praët (eds), *La muséologie des sciences et ses publics*, Paris: PUF, 2000, pp. 159–79.

Poulot, D., *Patrimoine et musées: l'institution de la culture*, Paris: Hachette, 2001, pp. 99–104.

Roger, J., *Buffon, un philosophe au Jardin du Roi*, Paris: Fayard, 1989.

Roux, C., 'Un exemple d'architecture publique muséale des années 1830. La galerie de Minéralogie et de Géologie au Jardin des plantes à Paris', unpublished master's thesis, Paris: Université Paris IV, 1991.

Spary, E. C., 'Le scalpel et l'Etat. Le Museum de Paris', *La Recherche*, 300, 1997: 50–3.

Taquet, P., 'De l'évolution de ses galeries à la galerie de l'évolution, genèse d'un projet', in Mission Musées, DAGIC, MNHN (eds), *La Galerie de l'Evolution: concepts et evaluation*, Paris: MNHN, 1990, pp. 7–16.

Van Praët, M., and Fromont, C., 'Eléments pour une histoire des musées d'histoire naturelle en France', *Musées et recherche*, Dijon: OCIM, 1995, pp. 55–70.

——, Demaret, H. and Drouin, J.-M., 'L'esprit du lieu, un concept muséologique', in J. Eidelman and M. van Praët (eds), *La muséologie des sciences et ses publics*, Paris: PUF, 2000, pp. 15–29.

Vareille, E. and Fromont, C., 'Les mémoires de la visite', in J. Eidelman and M. van Praët (eds), *La muséologie des sciences et ses publics*, Paris: PUF, 2000, pp. 95–121.

Viel, C.-F., 'Projet d'un monument consacré à l'histoire naturelle. Dédié à Monsieur le Comte de Buffon, intendant du Jardin du Roi (1776)', in D. Bezombes (ed.), *La Grande Galerie du Museum national d'Histoire naturelle. Conserver, c'est transformer*, Paris: Le Moniteur, 1994, pp. 22–4.

8

Producing a public for art

Gallery space in the twenty-first century

Helen Rees Leahy

There is no question that during the past ten years the landscape of museums and art galleries across Britain has dramatically expanded and diversified.[1] Many new, expanded and refurbished projects were the direct result of the intense period of Lottery-funded architectural patronage that marked the start of the millennium.[2] In effect, the nation's cultural map has been redrawn as landmark contemporary art galleries have opened in towns and cities such as Walsall, Milton Keynes, Gateshead and Dundee, which were not previously members of the gallery 'club'.[3] At the same time, the creation of new institutions in hitherto derelict sites, such as Salford Quays and Bankside, has disrupted the urban syntax in which the art gallery was traditionally located. As part of an explicit strategy that allied the development of cultural facilities with programmes of economic regeneration and social inclusion, cultural capital has been displaced from the monumental city centre and resited in disused power stations, warehouses and mills.

(Re)locating the gallery is just one way in which National Lottery funds have been spent on capital infrastructure with the aim of triggering a renewal of the relationship between the institution and its publics. For example, the creation and refurbishment of gallery space has been invariably designed to accommodate an expanded repertoire of cultural and commercial consumption, in response to public policy targets for increased access, the amelioration of social exclusion and the promotion of lifelong learning.[4] This chapter examines the ways in which the contemporary ideology of the art gallery is legitimized and concretized through its spatial form and politics of location and how, in turn, the meaning of gallery space is continuously renegotiated both through visitor use and behaviour and also institutional practice. The apparatus of physical access (ramps, automatic doors, lifts, handrails and so on) is now commonplace. Similarly, the architecture of educational access is signalled by the increasingly familiar vocabulary of 'discovery' and 'interactivity' within the gallery. But how is the institutional objective of cultural access embodied and accommodated in the new art gallery? What kinds of social relations and individual experiences are produced in these spaces, and how, if at all, do they differ from their predecessors?[5]

In order to address these questions, this chapter both focuses on the particular and also surveys the general. First, a short study of the redeveloped Manchester Art Gallery indicates how the renewal of a nineteenth-century art gallery with the aim of attracting an enlarged and differentiated public has not fully resolved the tensions between the institution's elite past and inclusive present. The Gallery now comprises an ensemble of neo-classical, palazzo-style and modernist buildings (finished in 1834, 1839 and 2002 respectively), which are linked by a steel and glass pavilion that 'acts as a junction box' connecting all three elements.[6] However, inside the Gallery, the visitor experiences these shifts in the architectural register as a series of physical and symbolic thresholds that must be crossed if he or she is to penetrate its deepest spaces. Only by crossing these thresholds to reach the furthest sections of the Gallery is its ambitious interpretative regime fully disclosed. Whereas prior to the enlargement of the Gallery, the visitor's path centred on the axis of the art historical canon, today he or she encounters a much more complex curatorial repertoire in which the priority previously afforded to chronology of art history has been displaced within the expanded architectural frame.

In the second part of the chapter, issues raised by the case of Manchester Art Gallery are discussed in a wider context of four new art galleries, each of which opened between 2000 and 2002. Both the New Art Gallery Walsall and Tate Modern in London opened in 2000; the Millennium Galleries, Sheffield, opened in 2001; and, finally, Baltic in Gateshead opened in 2002. Together with Manchester Art Gallery, these institutions instantiate the complex geography of art galleries in England today. They also represent a spectrum of display and interpretative practices within diverse physical structures, from new, purpose-built galleries in Walsall and Sheffield, to reused industrial buildings on the banks of the River Thames and Tyne in London and Gateshead respectively, as well as the expanded nineteenth-century gallery in Manchester. Five different architectural practices[7] were responsible for the five projects, but this chapter is not about the specific response of an architect to a client brief, nor is its purpose to provide detailed or technical descriptions of each of the buildings; instead, it addresses the operation of architecture as both 'representation and instrument' for the display and interpretation of works of art.[8] What kinds of experiences of art are accommodated and produced by these new spaces? How is the scopic regime of the art gallery constructed by the encounter both with the materiality of the work of art *and* with bodies moving through space? How is its ideology legitimized and concretized through its geographical location, external appearance and internal spatial syntax?

A study of these new and renewed art galleries suggests that a new typology of gallery space has emerged in Britain at the start of the twenty-first century, in which the postmodernist construction of the museum, 'as mass medium . . . a site of spectacular mise-en-scène and operatic exuberance'[9] has formed an uneasy alliance with the contemporary orthodoxy of the museum as a site of learning and the management of cultural diversity. This typology is characterized by the dislocation and decentring of the canon of art history within the architectural frame, and the substitution of linear narrative on a horizontal plane[10] with a new syntax of verticality, transparency and spectacle. Within these spaces, the gallery's ambition to construct its visitors as learners is always at risk of subversion by an architectural play of disorientation and distraction. At the same time, the relationship between gallery and city has been renewed via strategies of spectacular viewing, ocular dominance and architectural metaphors of transparency and permeability.

Decentring the canon at Manchester Art Gallery

In 2002, the arts marketing agency Arts About Manchester published a small book of comic strip tales by the Kartoonkings, otherwise known as artists Christopher Sperrandio and Simon Grennan.[11] Entitled *What in the World?*, the book contains nine 'real-life' stories, each of which is a little parable of the transformatory potential of museums. They are tales of individual rediscovery, revelation and re-enchantment in Greater Manchester's mixed economy of museums, including the recently expanded and rebranded Manchester Art Gallery. All of the stories' protagonists are either Black or Asian: each therefore embodies a community that was previously excluded from the museum's public.

The parable of Manchester Art Gallery is called 'Bridging the Past' and is based on the story of Lisa Mok, who came to live in Manchester from Hong Kong in the early 1990s. When Lisa first visited the Gallery, she thought it was 'sunk in the past', but now, ten years later, it has been transformed – the result of four years' closure and a substantial Lottery grant. Above all, Lisa is delighted with the physical renewal of the Gallery and, in particular, by a new glass bridge that links the original gallery building with the new extension designed by Michael Hopkins & Partners. As Lisa says, the bridge has a symbolic, as well as a physical, function: it not only joins together the old and new parts of the building, its modernity symbolizes the transformation that has taken place within the institution. By linking the nineteenth-century gallery and the new extension, the bridge creates an apparently seamless continuity between the Gallery's past and present. In turn, Lisa's presence in the story vindicates the central aspiration of the capital development project: namely, the production of an enlarged, more inclusive and more diverse public for the gallery.

The redevelopment of Manchester Art Gallery, between 1998 and 2002, exemplifies the use of capital funding for museums as a driver both for internal organizational change and for the renewal of the relationship between the institution and its public. A combined package of Lottery, European Union and local authority funding[12] for its refurbishment and extension was predicated on the delivery of social and economic benefits, including targets for the amelioration of social exclusion and job creation. As elsewhere, new spaces for exhibitions and education are incorporated into the enlarged Gallery to accommodate an expanded repertoire of curatorial and interpretative practice, with the objective of promoting access, audience development and lifelong learning. At the same time, the Gallery's need to maximize revenue from its visitors is reflected in the location and size of its shop and café, both of which occupy prominent positions on the ground floor. Today, a snapshot of Manchester Art Gallery reveals a self-portrait of the Gallery as a site both of education and of virtuous consumption, in which the visitor is hybridized as learner and customer. However, closer scrutiny of the effects of structural renewal of galleries such as Manchester Art Gallery shows that they are more complex, and more conflicted, than the ostensible recoding of the building and its public suggests. To take a simple example: research on visitors to the Gallery during 2002 revealed a more ambivalent response to the thresholds marking the crossing points between different parts of the building.[13] Among a substantial number of visitors, the glass bridge between the nineteenth- and twenty-first-century buildings produced a sensation of unease and mild vertigo, and thus for these visitors became a barrier, rather than a link, between the old and new sections of the Gallery.

Of all the galleries discussed in this chapter, only Manchester Art Gallery occupies a monumental building in the centre of the city. The neo-classical premises of the Royal Manchester Institution (RMI), designed by Charles Barry and opened in 1834, still provide the main entrance to the Gallery. In fact, it had been intended that the door leading to the central glass pavilion would form a new entrance to the building, but the decision was made on financial grounds to retain the RMI door as the only general entrance to the building. For many visitors, unaware of the operational constraints, it is a baffling decision.[14] Prior to the redevelopment of the Gallery, Barry's neo-classical building had stood proud of its neighbours – an archetype of the nineteenth-century art gallery. Access to the building was – and is – up a flight of stairs (now supplemented with a gentle ramp) and through a small door beneath a portico of Ionic columns.

Once inside, visitors enter Barry's grand hall, dominated by a massive staircase leading to the first floor galleries, whose upper walls are decorated with casts of the Parthenon marbles (donated by George IV). Above and below the casts, the walls were further embellished in the 1840s with red and gold decorative stencilling and gilding. In addition, paintings from the collection were hung around the staircase landings. In effect, this was the cardinal space around which the collections galleries were ranged in a single loop, starting and finishing on either side of the staircase. The ascent through the building was thus contrived as 'an experience of grandeur [which] entails both a display of largesse and a rite of passage'.[15] Today, however, that display of largesse is diminished because the walls have been stripped of the paintings that used to decorate them on the grounds that they are inaccessible to those visitors who cannot climb the stairs. As a result, many visitors have commented on the rather bare and cold effect of the blank, grey walls that they encounter on entering the Gallery.[16]

The spatial regime at Manchester was characteristic of the nineteenth-century art gallery: the power of culture was signalled by the movement of bodies up, into and around the sequence of rooms in which the history of art unfolded in perfect synchronicity with the movement of the visitor. The flow of rooms

111

carried visitors – attentive or bored – in a single direction on a horizontal plane, and there was no escape from the canon for the visitor who was physically incorporated within the spatio-temporal logic of display.[17] By contrast, the space syntax of the Manchester Art Gallery is now no longer ordered by the chronological display of art history, and the authority of the canon has been subverted by its reorganization into periodized-thematic displays on two floors (instead of one). Similarly, the provision of alternative access to Barry's long flight of stairs means that the physical exertion of the ascent to art is not required: glazed lifts in the central atrium carry visitors on to the glass bridge and through a new doorway, which punctures the enfilade of galleries at the halfway point in the sequence. Entering at this point, the visitor no longer apprehends the clockwise direction of rooms starting from, and leading to, the grand staircase, and is quite likely to walk in the 'wrong' direction around the clockwise circuit and against the flow of the curatorial argument. Having entered the narrative at an arbitrary point, opportunities to double back, reverse and exit early no longer appear transgressive, and the logic of the thematic-chronological sequence is undermined.

Visitor research in the Gallery suggests that most first-time visitors are not aware of a curatorial or art historical route through the collection displays.[18] Disconnected from the logic of the space, and frequently distracted by the 'continual pull of something else' they move fairly quickly through the galleries, as either browsers or butterflies.[19] Browsers are like window shoppers whose interest in the displays is never fully engaged, but whose eye takes in the general effect and occasionally alights on a particular object. Butterflies flit from one exhibit to the next, focus on the particular, rather than the general, and are easily distracted when another, more alluring exhibit catches their eye. Neither browsers nor butterflies follow a planned route through the building: architectural cues – such as openings and vistas of different spaces and other displays – prompt them to change course and so deviate from the imagined path of curatorial intention. Now that the historical collection is just one element in a complex menu of displays and exhibitions, it no longer occupies either the spatial or programmatic core, and the Gallery visit is no longer structured around the axis of the art historical canon. The effect can be disorientating: many visitors commented that they found the Gallery confusing and were worried that they had missed 'something important'.[20]

Towards a new architectural typology

The same process of decentring the collection within Manchester Art Gallery is even more marked in the contrasting spaces of Tate Modern and the Millennium Galleries, Sheffield. At Tate Modern, the galleries that house both the collections displays and temporary exhibitions are stacked up on three floors above the shop, café and auditorium on the north side of the building (the Boiler House) overlooking the River Thames, thereby preserving intact the massive verticality of the Turbine Hall, which dominates the building interior. The galleries themselves are not only invisible from the axial Turbine Hall, but their location is peripheral and, according to the architect, Jacques Herzog, visiting them is optional: 'You can go into the great hall and spend time there without coming into contact with the museum.'[21] Thus freed of the 'museum' function of the institution, the Turbine Hall is, above all, a space for promenading – walking as performance and display – under the gaze of people looking down from the glazed balconies that run along the sides of the galleries, high up on the edge of the building.

Inevitably, the Turbine Hall has been compared with a nineteenth-century Parisian arcade,[22] but the analogy is even more apt in the case of the Millennium Galleries, which comprise four quite separate gallery spaces, each of which is entered via its own front door from a central corridor – just like shops off an arcade. And, like a shop, each gallery has its own window display and sign: Exhibitions, Craft and Design, Metalwork and the Ruskin Gallery. In fact, the corridor (or arcade) has a dual function: to provide access to the galleries and also to serve as a handy pedestrian shortcut to the city centre. It is easy to cut through the building without ever entering one of the galleries ranged along its side; it is as a pedestrian thoroughfare (and street-front café) that the Millennium Galleries are physically integrated into the fabric of the city. But in a twist on the conventional form of the arcade, here the gallery shop is located *within* the arcade itself: as in Tate Modern, the art galleries are optional, but the shop is unavoidable. Both the Millennium Galleries and the New Art Gallery Walsall are deliberately embedded in a city centre landscape of consumption: the Sheffield gallery is physically linked to the Winter Garden, lined with cafés and shops, which, in turn, leads into the central shopping district. In Walsall, the gallery is located at the top of a pedestrian precinct: in the words of its founding Director, Peter Jenkinson, it is, 'next to Woolworths and British Home Stores. What better location can you have?'.[23]

The arcade in Sheffield is brightly lit, and the hard, white marble floors are reflective and smooth, reminiscent of a department store or airport: it is a space of transit as well as consumption. Access to and from the arcade (from the lower level entrance and café) is by an escalator or a glazed lift: in Sheffield, stairs are for emergencies only; elsewhere, they are not only the least attractive means of ascent, but also the least evident. Although the galleries at Tate Modern can be reached via the so-called Grand Staircase, this is the least obvious means of ascent. The black walls and rough wooden floors do little to relieve the cramped proportions of the stairwell, with its varying levels of headroom.[24] Similarly, at Baltic, the public stairs are tucked into a corner of the building: the staircase is an enclosed space, shut off from both the interior core of the building and from an exterior view. By contrast, the transparent lift shaft occupies centre stage above the entrance to the building, and the constant motion of the lifts rising above the River Tyne defines the dominant vertical axis of the building, which is topped by the viewing platform that visually reconnects the gallery with the city. Displays within the gallery compete for visitors' attention with the periscopic view of the city laid out beneath them. At the New Art Gallery Walsall, too, the long, narrow staircase is buried in the middle of the building, lined in wood and largely concealed from view: it is enclosed, secretive and arduous to climb. Again, the visitor is really intended to travel up through the building by lift, watching the rather bleak urban landscape of the West Midlands unfold through the windows punched through the lift shaft.

The transformation of the conditions of vertical mobility through the gallery was motivated by the need to increase physical access, but what are its *effects* on the ways in which visitors experience and apprehend the space of the gallery? Ruskin's museum was built on a hill outside Sheffield, so that its visitors would always be aware of the effort required for the acquisition of educational capital.[25] Today, the exertion of climbing has been replaced by physical stasis on an escalator or inside a lift, from which the visitor can see the interior of the gallery and/or the exterior of the city unfold as he or she effortlessly ascends. Within the multi-storeyed gallery, the kinaesthetics of viewing art has been transformed by replacement of physical exertion with visual diversion, exemplified by the static ascent via escalator or transparent lift. Viewed from above, the gallery is consumed as a spectacular ensemble of art, architecture and bodies. The architecture of arcades and vistas produces spaces that are both performative and distracting; and the interior building itself becomes an event that is continuously (re)produced by the motion of people within it.

Travelling on an escalator is as prescriptive as walking through the enfilade: you cannot get off until you reach the top and, in this sense, it is its vertical equivalent. Once each work of art, instantiating a moment in art history, was revealed through horizontal walking; now the *gallery itself* is revealed through vertical ascent through the building. Visual (as opposed to physical) movement is further stimulated and accommodated by the apparatus of balconies, mezzanines, internal windows and viewing platforms that characterize the contemporary gallery. Looking down on and through gallery space produces a view of art as an ensemble effect; it distracts attention from the individuated work of art.[26] In a variation on this theme, the installation of the Garman Ryan collection in Walsall borrows from the architecture of domesticity, including internal staircases, windows and balconies. The collection as biography is displayed in a house within a house; the gallery encloses the collection as an object in itself, and, viewed from the internal balconies and landings, the collection is apprehended as the sum of its parts.

The ease of travelling by lift or escalator appears to erase the hierarchy between floors, but this erasure is, in fact, illusory. The linear sequence of the enfilade has been replaced by diverse vertical systems in which the status of different kinds of practice is affirmed and encoded. Temporary exhibition galleries are located above the collections displays at Manchester Art Gallery and Walsall: their distance from the front door entails either a familiarity with the building layout or a concerted effort to reach them. In both cases, the exhibition is structurally coded as a cultural destination, rather than a casual encounter. At Tate Modern, exhibitions are sandwiched between two floors of collections. Here the collections displays have adopted the features of exhibitions; that is, they are overtly curated in the form of signed, thematic installations. Reflecting a strategy of physical change, canonical revisionism and multi-vocality, Tate Modern blurs the conventional display distinctions between collection and exhibition – except, of course, for the exhibition admission charge.

A common vertical move within the twenty-first-century art gallery is the emergence of education spaces from the basement, where they have typically been housed, to the ground and upper floors. The institutional structures of power and authority that were previously encoded in the 'upstairs downstairs' division of curatorial and educational spaces have been realigned in new buildings that simultaneously concretize and accommodate the increasing emphasis on the educational function of the gallery. New interactive galleries, designed for both adults and children, are prominent in both Manchester and Walsall, where they are located on the first floor and close to the main entrance respectively. In these spaces, learning about art is constructed as both play and performance: many of the 'interactives' encourage joint participation, and even those that invite solitary engagement are calculated to attract an audience. How do these spaces affect the meaning of the gallery space as a whole? Research at Manchester Art Gallery suggests that they signal informality and give permission to move around, double back, try again, make a noise and watch and talk to other people – behaviours that subvert the conventions of strolling and quiet conversation through linear displays.[27]

Vertical structures at Tate Modern, Baltic and Walsall also encode a hierarchy of consumption, based on the visitor's ability to pay. In each of these buildings, the most spectacular views of the city laid out down below is available to those who can afford to eat in their rooftop restaurants; invariably, a more formal and expensive option than their ground floor cafés. The success of these restaurants of course depends on the custom of a sufficiently large and/or regular clientele of well-heeled diners; already, the restaurant at Walsall has shut to the public and is now only available for hire. Thus access to one of the spaces which was most celebrated when the gallery opened has since been effectively privatized.

Conclusion

The architecture of access, exemplified by all five galleries discussed here, is also an architecture of performativity and distraction, the effect of which can be both compelling and disorientating. What the view through the gallery reveals is a process of decentring the canon within both the spatial syntax and the curatorial programme of the institution. Not for the first time in gallery history, these buildings function simultaneously as destination and artefact: frequently, the plan or silhouette of the building is used to promote the gallery as a cultural brand, and is further commodified in the production of souvenirs for sale in the gallery shop. Yet the meaning of gallery space is continuously reproduced by the behaviour and experiences of its visitors, be they butterflies, browsers or simply diners, as well as by (and sometimes at odds with) institutional practice and architectural design.

Notes

1 S. Martin and S. Nordgren (eds), *New Sites – New Art*, Newcastle: BALTIC and University of Newcastle, 2000.
2 A. Stetter (ed.), *Pride of Place: How the Lottery Contributed £1billion to the Arts in England*, London: Arts Council of England, 2002.
3 Martin and Nordgren, *New Sites – New Art*, p. 83.
4 Department for Culture, Media and Sport (DCMS), *Museums for the Many*, London: HMSO, 1999; Department for Culture, Media and Sport (DCMS), *Centres for Social Change: Museums, Galleries and Archives for All*, London: HMSO, 2000; Department for Culture, Media and Sport/Department for Education and Employment (DCMS/DfEE), *All Our Futures: Creativity, Culture and Education*, London: HMSO, 1999; Department for Culture, Media and Sport/Department for Education and Employment (DCMS/DfEE), *The Learning Power of Museums: A Vision for Museum Education*, London: HMSO, 2000.
5 Of course, these questions are also pertinent to other kinds of museums, as well as art galleries. However, Bourdieu's contention that, of all collecting institutions, the contents of the art gallery require the greatest deployment of cultural and educational capital in order to be decoded and thus fully enjoyed suggests that these issues are least susceptible to resolution there. P. Bourdieu and A. Darbel, *The Love of Art: European Art Museums and the Public*, Oxford: Polity Press, 1969 (trans. C. Beattie and N. Merriman, 1991).
6 J. Glancey, 'A dream come true', *The Observer*, 12 May 2002, p. 32.
7 The five architectural practices were: Caruso St John (The New Art Gallery Walsall); Herzog and De Meuron (Tate Modern, London); Pringle Richards Sharratt (Millennium Galleries, Sheffield); Michael Hopkins & Partners (Manchester Art Gallery); and Dominic Williams (Baltic, Gateshead).
8 A. Vidler, *The Architectural Uncanny*, Cambridge, MA, and London: MIT Press, 1992, p. 96.
9 A. Huyssen, *Twilight Memories: Marking Time in a Culture of Amnesia*, New York and London: Routledge, 1995, p. 14.
10 This is what Nicholas Serota calls 'the conveyor belt of history'. N. Serota, *Experience or Interpretation: The Dilemma of Museums of Modern Art*, London: Thames and Hudson, 1996.
11 Kartoonkings, *What in the World?*, 2002. Available at: www.kartoonkings.com (accessed 13 August 2004).
12 The total budget for the Manchester Art Gallery capital development project was £35 million.
13 H. Rees Leahy, *Researching Learning at Manchester Art Gallery*, 2003. Available at: www.art.man.ac.uk/museology (accessed 13 August 2004).
14 Ibid.
15 I. Scalbert, 'The New Art Gallery and its geography', in D. Smith (ed.), *The New Art Gallery Walsall*, London: Batsford, 2002, pp. 40–57.
16 Rees Leahy, *Researching Learning*.
17 C. Duncan and A. Wallach, 'The Universal Survey Museum', *Art History*, Vol. 3, No. 4, 1980: 448–69; C. Duncan, *Civilizing Rituals: Inside Public Art Museums*, London: Routledge, 1995; R. Krauss, 'Post-modernism's museum without walls', in R. Greenberg, B. Ferguson and S. Nairne (eds), *Thinking about Exhibitions*, London and New York: Routledge, 1996, pp. 341–8.
18 Rees Leahy, *Researching Learning*.
19 Krauss, 'Post-modernism's museum', p. 347.
20 Rees Leahy, *Researching Learning*.
21 G. Mack, *Art Museums into the 21st Century*, Basel, Boston, Berlin: Birkhauser, 1999, p. 42.
22 Ibid., p. 17.
23 Martin and Nordgren, *New Sites – New Art*, p. 87.
24 K. Sabbagh, *Power into Art*, London and New York: Allen Lane, 2000, p. 230.

25 J. Barnes, *Ruskin in Sheffield*, Sheffield: Sheffield Arts and Museums Department, 1985.
26 Krauss, 'Post-modernism's museum'.
27 Rees Leahy, *Researching Learning*.

References

Barnes, J., *Ruskin in Sheffield*, Sheffield: Sheffield Arts and Museums Department, 1985.
Bourdieu, P. and Darbel, A., *The Love of Art: European Art Museums and the Public*, Oxford: Polity Press, 1969 (trans. C. Beattie and N. Merriman, 1991).
Department for Culture, Media and Sport (DCMS), *Museums for the Many*, London: HMSO, 1999.
——, *Centres for Social Change: Museums, Galleries and Archives for All*, London: HMSO, 2000.
Department for Culture, Media and Sport/Department for Education and Employment (DCMS/DfEE), *All Our Futures: Creativity, Culture and Education*, London: HMSO, 1999.
——, *The Learning Power of Museums: A Vision for Museum Education*, London: HMSO, 2000.
Duncan, C., *Civilizing Rituals: Inside Public Art Museums*, London: Routledge, 1995.
—— and Wallach, A., 'The Universal Survey Museum', *Art History*, Vol. 3, No. 4, 1980: 448–69.
Glancey, J., 'A dream come true', *The Observer*, 12 May 2002, p. 32.
Huyssen, A., *Twilight Memories: Marking Time in a Culture of Amnesia*, New York and London: Routledge, 1995.
Kartoonkings, *What in the World?*, 2002. Available at: www.kartoonkings.com (accessed 13 August 2004).
Krauss, R., 'Post-modernism's museum without walls', in R. Greenberg, B. Ferguson and S. Nairne, *Thinking about Exhibitions*, London and New York: Routledge, 1996, pp. 341–8.
Mack, G., *Art Museums into the 21st Century*, Basel, Boston, Berlin: Birkhauser, 1999.
Martin, S. and Nordgren, S. (eds), *New Sites – New Art*, Newcastle: BALTIC and University of Newcastle, 2000.
Rees Leahy, H., *Researching Learning at Manchester Art Gallery*, 2003. Available at: www.art.man.ac.uk/museology (accessed 13 August 2004).
Sabbagh, K., *Power into Art*, London and New York: Allen Lane, 2000.
Scalbert, I., 'The New Art Gallery and its geography', in D. Smith (ed.), *The New Art Gallery Walsall*, London: Batsford, 2002, pp. 40–57.
Serota, N., *Experience or Interpretation: The Dilemma of Museums of Modern Art*, London: Thames & Hudson, 1996.
Stetter, A. (ed.), *Pride of Place: How the Lottery Contributed £1billion to the Arts in England*, London: Arts Council of England, 2002.
Vidler, A., *The Architectural Uncanny*, Cambridge, MA, and London: MIT Press, 1992.

9

Towards a new museum architecture

Narrative and representation

Lee H. Skolnick

Introduction

The new century finds museums in yet another life cycle transition. Issues of varying new media for high-speed access to information, evolving roles and programmes of civic institutions within society and changing styles of teaching and learning – including the long-term cognitive effects of new media/information technologies – have had an unexpected impact on the role of museums in their immediate communities and in the world. Interestingly, they have only become more popular. This is due to a myriad of factors, including an increase in the appeal of social environments for learning, and the growing distrust of other public sources of information. Obviously, this combination of conditions represents a double-edged opportunity for museums: they have the perfect chance to experiment with new ways of interpreting information for an ever growing audience, and a greater risk of being held accountable if they don't get it right.

The challenge for designers, architects and other museum professionals is to collaborate in leading the way towards new methods of conceiving, and executing, visitor experiences that take into account constantly shifting and progressing modes of thought and understanding. It is also incumbent upon us to find new strategies that serve to render those experiences fresh and invigorating, while realizing that certain aspects of visitor behaviour and comfort are in fact more predictable and fixed.

In this chapter, I will explore the role that narrative can play in the conceptualization, planning and design of the overall museum experience, including its potential to encompass and integrate site, architecture and exhibition. Over the course of 25 years of practice, Lee H. Skolnick Architecture + Design Partnership has used 'narrative' as a means of tapping into the power of an innate human tool used for understanding: as a design generator, as an organizational device, and as a method of embodying the conceptual and thematic within the spatial and experiential.

Through reference to historical and contemporary examples, I will make a strategic and qualitative distinction between the concepts of 'Embodiment' and 'Representation' as they refer to architectural design in general. I will then demonstrate why an understanding of these points, their particular significance to the field of museum design, and their relationship to the use of an expanded definition of narrative, constitutes a promising and fertile area for creative exploration and inquiry. Finally, I will discuss how this potent mix, inherently inclusive of the many voices (curator, designer, educator, etc.), which can contribute to the ultimate success of the visitor experience, offers a new dimension in the creation of meaning.

Before going forward, permit me to start with an apology (something architects rarely do) inside a deconstruction (something architects did for a short time, but have largely stopped doing). All of this relates to the title of my chapter: 'Towards a new museum architecture: narrative and representation.' I must beg forgiveness for a bit of petty larceny to two writers who came before me, and whose titles I have borrowed and bastardized.

In 1923, the Swiss-born architect who called himself Le Corbusier published a revolutionary manifesto on architecture, technology, philosophy and society. He called it *Vers Une Architecture*, or *Towards an Architecture*. For some reason, when it was translated into English, it morphed into the perhaps more apt *Towards a New Architecture*.[1] In it, Le Corbusier prophesied an architecture that took as its inspiration the no-nonsense, yet sublimely beautiful formal solutions to functional problems that advances in technology and mass production would make possible. He equated democracy with equal access to stripped-down 'machines for living' and envisioned 'radiant cities', which would promote physical, mental and spiritual health amid communities of serene sameness.

In 1998, the American connoisseur and architectural writer Victoria Newhouse published *Towards a New Museum*.[2] Far from offering a bold manifesto, Ms Newhouse proposed to 'observe and assess what others have done', and 'to report on the direction museum architecture is taking'. She further limited her brief by taking as the object of her analysis the art museum only.

In a review of Ms Newhouse's book that I wrote for *Curator* magazine, I noted that 'the book on the future of architecture and museums is still being written'.[3] While that statement is perhaps more true than ever, and while I do not propose to offer that book up now, I would like to focus on a particular opportunity for vivid communication that museum design affords. I would call your attention back to my introduction, where I wrote that in the face of constant and rapid change, and the growing need for new approaches to the crafting of experiences, we must remember that certain aspects of visitor behaviour and comfort are in fact more predictable and fixed. Here, one must make a connection back to something which is a very basic human instinct as well as a strategy and structure common to many types of communication and learning: narrative. And while there seems to be an undoubted trend these days to ascribe narrative significance to everything from philosophy to medicine, I would submit that narrative has had, and continues to have, a particularly significant place in the making and experiencing of both architecture and museums.

Narrative

To substantiate the foundational role of narrative in creating human culture, let us look at its roots in storytelling, and cite the work of psychologist Jerome Bruner (e.g. his book, *Acts of Meaning*)[4] by way of a wonderful paper on this subject by museum specialist Leslie Bedford. Bruner observed that human beings are natural storytellers, that they make sense of the world and themselves through narrative (in other words, learn), and that, as such, storytelling is a primary instrument for making meaning. Leslie Bedford goes on to put a cap on it by saying:

> storytelling is an ideal strategy for realizing the constructivist museum, an environment where visitors of all ages and backgrounds are encouraged to create their own meaning and find that place, the intersection between the familiar and the unknown where genuine learning occurs.[5]

Or, as the late Arthur Rosenblatt, founding Director of the US Holocaust Memorial and Museum in Washington, DC, offered in his foreword to a recent book on museums: 'architecture can be both evocative and moving in the development of a "storytelling museum".'[6]

So, in explanation of why I chose to reference and plunder the titles of the previously cited authors, Le Corbusier and Newhouse, let me propose that I intend a mild manifesto, supported by observation and assessment of what some others have done. At the very least, I hope to provide some food for thought to those whose work is devoted to imagining and moving us 'Towards a new museum architecture'.

Narrative is good. Representation is not as good. Embodiment is ideal.

This might have been a more appropriate sub-heading for this chapter. Actually, I left 'embodiment' out of my original title because I was afraid that it might already be too obscure and I didn't want to confuse people any more than necessary. Nonetheless, embodiment is, from my point of view, the highest and ultimate goal. For, while architecture certainly deals in the fourth dimension – time – it is not film or music (frozen or otherwise) or writing; it exists all at once, while unfolding and revealing itself in time. So, with apologies to 'narrative', I like 'embodiment'.

Representation

Well, then, what's wrong with 'representation'? In truth, it's certainly not terrible. Some very nice buildings use metaphor and symbol to great poetic effect. This is especially true in recent times, when formal architectural vocabulary has been freed from the formulaic constraints of strict stylistic convention, and as technological advances in both design tools and construction methods have allowed for greater freedom in imagining buildings and in building them (although in many cases the ways people actually use buildings may not have undergone the same revolutionary changes). I think the operative point for us is that often these exuberant expressions bear very little relation to the ostensible or real purpose of the building, and that they sometimes actually impede rather than enhance their natural and proper function.

In Frank Gehry's Guggenheim Museum, Bilbao, the light, curvilinear forms of walls and roofs have been said to evoke sailing ships on the water, and are themselves sculpturally expressive. Further, they refer to Bilbao's geographical position and historical role as a port city. This does not necessarily qualify them, or the interior spaces they enclose, as the most beneficial places to display art. Similarly, Santiago Calatrava's boldly expressive new Milwaukee Art Museum, with its birdlike form and retractable roof, is a blockbuster in its own right, but neither particularly expressive of, nor supportive to, the artwork stored and installed inside. And while Renzo Piano's New Metropolis Museum in Amsterdam may be photographed strategically in juxtaposition with the ships' prows from which it takes its form, it is difficult to understand what relationship this is intended to have with the science activities that are at the heart of the museum's programme and raison d'être. Before leaving this aspect of 'representation', we might compare these buildings to Jorn Utzon's iconic Sydney Opera House, whose forms manage to refer to both the sails of the harbour and to the theme of music, while having the added advantages of clearly delineating the concert halls and offering them notably euphonic acoustics.

Of course, sometimes the 'representation' is quite literal. Throughout history there have been buildings and structures that were, if not actually figurative, at least referring in their visual message to nothing so strongly as the function and/or subject for which they were created. And if they didn't always work perfectly as integrated experiences or as beautiful objects, they nevertheless gave people a pretty good idea of what they were for. The Long Island Duck, of 'Complexity and Contradiction' (Robert Venturi) fame, wears its function and subject on its sleeve (or wing). You bought ducks there. The forms of Frank Gehry's Experience Music Project in Seattle are said to have been developed by smashing up electric guitars and then rearranging them until an optimal composition was found. (It is widely held that the usually masterful Gehry may have hit a 'clinker' on this one. Herbert Muschamp, architecture critic for the *New York Times*, recently likened it to 'something that crawled out of the sea, rolled over and died'.)[7] Much of the music venerated at EMP was played on the guitar, mostly the electric guitar, and groups from The Who to The Jimi Hendrix Experience enjoyed smashing them. Unfortunately, the interior of the building gains little other than spatial bombast for all the trouble. It might get at the fracturing rebelliousness of rock music, but it doesn't capture any of its other qualities. On the other hand, in that regard it beats I. M. Pei's Rock and Roll Hall of Fame in Cleveland by miles and miles. Some can see the supposedly intentional reference to a record player there, but I'm not that creative. Further, it feels like nothing so much as Pei's East Wing addition to the National Gallery of Art, in Washington, DC, and manages to freeze any of the heat of rock and roll, while sticking the exhibits in the basement and the mausoleum-like Hall of Fame way up in its darkened peak. Dominique Perrault's infamous Bibliothèque Nationale in Paris (the one that baked the books) is defined by the four glass towers at its corners (wherein books are stored behind large sheets of glass), each in the shape of an open book. Books within books, get it? Ranging from the sublime to the ridiculous (you decide which is which), there are Claude Ledoux's project for a Cenotaph for Newton, whose neo-Utopian/neo-Platonic design refers to the planets and/or the cosmos/universe; James Stewart Polshek's Rose Center for Earth and Space in New York, which although a naturally literal and cool visual reference is not known to be a great place to design or experience exhibits on the subject; and, of course, Lucy (the Elephant), standing proudly near the Jersey Shore. One could go on.

There have been more ingeniously sophisticated examples of 'representation' as well. Here, a modern sensibility has filtered and translated historical, cultural or other subject matter information into an essentially contemporary design vocabulary. Still, in these buildings the references frequently appear to be somewhat applied, and as such have less influence on the depth and specificity of the experience in and around them. Two come to mind immediately. There is Jean Nouvel's Institut du Monde Arabe in Paris, one of whose glass façades is fitted with a pattern of Islamic-inspired mechanical irises that open and close based on sensors that measure the sunlight hitting them. This late twentieth-century tour de force sends a message about Islam's traditional art and its marriage with a heritage of mathematics and science, and also serves as a forward-looking comment regarding the Islamic world's relevance and vibrancy in an age of technology. It has the added advantage of modulating the light entering spaces devoted to work and study. James Ingo Freed's US Holocaust Memorial and Museum in Washington, DC, adapts a visual language referring to Hitler's Second World War death camps for some of its interior and exterior forms and details (although far too slickly and exquisitely for my taste), and in an ironic twist for a building in our nation's capital, collides and juxtaposes it with an overtly hulking and conventional institutional building. Its almost covert insertion into its federal context provides a subtle but subversive commentary on the dangers of government-sanctioned atrocities. In this building, one must note that the staggering power of the total visitor experience is the result of a clear desire on the part of both the architect and the exhibit designer to imbue their separate parts with meaning and association. And, although the integration between architecture and exhibits could be both more intentional and more seamless, there is an undeniable emotional impact that owes itself to the largely successful attempt to let design help tell the story.

Embodiment

Well, we're getting closer and closer to our goal, so why not just cross the threshold? The problem with many of the very good – in some cases great – buildings that I have cited thus far is simply that, in general terms, they just don't allow their story – their narrative – enough of a role in defining the experiences they offer. They miss the full opportunity to infuse their core mission, themes and concepts into all aspects of their sites, buildings and exhibits, thereby instilling a sense of specificity, an organic rightness unique to their situations. In other words, they don't venture past 'representing' these ideas to the more fertile ground of 'embodying' them.

When Louis Sullivan told the world that form should follow function he was interpreted by different people in different ways. On the most mundane level, the phrase is understood to mean that a building should do no more nor less than be designed to facilitate its most pragmatic purpose. Storage facilities need big, open spaces. Prisons need lots of cells (perhaps), good lines of sight for security, and should be hard to get out of. Offices benefit from easy access to light and air, and the provision of certain types of workspace and communication. It is easy to be reminded of Le Corbusier's 'machines for living'. However, Sullivan's declaration and edict is widely interpreted in architectural and academic circles as proposing something that is both more profound and more creatively challenging. It is understood to demand that the design of a building stem from an initial set of ideas that inform, to the greatest degree – and extent – possible, the creative problem-solving that is embodied in the myriad of decisions regarding how it looks, functions and is made. The idea is that, by being clear regarding one's intent, and by carefully integrating each part of the building through adherence to rules and referents that support that intent, a unique harmony – that 'organic rightness' I mentioned earlier – can be achieved. And it strongly suggests, I believe, that those guiding concepts be derived from the project's purpose, in a range of both general and specific terms.

Thus, a church, while designed to comfortably seat its congregation, must also speak to themes of inspiration, and do so in ways that are evidenced in its materials, acoustics and ventilation no less than in its space, light and 'decoration'. (I use this term guardedly, for while Sullivan and his contemporaries felt comfortable in ascribing organic significance to decoration and ornamentation, subsequent history has gone through a sequence of banning it as impure and perverse, reintroducing it as symbolic pastiche and, more recently – as seen in some of the previously cited examples – making it the guiding principle or image of the overall design – a big duck, a big bird, smashed guitars, boats of all sorts.)

A hospital, in order to fulfil its mission of healing and wellness, must augment its technical specificity with the provision – at every level of the design and decision-making process – of those elements that promote physical, mental and spiritual health. These should manifest themselves in the overall look and feel, in the treatment of the site, in the approach and entry, in the spaces and modes of reception and admittance, and so on. But it should also influence the construction materials and finishes, the treatment of light and air, the acoustics, the sense of privacy and the access to community.

The example of a hospital, or health centre, is perhaps one of the most programmatically complex that one can tackle. So let's look at some very simple ones to illustrate the notion of successful 'embodiment'. The fact that they are notable examples of modern architecture frequently cited by historians should not, for our purposes, bestow upon them undue imprimatur or censure. The Penguin Pool at the London Zoo (1933), designed by Ove Arup and others, is a perfect poster child for 'embodiment'. It is meant to enhance the viewing of penguins by offering them a place to congregate, to walk down a ramp and to jump in the water. It affords the viewing public multiple unobstructed views of the proceedings and does so in a simple, elegant and straightforward manner. It doesn't refer to anything else. Some may say that it doesn't refer in a strongly literal enough way to the penguins' natural habitat, but that may be seen as a more subjective question of interpretive style.

Alvar Aalto's Sawmill in Vancas, Finland, of 1945 is another good case in point. It celebrates its purpose and the processes it houses, enhancing one's appreciation of them, while facilitating its function. It doesn't look like logs(!). However, through its gracefully sculptural design, it artfully elevates this relatively mundane process by clarifying and highlighting it, thereby increasing understanding.

To begin to come back around to our own subject of museums, it is fruitful to look at Daniel Libeskind's Jewish Museum in Berlin (2001). Although not universally revered, its jagged, slashing design is unquestionably successful at evoking the wrenching, irrational and disorienting chaos of the Holocaust on the most visceral and experiential level. Though it has gained the perhaps igno-minious distinction of either obviating the need for actual exhibitions, or at least making them notoriously difficult to mount in its highly architecturally specific spaces, at least these spaces are interpretive of the subject at hand rather than something completely unrelated (although as Libeskind has since come to enjoy having international commissions piled on, one does begin to question how this visual vocabulary, so appropriate to the Holocaust and to other wars and tragedies – The Imperial War Museum in Manchester, Ground Zero in New York City – relates to less highly charged projects, such as his designs for the Victoria and Albert Museum in London and his addition to the Royal Ontario Museum in Toronto).

Towards embodiment

For those of us who labour and dwell in the world of museums, who believe in their potential and are committed to making them better, the challenge is to take up the tools – of embodiment, of narrative, of the broadest interpretation of function – and to exploit their still untapped capabilities in order to enrich the museum experience for the broadest range of visitors.

At Lee H. Skolnick Architecture + Design Partnership, we have spent 25 years pursuing this challenge. Through projects ranging from master planning and site design, through the architectural design of new buildings, renovations and additions, to exhibition design, graphics and educational programming, we have explored new ways of creating seamlessly integrated experiences that embody the mission, goals and objectives of each institution, combining an understanding of their specific target audiences with the unique stories these organizations seek to tell.

The brief project descriptions that follow are not meant to be held as exemplars of the perfectly successful achievement of the goals I have espoused. In fact, one might easily and rightly question whether that ideal has yet been attained anywhere. Rather, the best reason for citing examples of our own work is simply that I am intimately familiar with what our objectives were, and the means we undertook to meet them. These processes and methods are not meant to be prescriptive. If they are in some way instructive and useful, we will h contributed something to the cause.

A key indication of our commitment to the values of interpretation and a. ence is the fact that I believe we were the first design firm – certainly the fi architecture firm – to have a full-time museum services division, led and staffed by trained museum educators, as an integral part of our design team. One impact of this is that we are uniquely equipped to engage the interest, expertise and perspectives of the full range of players necessary to ensure a project's success: the museum board and administration, the curators and subject area specialists, the educators and programming personnel, the registrars and conservators, and the facilities and maintenance staff. And, most importantly, the visitor.

There are a few fundamental aspects to our approach to any project. First, we try and put ourselves in the position of the potential anticipated participant: What do they know about this subject? How interested might they be? We try to learn as much as we can both about them and about the subject itself in order to find connections between the two. This involves research, close collaboration with curators and content experts, educators and interpreters, as well as the implementation of any range of interviews, focus groups and other forms of front-end evaluation. Second, we look at all the interpretive opportunities that the situation might offer – from its location within a larger architectural or geographic context, to the potential for narrative expression in the building design, and finally to the marriage of site, building and exhibitions into a cohesive visitor experience. These explorations eventually lead us to the development of a highly particularized, yet consistent, visual and communicative vocabulary, including forms, space, materials, details, graphics and media. Finally, through various evaluative means, we test our assumptions and refine them along the way in order to ensure that the story we are telling is as vivid, as compelling and as understandable as we can make it. Throughout the process, we continually challenge ourselves, and our collaborators, to unearth, identify and exploit any aspect and/or component of the project that has a narrative potential that can contribute to the complete embodiment of the content. In each of the projects described, I will note something about it that attempts to get at the notions of narrative or embodiment to which I have been referring. Where appropriate, I will also highlight some of the methodological approaches used to address that goal.

Figure 9.1 The Creative Discovery Museum in Chattanooga, Tennessee. Photograph ©
Peter Aaron/Esto.

Figure 9.2 The interior of the Creative Discovery Museum in Chattanooga, Tennessee.
Photograph © Peter Aaron/Esto.

126

The Creative Discovery Museum in Chattanooga, Tennessee, was conceived to be a place where children and families are invited to become actively involved in a creative exploration that integrates the arts and sciences; a place that da Vinci would have loved. The Museum was placed within Chattanooga's downtown riverfront to enhance its redevelopment as a centre of cultural and recreational activity. The building is only part of a procession that links the city and the inner workings of the Museum's internal exhibition programming. Along the way, from discovering the building's tower on the skyline, to the participatory pathway that leads to the entry, to encountering the interactive water sculpture from first outside and then inside, the visitor is drawn deeper and deeper into the mission and programme of CDM, finally realizing that it is they who are the creators and discoverers who make the entire Museum come alive.

For the Marine Park Environmental Center in Brooklyn, New York, situated in a sensitive wetlands area at the junction of land and water, the processional pathway led to a series of sequential revelations and an ultimate goal. As visitors strolled through a public park, the walkway transformed imperceptibly into a bridge, focusing attention on the transition from land to water. At the same time, the ground plane tilted up and the path continued, inviting visitors into the space between land and water, the glass-enclosed exhibit and workshop spaces under the planted roof. From here, breathtaking panoramic views of the wetlands and the bay beyond beckoned visitors back on to the path, now leading out of the building to ramps and floating docks from which to board the boats that would take them to engage in further exploration out in the unspoiled nature.

Figure 9.3 The Marine Park Environmental Center in Brooklyn, New York. Photograph Lee H. Skolnick Architecture + Design Partnership.

At the Sony Wonder Technology Lab in New York City, the story was the breakthroughs in media and technology that have permitted great advances in the ability to create, alter and share content. This paramount message, combined with the evolution from analogue to digital media and the freeing of presentation from the confines of the traditional screen, led us to create an environment where architecture and media merge, and visitors hold the power to transform their surroundings through unleashing their own imaginations.

Congregation B'nai Yisrael in Armonk, New York, is not a museum, but it offers a lesson on how a strong narrative concept can inform the design of a building. In this case, the key ideas are the Jewish religion's focus on the quality of how one lives one's life on earth, the cycles and journey embodied in that life, reverence for God's creation, and the primacy of community, study and observance. Congregants and visitors come upon a garden wall, which, though level on top, appears to grow taller as the land slopes down to the building's entry. After passing through the transition space of a small, wooden vestibule, one finds oneself under the shelter of an ethereal tent-like curved canopy. After advancing through the lobby, one emerges into the Sanctuary and an unobstructed view of the Torah Ark set into a large, glass façade: the permanency of the Laws amid the ever changing landscape. The cycle is completed from nature, through study, gathering, observance and communion, back to nature.

When invited to compete to design a headquarters and visitor centre for the Mohonk Preserve, New York State's largest private, non-profit land preserve, one thing was clear: they really didn't want a building. Through retreats and interviews with the Board and staff, we came to realize the obvious. What was called for was not a destination, but a gateway. Thus was born the Trapps Gateway Center, an experience and a building of and for the land. Everything about the siting, physical approach, land development, architectural design, and exterior and interior interpretation tells a story about the land. Themes of geology, geography, biology, ecology, cultural history and responsible land stewardship combine through careful attention to the individual experiential and physical components and the messages they send.

The building is almost hidden upon approach; it disappears into the landscape and is made from the site's native stone and the few trees felled to create its footprint. When it finally emerges, it appears as a modest gateway, concealing its 11,000 square feet of floor space by being cut into the slope of a land ridge. It bespeaks environmental awareness through the incorporation of local and recycled materials and derives most of its climate control through a geothermal heating and cooling system. The building and site further cooperate in telling their stories by sending the visitor, first through views and then through circulation, back out to the interpretive trails and the land, which are the true focus and destination.

To honour and further the humanitarian achievements of 'The Greatest', the Muhammad Ali Center in Louisville, Kentucky, had to embody the strength, power, lightness, speed and grace that Ali brought to 'the ring' and to the field of human empowerment, respect and understanding. The form of the Center,

Figure 9.4 The Muhammad Ali Center in Louisville, Kentucky. Photograph Lee H. Skolnick Architecture + Design Partnership/Beyer Blinder Belle Architects and Planners.

referring to Ali's famous dictate to 'float like a butterfly, sting like a bee', juxtaposes a solid masonry base, firmly rooted to the ground, with a light and aerodynamic winged roof canopy. The narrative is further enhanced by the façade's use of digitized photographic images of 'the most recognized face on earth' to impart its distinctive identity. The man whose ascendancy paralleled the proliferation of mass media within our culture will forever be remembered through the medium that helped to immortalize him. On a substantive experiential level, the story of Ali's evolution as a professional, as a world ambassador and as a man is traced through a spatial organization that uses the timeline of his life as an armature. Along it are hung both the key moments in his development and the broader themes that they represent, and that tie his experiences to the lives of each visitor. In ascending through the space along with Ali, we are all encouraged to be the greatest we can be.

Onwards, towards . . .

The preceding illustrations represent but a few ways that 'embodiment' might be pursued in the realm of museum design. The hope lies in the possibilities to be mined from the raw materials of the human tendency to understand the world through the stories it can tell, and the potential that design holds to

129

translate those tales into real-time, spatial experiences. If architects, designers and museum professionals rally together towards these ideals, museums may continue to become more engaging, more meaningful and ever more well-attended cultural resources.

Notes

1   Le Corbusier, *Towards a New Architecture*, London: Dover Publications, 1986.
2   V. Newhouse, *Towards a New Museum*, New York: Monacelli Press, 1998.
3   L. H. Skolnick, 'Review', *Curator: The Museum Journal*, Vol. 42, No. 1, 1999: 58.
4   J. S. Bruner, *Acts of Meaning*, Cambridge, MA: Harvard University Press, 1992.
5   L. Bedford, 'Storytelling: the realwork of museums', *NEMANews*, Summer, 2000: 8.
6   J. Henderson (foreword by Arthur Rosenblatt), *Museum Architecture*, Gloucester, MA: Rockport, 1998, p. 9.
7   H. Muschamp, 'Architecture: the library that puts on fishnets and hits the disco', *New York Times*, 16 May 2004, p. 2.1.

References

Bedford, L., 'Storytelling: the realwork of museums', *NEMANews*, Summer, 2000: 8.
Bruner, J. S., *Acts of Meaning*, Cambridge, MA: Harvard University Press, 1992.
Henderson, J. (foreword by Arthur Rosenblatt), *Museum Architecture*, Gloucester, MA: Rockport, 1998.
Le Corbusier, *Vers une architecture (Towards an Architecture)*, New York: Payson & Clarke Ltd., 1927.
——, *Towards a New Architecture*, London: Dover Publications, 1986.
Muschamp, H., 'Architecture: the library that puts on fishnets and hits the disco', *New York Times*, 16 May 2004, p. 2.1.
Newhouse, V., *Towards a New Museum*, New York: Monacelli Press, 1998.
Skolnick, L. H., 'Review', *Curator: The Museum Journal*, Vol. 42, No. 1, 1999: 58.

Part III

Inside spaces

10

Building on Victorian ideas

Lawrence Fitzgerald

Kelvingrove Art Gallery and Museum is a 100-year-old, grade A listed building described as housing 'one of the supreme European civic collections' by Neil MacGregor, Director of the British Museum. By the 1990s, the building's services, infrastructure and facilities were succumbing to the passage of time and the displays and education facilities were failing to meet the needs of the Museum's increasingly diverse prospective audiences. In 1998, Glasgow City Council staff embarked upon the largest research and consultation exercise in the Museums Service's history to shape redevelopment proposals. Many large-scale museum projects fix the content, design and intellectual rationale in so-called 'permanent' displays and thereby act not as repositories just for old objects but for old ideas. This chapter will suggest one model of how to create museum display spaces and displays that are more accessible and responsive to visitors' and potential audiences' interests, needs and aspirations.

Figure 10.1 The Art Gallery and Museum, Kelvingrove, Glasgow. Photograph Glasgow Museums, with permission.

Kelvingrove New Century Project

The Art Gallery and Museum, Kelvingrove, is the most visited museum outside London in Britain and, as part of Glasgow Museums, can draw upon some of the finest collections of British and European paintings, arms and armour and Scottish natural and social history. It is also Glasgow's most popular building.[1] But, like many splendid Victorian Gothic museums, it was creaking at the joints with permanent displays and building services no longer meeting the needs or expectations of today's visitors. A project was needed that would, literally and metaphorically, build upon the success of the existing museum and create a museum for the twenty-first century, the Kelvingrove New Century Project (KNCP).

Kelvingrove Art Gallery and Museum, like many other Victorian museums in Britain, was formed through the efforts of local government, industrial and mercantile benefactors, educational and social reformers and academic and amateur collectors. The main aims of Kelvingrove's creators were to: informally educate the public through the display of material culture; display and validate the fruits of object-based research; show the latest and best products of industrial and engineering design; accommodate and display public collections; and act as a focus for civic and cultural pride.

The design of Kelvingrove in many ways embodies these aims – in the grandeur of the building and in name checks for the great and good of the period on plaques around the east and west courts. Today, these aims are still important, but there is a different emphasis in the way in which collections are displayed and made accessible. At the turn of the century, simply placing objects on display within a fixed typological group and with a short descriptive label reflected contemporaneous theories of knowledge and practice. It conformed to the general belief in education through exposure to a fixed body of knowledge and a shared culture. We now recognize, however, that people learn in different ways and through a variety of media, that knowledge is constantly developing, that the museum is a social as well as educational space and that visitors come from a range of backgrounds and cultures. The public's interests and needs and the relevance of museums to people's lives are also constantly changing and evolving. Understanding the public and creating displays and facilities that respond and are responsive to different audiences, as well developments in research, is thus vital in defining the new museum.

What they really really want: understanding and involving stakeholders

Understanding stakeholders' disparate interests and involving them in the formulation of project objectives is considered good project management[2] and is, today, an essential part of the process of receiving grants from public bodies.[3] Front-end evaluation and research and formative evaluation of visitors and stakeholders have been promoted for many years in museological literature as the cost-effective way of ensuring an exhibition or museum programme's success.[4] A commitment to such evaluation underpins the KNCP and, to inform the project objectives and proposals, Glasgow Museums service embarked upon the largest exercise in public consultation and research in its history. This included:

- A survey, using self-completion questionnaires, of visitors to Kelvingrove to gauge general views on plans to refurbish the museum.[5]
- Three large-scale quantitative surveys of visitors to Kelvingrove to establish demographic profile and preferences for both the current and the proposed displays.[6]
- Qualitative focus group research with five key groups of visitors and non-visitors to understand current display preferences and reaction to possible changes.[7]
- A building usage survey of visitors to Kelvingrove by interview and observation.[8]
- A large-scale quantitative survey among Glaswegians to assess the popularity of the Kelvingrove Art Gallery and Museum when architecturally compared to other important buildings in the city.[9]
- Formative evaluation of the prototype 'story display' system through interview and observation of visitors and non-visitors to the Museum.[10]
- Formative evaluation of the prototype 'object cinema' by visitors to the Museum using self-completion questionnaires.[11]
- A large-scale self-completion survey of the Friends of Glasgow Museums to establish demographic profiles and preferences for current and proposed displays.[12]
- Formative evaluation, using large-scale quantitative surveys of current visitors and the Glasgow general public, of proposed themes, 'story displays' and preferred methods of interpretation.[13]
- An access audit of the current building and proposed changes.[14]
- Expert advice on orientation from Dr Chris Moore, Retail & Marketing Department, Strathclyde University.

In addition to this research, three panels were also established to suggest and comment on project proposals. These were:

- An education panel made up of formal education professionals from across the spectrum of education provision from nursery to university.
- A community and access panel made up of representatives from, and professionals working with, socially excluded groups, such as sight-impaired people, ethnic minorities and young adults from deprived parts of the city.
- A junior board made up of up to 15 schoolchildren aged 9–11 years.

In addition, three peer groups of museum and related professionals from throughout Britain were formed to comment on display and facility proposals:

- Museum directors and senior managers of museums and museum services.
- Natural history and environmental science curators and academics.
- Social history and ethnography academics and curators.

This substantial and wide-ranging stakeholder research emphasized the need to enhance the wide variety of collections and display themes in the Museum as well as the range of interpretative techniques utilized. Display themes had to be more relevant to the public's own passions and interests and illustrate the object's real significance, context and human story. Regular visitors had expectations and opinions about what they felt was appropriate in the Kelvingrove Art Gallery and Museum. For example, almost 50 per cent said they were fairly or very interested in politics and 61 per cent were similarly interested in sport and leisure. However, of these groups, only 1 per cent and 4 per cent respectively chose these as suitable subjects for display themes.[15] Art, Scottish history and local and Scottish identity were clearly popular themes, but there was also support for displays that might be of minority interest to attract and cater for a diverse audience.

Kelvingrove Art Gallery and Museum attracts a high proportion of regular visitors – around 50 per cent have been ten times or more.[16] As Glasgow's most popular building, it is clearly held in great affection by a large number of local people. Although many of these visitors, and other regular visitors such as the members of the Friends of Glasgow Museums, liked aspects of the current displays, they also welcomed change and the prospect of continually changing displays.[17] The qualitative research revealed that non-traditional themes and changing displays were more likely to attract non-visitors and new audiences.[18] Most stakeholders were also keen on introducing more active, lively and hands-on displays alongside traditional passive displays in reflective and quiet spaces.

Permanent displays and temporary solutions

How did the KNCP team respond to these findings? Lottery and millennium funding has enabled many museums to deliver long-overdue capital projects. This has often meant an opportunity to invigorate dated 'permanent displays' of the core collections. The problem is that many of these permanent displays end up literally being just that, with inflexibility built into not just the display architecture but the display themes and rationale. With a long gestation period for large capital projects,[19] 'permanent' displays are often out of date, both intellectually and aesthetically, and in need of renewal a few years after completion. For this reason, museums and galleries have a reputation for unchanging preserved displays as well as preserved objects. Some visitors can find this reassuring and part of the pleasure of visiting. When Dali's *St John on the Cross* moved from the Kelvingrove Art Gallery and Museum to the St Mungo Museum of Religious Art and Life across town, visitors to Kelvingrove enquired of its whereabouts or complained about its absence, years after the painting's move to its new home. However, for many visitors, particularly local visitors, their interest is maintained and they are encouraged to embark on repeat visits only if there is something new to see and do.[20]

To provide the 'new' and overcome the perceived expense of changing permanent displays, museums and galleries adopt a number of strategies. The most common is the temporary exhibition where displays using in-house and loaned collections are created, or touring exhibitions of almost entirely loaned collections are accommodated, typically for a period of three to six months. Temporary exhibitions have enormous advantages. They encourage co-operation and networking among staff of different museums and the exposure of sometimes significant collections to new audiences. They can be used to respond to current issues, anniversaries and events and, at their best, are used to involve different voices or specific audiences in the development or creation of displays. The very temporary nature of the exhibition can positively encourage museum staff, funders and other stakeholders to be more experimental than they otherwise might be. It is no coincidence that some of the most challenging, innovative or even the downright populist displays are temporary ones.

The two largest drawbacks to traditional temporary exhibitions is that, in the main, they do not feature the very things that give a museum or gallery its identity and meaning – its most significant objects and collections. They are also relatively resource intensive and typically have a high cost per visitor. Permanent displays are, not surprisingly, usually centred around the high points of a museum's holdings and the way in which galleries are themed mitigates against these collections being used elsewhere. Art galleries with large collections of flat art can, in relative terms, 'rehang' galleries or create new temporary exhibitions at a lower cost, but only if they do not require expensive cases or supporting structures, or, for that matter, if the galleries choose not to cater to a wide range of audiences and learning styles. Of course, art galleries are not alone in creating displays of 2-D material with minimal interpretation. History and technology museums resort to relatively inexpensive temporary displays of photographs, advertising posters, postcards and other works on paper. This is not to say that these are not intrinsically significant and of interest to many visitors, but the low cost is also undoubtedly an important factor in their justification.

Events, workshops, activity trails, tours and performance are effective ways of adding fresh and responsive interpretation to jaded permanent galleries. They can be relatively inexpensive to produce and deliver and, as with temporary exhibitions, their short life and relative inexpense compared to permanent galleries can encourage experimentation with interpretative methods and the targeting of non-traditional audiences. But their temporary nature is also their main shortcoming. When the tour guide is at lunch or the workshop has ended, the visitor is left alone with the ten-year-old label or the worn-out interactive. So is there an alternative?

Flexible and responsive galleries: themes

Before the KNCP, collections at Kelvingrove Art Gallery and Museum were displayed in traditionally themed galleries – arms and armour, archaeology, musical instruments, Egyptology, ethnography, natural history and fine and decorative art. These gallery themes tend to limit both the range of information and stories that can be conveyed about objects and the types of objects displayed. We know from stakeholder research that the sheer range of material and themes has been a key factor in the success of Kelvingrove and there is a multitude of important information and knowledge we can convey about the collections. There are also very significant objects and collections in store which fall outside the existing display themes.[21] Why then, choose to impose unnecessary constraints by using themes that limit that variety?

To create flexible and responsive displays, the new theming structure for galleries or choice of displays would be based upon two criteria: visitor and audience interest and the significance and strengths of the collections. What was required was a range of themes that built upon the encyclopaedic approach of the Victorians and encompassed these criteria. Twenty-eight themes were originally chosen, but after evaluation these were later rationalized to 25: Ancient Egypt, Animals on the Edge, Animal Recordbreakers, Armed and Dangerous, Cultural Survival, Italian Old Masters, Early Settlers of Western Scotland, Every Picture Tells a Story, Flight, French 19th Century Paintings, Gifts to Glasgow, Glasgow and its World, Italian Renaissance Art, Looking at Art, Design for Life, Mackintosh and the Glasgow Style, Dutch Old Masters, Prehistoric Animals, Scottish Art, Scottish Battles, Scottish Wildlife, The Earth, The Story of Kelvingrove, What is Beauty? and Words and Music.[22]

Some of these themes will occupy an entire gallery, others only a part. The task of the theme titles is to resonate with subject areas of interest to the public and to suggest possible content, not to imply an all-encompassing narrative or historical perspective. They will function as orientation signs to help visitors find their way around the Museum and so for very practical reasons have to be comprehensible and short.

Flexible and responsive displays: stories

What sort of displays will feature within these new interpretive themes? In order to be responsive to new research, new acquisitions and our visitors' and communities' changing interests and needs, displays will have to be easy to change. Within any one display theme the individual displays will tell a 'story', which is self-contained, focused on the object's real significance and relevant to the target audiences' knowledge, experiences and interests.

Each island 'story display' will be as large or as small as it needs to be, ranging from a single significant painting, such as Rembrandt's *Man in Armour*, or a small group of paintings showing a particular style or movement with interpretation appropriate to the target audience. This means focusing the displays on the most significant collections and not attempting to tell a larger narrative that will result in filling in the gaps with graphics or other media because the relevant collections are missing. Objects will not be shown as illustrations in a wider story, or to make a tangential historical point. The displays will go directly to the story of the objects. There may, of course, be many stories inherent in each object, but the key point is that the story will arise out of the object and not vice versa.

Curators were invited to suggest ideas for story displays and over 150 were received. Using evaluation this was reduced to 100. Each theme will therefore contain an average of four separate story displays, each with one or two key messages derived from the objects. Each of these self-contained story displays within a theme will be related to its neighbour only by virtue of the theme title. Thus, within Scottish Wildlife there will be story displays such as 'Life in a Scottish loch', 'Birds from a window' and 'Animal camouflage'. In response to stakeholder evaluation or new research, any story display can be entirely replaced, or the key message and objects changed, without disrupting any larger narrative.

Once Kelvingrove Art Gallery and Museum is reopened, staff will aim to completely replace or change eight story displays a year, based on the twin principles of visitor interest and collection significance. This means almost 50 per cent of the display space will alter over a six-year period and the remaining displays will be those considered by evaluation to be of continuing relevance to visitors.

Redefining permanent galleries through flexible story displays will not banish the need for a temporary exhibition space. The city requires, and the new museum will incorporate, a large temporary space, but this will be for brought-in 'blockbuster' touring exhibitions rather than in-house displays. Staff resources will be directed towards changing the story displays, and events, performance, workshops and guided tours based around the story displays will provide a complementary interpretation, rather than substituting for change as in traditional permanent displays.

Themed galleries and story displays will occupy 80 per cent of the display space in the new Museum, but the educational benefits and demand for supervised and 'hands-on' group activities and events and study areas is also recognized. For that reason, in separate galleries alongside the story displays, the new Museum will incorporate three 'discovery centres', a 'display study centre' and an 'object cinema'.

Discovery centres in museums are a well-established method of providing a more interactive experience of objects, particularly in History, Science and Technology. Kelvingrove Art Gallery and Museum will feature an 'Art discovery centre', an 'Environment discovery centre' and a 'History and technology discovery centre'. The 'display study centre' will provide an object, IT and publication-based further study and research facility for all visitors. An object cinema is a very effective and inspirational way of telling an in-depth story about a highly significant object or group of objects using tried and tested multi-media in conjunction with the real objects themselves.

Prototyping solutions

Based on this new plan, a number of questions arose. Individual story displays within Kelvingrove Art Gallery and Museum could be designed and produced as one-off elements of the overall gallery theme and design. As already noted, the lack of an overarching narrative will mean that galleries could, potentially, be changed in an achievable incremental fashion. Although this provides flexibility, what if the object or objects were to remain the same and the only thing being changed was the message? Is there a quicker and more cost-effective way to change text, labels, multimedia, audio or other interpretative media (or even for that matter individual objects, mounts or the display appearance) without resorting to dismantling the whole story display?

To explore possible solutions, Glasgow Museum's staff worked with an external architectural practice and a display case and structure manufacturer. Between October 1998 and August 1999, the first phase of a prototype flexible story display system was developed and evaluated in Kelvingrove Art Gallery and Museum. This involved creating two prospective 'story displays' – a fine art display entitled 'Introduction to Italian Renaissance Art', and a social and natural history display entitled 'St Kilda: Living with the Land'. The solution to providing flexibility appeared to lie in some form of standardized modules that could be arranged in different ways, were capable of containing a mix of all likely objects and media, but could also accommodate bespoke finishes and graphics to avoid a 'trade show' look. The key modules of the prototype flexible story display system were the case, table, bench, screen and slab, designed to be as physically accessible as possible. Other flexible elements evaluated included object labels, text and image panels, an interactive IT facility, a scripted audio and lighting presentation, a video presentation, a power and lighting track, a drawer-mounted object display and a hand-held audio guide.

Figure 10.2 The prototype flexible 'story display' system, the Art Gallery and Museum, Kelvingrove, Glasgow. Photograph Glasgow Museums, with permission.

The prototype displays were well received by respondents of different sexes, ages, needs, backgrounds and levels of interest in the chosen subject matter. As intended, the displays appealed to most learning styles. A major concern of the staff was the reaction of the public to the modular look of the system, particularly within the context of a late Victorian gallery space. The overall design of the displays proved very popular, however, with over 75 per cent of respondents in the evaluation rating the design as good or very good.[23] Where the prototype display system failed was in providing practical modular elements that were inexpensive, easy to change and maintain and that met all conservation requirements. This may be too harsh a criticism, as the prototype display system was never meant to provide definitive solutions to all the KNCP flexible display requirements, being, rather, a step towards achieving that goal.

Compromising with reality

The results of both the public and technical evaluation of the prototype flexible story display system was to inform a second phase of development and evaluation that would test additional elements and refine the production brief. This work was planned originally for March 2000. However, the KNCP team's attention was directed to other project priorities, not least the need to secure Heritage Lottery and European funding for the project, and it is fair to say that the development of the flexible display system also took a backseat to other aspects of the project's development, such as curatorial and education display content definition and the complexities of refurbishing a grade A listed building. HLF finally approved £12.7 million for the project in January 2002, the largest ever HLF award in Scotland, and this funding also helped to lever in an additional £2.2 million in European funding. Redman Design was procured as the designer for the main gallery displays and the flexible display system in 2002 and was replaced by Event Communications in 2003. The KNCP client team has now taken the display system design partly back in-house and, in retrospect, the need for this could have been anticipated. It was always going to be a challenge for external designers to develop a flexible display system on their own and in the time the schedule allowed. The flexible display envisaged during the prototype display development was one in which 80 or 90 per cent of the display structure and elements could be reused. It was always understood that, to ensure that story displays looked different from each other and that visitors could tell where one display ended and another began, bespoke elements would be required for each display. These bespoke elements were the structure finishes, colour, text font and the free-standing interactives. Flexibility is not cheap to build into a system – structures and key parts have to be rugged, high quality, easy to maintain and reliable. There is always going to be a trade-off between very flexible displays that are expensive to produce, but relatively cheap to change and look similar if not alike, and less flexible displays that are cheaper to produce, more expensive to change and have a more individual appearance. A compromise in the brief for the flexible display system was agreed to allow a more bespoke design for each story display, resulting in around 60 per cent of any one display being reusable and incorporating some modularity, thus reducing production costs.

In reaching this compromise, two other important influences, other than cost, come into play. In my experience there is an understandable reluctance among some designers to produce more uniform and, maybe to some eyes, less imaginative displays – which a modular design seems to imply – and to design themselves out of future work. After all, what museum display design is going to be favourably judged by peers or win design awards on the basis of flexibility and ease of maintenance? In addition, if all museums had flexible display systems that were even 60 per cent reusable, there would potentially be a lot less work for designers.

Understanding the building and getting visitors around

In addition to informing the development of more interesting and responsive displays and facilities, stakeholder evaluation revealed the need for greatly improved access between floors and around the galleries.[24] The Kelvingrove Art Gallery and Museum is an almost symmetrical building along two axes and both the focus group research[25] and the Cardiff University's building usage survey[26] found that physical access, particularly to the first-floor galleries, was a major problem. The building was also essentially designed to display flat art in the first-floor galleries and museum objects on the ground floor. Amazingly, only one in five visitors were found to use the upper galleries. While this may in part have been due to the specific content of the first floor, Cardiff University analysis showed that the first floor of the building is inherently less accessible due to the limited number of clear access points, especially for families with children and people with mobility problems.

This piece of research also revealed that the building affects use patterns in other ways. The building was originally designed so that visitors could access, in sequence, the Museum's ten public galleries on each floor and effectively follow a circular route around the Museum, with each main gallery on the ground floor providing views on to the impressive Kelvingrove Park. Over time, however, some of the galleries were converted to other non-public uses, such as a print storage room or meeting room, effectively blocking this 'natural' route. With many galleries of a similar size and appearance, orientation became more difficult, making it harder to find a way around the Museum.

Informed by this research, the Education Panel suggestions and an access audit, the KNCP team decided to intellectually split the building east and west with 'Expressive art'-based themes on one side and 'People and the environment' themes on the other. The galleries will be cleared of all accretions and non-display activities – meeting rooms, staff facilities, café – so that the original 'natural' route around the museum can be reinstated. Non-display activities will in general be moved to the 'basement' area, which had previously been used for storage and staff accommodation and had been out of bounds to the general public.

Confusingly, the 'basement' is in fact the real ground floor of the building, as two typically grand Victorian staircases take visitors up to the 'ground' floor main entrances. A new ground-level main entrance will be created into the 'basement' to allow level access into the building for the first time. Two large-capacity lifts will run from the basement up through the central core of the building and two staircases will connect the basement with the ground floor, greatly improving access between floors.

As well as the building usage survey, in February 1999 Dr C. Moore, a lecturer in Retail Marketing at Strathclyde University, was invited to discuss ways of improving physical and intellectual access to the building with the project team.[27] Although there are obvious differences between large multidisciplinary museums and large department stores, not least in visitors' or customers' motivations, they have a number of features in common. Both display a large variety of objects arranged in different themes in a building that may be unfamiliar to the visitor or customer. Both have to accommodate a large number of people who browse displays and stop when something interests or attracts them and both have to provide easy access and clear guidance to the most popular items, while encouraging visitors or customers to call at everything on display.

Two suggestions by Dr Moore that were vital to informing the final position of themes and displays in the building were to keep foyer areas or 'decompression zones' clear of displays and attractions and, crucially, to position popular displays throughout the Museum to draw people around the whole of the Museum. Thus, from the stakeholder evaluation we know that the hands-on discovery rooms and the object cinema, as well as particular themes such as Ancient Egypt, Mackintosh and Scottish Battles, will be popular with specific or all audiences and so these will be positioned in the far corners of the building or east and west galleries. Displays will be kept out of entrance and orientation spaces where possible.

Building work started in October 2003, elements of the new flexible story displays will be formatively evaluated during 2004, and the Kelvingrove Art Gallery and Museum is scheduled to open in summer 2006. Glasgow Museums is committed to delivering inclusive and responsive displays and services and, with this in mind, a masterplan has been developed for a £40 million new-build project to create a new Museum of Transport and Technology on the River Clyde, Glasgow.[28] The masterplan has been informed by extensive qualitative and quantitative evaluation and more is to follow as the project develops.[29] Central to this masterplan is the idea of flexible themes and story displays that address the interests and needs of our current and potential audiences.

Notes

1 Lowland Ltd, 'Large-scale quantitative survey amongst Glaswegians to assess the popularity of Kelvingrove Museum, architecturally, compared to other important buildings in the city', unpublished report for Glasgow Museums, 1999.

2 See, for example, Commission for Architecture and the Built Environment, *Creating Excellent Buildings: A Guide for Clients*. Available at: http://www.cabe.org.uk (accessed 12 August 2004).

3 See, for example, the Heritage Lottery Fund, Arts Lottery Fund, Wellcome Rediscover Grant or European Regional Development Fund application guidelines.

4 For example, E. Hooper-Greenhill, 'A new communication model for museums', in G. Kavanagh (ed.), *Museum Languages: Objects and Texts*, Leicester: Leicester University Press, 1991.

5 Glasgow Museums, 'A survey, using self-completion questionnaires, of visitors to Kelvingrove to gauge general views on plans to refurbish the museum', unpublished report, 1999.

6 Lowland Ltd, 'Large-scale quantitative surveys of visitors to Kelvingrove Art Gallery & Museum', unpublished report for Glasgow Museums, April 1998, October 1998, January 1999.

7 System 3 Ltd, 'Qualitative focus group research of five groups of visitors and non-visitors to understand current display preferences and reaction to possible changes', unpublished report for Glasgow Museums, 1999.

8 T. Grajewski, 'Building usage survey of visitors to Kelvingrove by interview and observation', unpublished report for Glasgow Museums, 1999.

9 Lowland Ltd, 'Large-scale quantitative survey amongst Glaswegians'.

10 Glasgow Museums, 'Formative evaluation of the prototype "story display" system by interview and observation of visitors and non-visitors to the Museum', unpublished report, 1999.

11 Glasgow Museums, 'Formative evaluation of the prototype "object cinema" by visitors to the Museum using self-completion questionnaire', unpublished report, 1999.

12 Glasgow Museums, 'Large-scale self-completion survey of the Friends of Glasgow Museums to establish demographic profile and preferences for current and proposed displays', unpublished report, 1999.

13 Lowland Ltd, 'Formative evaluation, using large-scale quantitative survey of current visitors and the Glasgow general public, of proposed themes, "story displays" and preferred methods of interpretation', unpublished report for Glasgow Museums, 2000.

14 ADAPT Ltd, 'Access audit of current building and proposed changes', unpublished report for Glasgow Museums, 1999.

15 Lowland Ltd, 'Large-scale quantitative surveys of visitors to Kelvingrove', p. 12.

16 Ibid., p. 10, n. 6.

17 Glasgow Museums, 'Large-scale self-completion survey of the Friends', p. 2.

18 System 3 Ltd, 'Qualitative focus group research', p. 14.

19 For example, the first display suggestions made by curators to inform the Kelvingrove New Century Project were in 1995. The refurbished Kelvingrove Art Gallery and Museum will reopen to the public in 2006.

20 System 3 Ltd, 'Qualitative focus group research', p. 10, n. 8.

21 For example, Glasgow Museums has in store one of Britain's most significant collections of British costume.

22 These working titles are yet to be evaluated.

23 Glasgow Museums, 'Formative evaluation of the prototype "story display"', p. 2.

24 ADAPT Ltd, 'Access audit', p. 15.

25 System 3 Ltd, 'Qualitative focus group research', p. 9, n. 8.

26 Grajewski, 'Building usage survey of visitors', p. 8. Dr Grajewski and colleagues had been researching the way in which the architecture of large public buildings affects the way people use them and find their way around.

27 Dr Moore is a researcher and consultant to the retail industry on how people use and find their way around shops and department stores.

28 Event Communications Ltd-led consortium, 'A new Museum of Transport', unpublished report for Glasgow Museums, 2003.

29 Scotinform Ltd, 'Large-scale quantitative survey of visitors to the Museum of Transport, five focus groups, 25 mini-groups and telephone survey of Glasgow schools, April–June 2003', unpublished report for Glasgow Museums, 2003.

References

ADAPT Ltd, 'Access audit of current building and proposed changes', unpublished report for Glasgow Museums, 1999.

Commission for Architecture and the Built Environment, *Creating Excellent Buildings: A Guide for Clients*. Available at: http://www.cabe.org.uk (accessed 12 August 2004).

Event Communications Ltd-led consortium, 'A new Museum of Transport', unpublished report for Glasgow Museums, 2003.

Glasgow Museums, 'Formative evaluation of the prototype "object cinema" by visitors to the Museum using self-completion questionnaire', unpublished report, 1999.

——, 'Formative evaluation of the prototype "story display" system by interview and observation of visitors and non-visitors to the Museum', unpublished report, 1999.

——, 'Large-scale self-completion survey of the Friends of Glasgow Museums to establish demographic profile and preferences for current and proposed displays', unpublished report, 1999.

——, 'A survey, using self-completion questionnaires, of visitors to Kelvingrove to gauge general views on plans to refurbish the museum', unpublished report, 1999.

Grajewski, T., 'Building usage survey of visitors to Kelvingrove by interview and observation', unpublished report for Glasgow Museums, 1999.

Hooper-Greenhill, E., 'A new communication model for museums', in G. Kavanagh (ed.), *Museum Languages: Objects and Texts*, Leicester: Leicester University Press, 1991.

Lowland Ltd, 'Large-scale quantitative surveys of visitors to Kelvingrove Art Gallery & Museum', unpublished report for Glasgow Museums, April 1998, October 1998, January 1999.

——, 'Large-scale quantitative survey amongst Glaswegians to assess the popularity of Kelvingrove Museum, architecturally, compared to other important buildings in the city', unpublished report for Glasgow Museums, 1999.

——, 'Formative evaluation, using large-scale quantitative survey of current visitors and the Glasgow general public, of proposed themes, "story displays" and preferred methods of interpretation', unpublished report for Glasgow Museums, 2000.

Scotinform Ltd, 'Large-scale quantitative survey of visitors to the Museum of Transport, five focus groups, 25 mini-groups and telephone survey of Glasgow schools, April–June 2003', unpublished report for Glasgow Museums, 2003.

System 3 Ltd, 'Qualitative focus group research of five groups of visitors and non-visitors to understand current display preferences and reaction to possible changes', unpublished report for Glasgow Museums, 1999.

11

Representing Enlightenment space

Beth Lord

There is a current trend for museums to represent Enlightenment museum spaces, recreating the displays of the eighteenth century. In this chapter I will ask why museums are representing Enlightenment spaces in the twenty-first century, suggesting that the answer has to do with the concept of representation itself. I will look at three recent exhibitions that manifest this trend: *Enlightenment: Discovering the World in the Eighteenth Century*, a major new permanent display at the British Museum; *Art on the Line: The Royal Academy Exhibitions at Somerset House 1780–1836*, a 2001–2 temporary exhibition at the Courtauld Gallery; and the new, permanent Darwin Centre at the Natural History Museum.[1] What these three exhibitions have in common is that they not only display the art and objects collected in the eighteenth century, but also show *how* these collections were understood, organized and displayed at the time they were collected. These exhibitions share an ambitious aim to increase visitors' understanding of the history of the museum space, and to challenge them to consider the nature of museum representation itself. I will argue that it is in this sense that they are truly 'Enlightenment' spaces, and I will consider the challenges this approach poses to museums and visitors.

If we were to ask what people associate with the historical period known as the Enlightenment, the range of answers would be fairly predictable. Some might associate the Enlightenment with rational humanism, political republicanism and the rejection of religious and monarchical authority; others might include developments in capitalism and colonialism, and the beginnings of the Industrial Revolution. It is likely, moreover, that any description of the Enlightenment would be of an era defined by independent thinking, scientific rigour, observation and experiment, and ordering and classifying information with the aim of building universal systems of knowledge. This is what people understand by 'Enlightenment'.

If we consider these defining characteristics of rationalism, experiment, order, classification and universality, however, we find them equally present in pre-Enlightenment thinking. Aristotelian philosophy was centrally concerned with determining the categories of the world so that nature might be better understood for the purposes of our practical, empirical engagements with it. Rational

Aristotelian system-building went on to dominate the medieval period, in which philosophers set out to discover the order of the universe put in place by God.

The striving for order, classification and universal systems that we associate with the Enlightenment is not new or unique to that era. What is new is that with the rejection of religious and monarchical authority comes a rejection of the idea that the universe has an essential or divine order. Because divine systems are thrown into doubt, a thing's place in a system can no longer be assumed simply to be part of the essence of what it is to be that thing. Instead, the systems are now thought to be the product of human understanding, and these systems are suddenly at odds with the world of *things* that are not humanly produced. The Enlightenment recognizes, for the first time, that there is a gap – a space, if you will – between nature and the systems we use to order it. This space is the space of representation, and I would like to argue that the age of Enlightenment is characterized by this space.

In *The Order of Things*, Michel Foucault defines representation as the space opened up by the separation of words and things – *Les mots et les choses* in the book's original title.[2] The problem of this separation is the driving force of seventeenth- and eighteenth-century thought. The major philosophical questions of the era concern the relation between mind and world – how is it that words, concepts and human understanding relate to the things that we experience? It is the problem that occupies Descartes, Hume and Locke, and the problem that Kant struggles with in every one of his texts. As Foucault argues, the problem of representation is fundamentally new to the age of Enlightenment. The problem simply does not exist for ancient and medieval thinking, for in a universe of things whose concepts are included in them by God, ready for human reason to discover, there is no space between the thing and its concept.[3]

Enlightenment, then, might be characterized in two points. First, it is characterized by the open rejection of blind reliance on systems handed down by authority, as exemplified by Descartes' method of starting from first principles, and by Kant's claim that Enlightenment requires the 'freedom to make public use of one's reason in all matters'.[4] Second, Enlightenment involves the creation of new systems based upon the recognition that there is a gap between the system and what it purports to describe. Kant's philosophy is the pinnacle of architectonic system-building, yet all his work is occupied with the question of what justifies us in ascribing human systems to the non-human world of nature. Enlightenment thinking struggles with the need to create new systems, for it is always aware of the gap between those systems and the things themselves.

The space of representation that originates with the Enlightenment manifests itself in the birth of the museum. The museum as understood in the eighteenth century is more than just a collection of particular things – it aims at universality. This is one way in which the museum differs from the private collection or the 'cabinet of curiosities', as exemplified by the founding of the British Museum in 1753 as a 'universal museum'.[5] The museum brings together disparate collections from different branches of knowledge and interprets them according to a system of classification, the guiding editorial principle of which is the assumption that they *can* be interconnected in a universal system.[6] Incidentally, this assumption is the same one that Kant says we must make when trying to interpret the vast diversity of nature – in order to make any sense of things at all, we must assume that nature does conform to 'a system our understanding can grasp', although we have no proof that nature actually does conform to such a system.[7] Systems of classification, for Kant, are artificial, invented by human understanding and interpreted into nature, in an attempt to bridge the gap of representation.

It is the role of the museum in the eighteenth century not only to study and display objects, but to study and display these human *systems* for understanding objects. This is another way that the museum goes beyond the private collection: from the start it is concerned with interpretation, with how objects are systematically represented. It is at this time that 'curiosity' becomes increasingly regarded as an outmoded way of thinking, in favour of methodical classification.[8] The museum is quite literally a space for representation – a space in which the representational system itself is put on display, and in which scholars and visitors, through looking at objects, can think about the adequacy of that 'artificial' system to nature. Of course, the expanding role of the museum in the eighteenth century must be attributed to a complex of social, economic, intellectual and political factors that it is not my intention to marginalize. However, the impulse among Enlightenment collectors to classify things and to make them publicly available in a certain systematic form is made possible by that era's new concern with the space of representation.

Foucault thus discusses the phenomena of amassing and displaying collections in the seventeenth and eighteenth centuries in the context of this Enlightenment mode of thought:

> It is often said that the establishment of botanical gardens and zoological collections expressed a new curiosity about exotic plants and animals. In fact, these had already claimed men's interest for a long while. What had changed was the space in which it was possible to see them and from which it was possible to describe them.[9]

For Foucault, it is not *primarily* the new European curiosity about the world that makes the museum possible in the Enlightenment era. This curiosity had already long been present, although the rise of capitalism and colonialism certainly gave more people the means to transform this curiosity into active collecting. As a result, the museum, botanical garden and menagerie become *materially* possible. Conceptually, however, they are made possible by the *space* between human systems of thought and the things themselves – the space of representation that governs Enlightenment thinking. Only when this space opens, when the relationship between things and the concepts we apply to them becomes problematic, is it possible to create a physical space for positing and questioning the nature of this relationship. Positing and questioning the relationship between things and systems is *interpretation*. Museums are fundamentally about interpretation – about attempting to bridge the gap between things and systems.

It is in this context that I'd like to look at the three museum exhibitions that recreate, represent or evoke Enlightenment museum spaces described above. I suggested that what these exhibitions have in common is that they not only display art and objects collected during the Enlightenment, but also show *how* these collections were understood, organized and displayed in the Enlightenment.

Figure 11.1 *Enlightenment: Discovering the World in the Eighteenth Century*, which opened in 2004 at the British Museum. With permission of the British Museum.

149

The exhibitions show us the Enlightenment museum, and are in different ways concerned with helping visitors to understand the principles of order, classification and universality that have governed museum collecting and display. But what is truly 'Enlightenment' about these exhibitions is that they challenge us to consider the nature of representation, and this challenge is at the heart of all Enlightenment thinking. These exhibitions are spaces for representing systems of representation themselves, asking visitors to consider what museum space is for.

The aim of the British Museum from 1753 to be a 'universal museum' is reflected in *Enlightenment: Discovering the World in the Eighteenth Century*, which opened in 2004 to mark the British Museum's 250th anniversary. It is a permanent display in the King's Library, the room designed and built by Robert Smirke in 1823–7 to house the library of King George III. The books were moved to the new British Library building in 1998 and the room was restored to its original condition to house 'a permanent display of objects selected from the rich stores of the Museum, arranged in an exhibition devoted to discovery and learning in the age of George III'.[10] The gallery is loosely divided into seven sections exhibiting the types of objects that would have been present in the Museum in the eighteenth century, organized according to the interests of eighteenth-century collectors. The central section, called Classifying the World, brings the themes together to consider methods of classification used by Enlightenment collectors and scientists, and by the British Museum itself.

Objects are exhibited in the Library's original nineteenth-century manuscript cases with sloping glass tops; glazed cabinets full of objects from the reserve collections line the walls. While the manuscript cases are accompanied by interpretive panels and labels, the cabinets are entirely without text (a guide to the objects is available on request). Extensively researched and painstakingly recreated, the room beautifully and effectively evokes an eighteenth-century museum space. The effect on a modern-day visitor can be remarkable. This is an exhibition where we are invited not only to look at and think about objects, but also to think about how they are organized and presented; to consider the governing principle behind their selection and arrangement; and to think about how and why museums represent things in certain ways. The text panels and gallery guide encourage visitors to think about the 'culture of collecting and classification', and how and why it arose in the Enlightenment.

The Darwin Centre at the Natural History Museum similarly aims to challenge visitors to think about museum representation. The Darwin Centre is different from the Enlightenment gallery in that it is primarily a research centre housed in a state-of-the-art new building, and does not outwardly look like an Enlightenment space. The space accessible to the visitor in Phase One features interactive terminals that explain the significance of the specimens preserved in formaldehyde, and the work undertaken in the Centre.

But if the physical space is not eighteenth-century, the interpretive space is. The rows upon rows of glass jars of preserved specimens of indeterminate age evoke

Figure 11.2 Display cabinets in the British Museum's Enlightenment gallery. With permission of the British Museum.

a quintessentially eighteenth-century mode of collecting and presenting nature. The oldest specimens date from the seventeenth century; labels on glass jars name the voyages on which specimens were collected, evoking the same sense of discovery present in the Enlightenment gallery. The numbers, too, are awe-inspiring: 22 million zoological specimens in 450,000 jars, holding 350,000 litres of alcohol in Phase One alone. The small number of jars visible to the public are closely packed on to shelves with minimal interpretation, resembling the glazed wall cases of the British Museum's Enlightenment gallery. Even the demonstration area, where scientists present the collections to the public, recalls eighteenth-century public lectures on science.

Furthermore, what the Darwin Centre presents to the public is fundamentally an Enlightenment idea: that all of nature – or at least as much of it as is physically and ethically possible – is brought together under one roof, classified according to the latest taxonomic and systematic thinking, and put on display more or less as-is. Researchers at the Darwin Centre specialize in taxonomy and systematics, and the fact that the Centre is focused on systems of classification comes through clearly in the interpretive panels and interactive displays. Through both the displays and the guided behind-the-scenes tours, visitors may reflect upon scientific methods of representing nature through systems of classification. Further, the Natural History Museum's description of the Darwin Centre as marking a 'new era' that will 'radically alter public perception of what a museum can be and bring people closer to the heart of its day-to-day work',[11] suggests an aim to challenge visitors to think about museum space and museum representation – to consider what museums are and how they work.

Art on the Line, a temporary exhibition shown at the Courtauld Institute in 2001–2, aimed even more explicitly to consider the nature of gallery space. This exhibition recreated a Royal Academy exhibition from the late eighteenth century in the Great Room of Somerset House, the same room in which the RA exhibition was held at that time. Paintings were hung frame-to-frame, floor to ceiling, as they would have been then, overwhelming today's visitor and conflicting with current expectations of the gallery space. The exhibition featured reviews and satirical drawings contemporary with these historical exhibitions, to show the visitor the social and economic context in which paintings were made and exhibited. This was a remarkable exhibition, for it put the audience *both* in the place of an eighteenth-century audience, looking at the paintings, experiencing the space and enjoying the social aspect of gallery-going, *and* in the reflexive position of a twenty-first century audience, looking at the way in which eighteenth-century audiences experienced exhibitions. The exhibition raised the question of what it is to be a gallery audience and what an exhibition of paintings is for, challenging audiences to think about systems of displaying art, and about the social function of museums and galleries.

Why are these exhibitions that return to Enlightenment modes of display opening today, at the beginning of the twenty-first century? There are a number of interrelated reasons. For the British Museum and Natural History Museum, the need to increase public access to collections previously in storage has been a major factor. These galleries allow great numbers of objects from reserve collections to be brought to public view, arranged closely together in cases with very little by way of interpretive text or labelling – both the Enlightenment gallery and the Darwin Centre present something akin to visible storage.

Helping visitors to orient themselves historically to the museum is also a factor: the Enlightenment gallery can function as an introduction to the British Museum through the history of its collectors and collections, while the Darwin Centre introduces visitors to the work of taxonomic researchers over the past 400 years that has been fundamental to the development of the Natural History Museum. It has also been suggested that these exhibitions represent a reaction against the trend for exhibitions led by designers and educators: Enlightenment displays return power to curators and restore *objects* as the essence of the museum.[12]

I have argued, however, that museums are not fundamentally about objects, but about the space of representation. The museum does not simply present objects; it presents and questions the space between objects and conceptual systems. I'd like to suggest, then, that the overriding reason for recreating Enlightenment spaces today is that the question of museum representation has become relevant again as it has not been since the late eighteenth-century. Questions of how and why we represent objects, from whose cultural perspective, and according to which set of presuppositions, are of enormous importance as the role of museums as centres for learning, inclusion and community-building is fully recognized. We are returning to an age of interdisciplinary learning that was lost with the fragmentation of disciplines in the nineteenth and early twentieth centuries. We are returning to the notion that the organizing principle behind museum display can be the theme, material or function of the objects as well as their chronology or geography. The recognition that there can be more than one 'correct' way of classifying objects, and that there can be a multiplicity of ways of interpreting them, leads us to question the very nature of classification systems and the very nature of interpretation. This above all marks a return to an Enlightenment way of thinking: questioning the very nature of representation, the way that we apply words, concepts and interpretive systems to things.

One role of the contemporary museum can be to challenge us to rethink the interpretive systems we do apply to things, and to encourage us to see things in a different way. I have suggested that these Enlightenment spaces, in being centrally concerned with the nature of representation, do just that. But the question of visitors' reactions to these galleries is another matter. What do visitors make of these spaces, that on the one hand seem to resemble the archetypal image of what a 'museum' is, and on the other hand encourage them to question that image? Kim Sloan, principal curator of the Enlightenment gallery, has said that, because audiences today are accustomed to museums providing hi-tech, interactive 'edutainment' experiences, they are pleasantly surprised to encounter an old-fashioned approach in the gallery.[13] The Enlightenment gallery allows them to spend time with the objects, without too much interpretive

153

mediation, and without any audio-visual mediation other than an optional audioguide. Visitors have expressed a desire to return to the Museum, because they did not have time to look at all the objects. This is a wonderfully positive public reaction to the gallery, and undoubtedly there are many audiences who do appreciate the old-fashioned display and the absence of computer screens. If museums *are* motivated by the desire to reassert curatorial power, these responses vindicate the decision to do so by seeming to affirm a public interest in objects over interpretation.

I think that there are challenges, however, with the Enlightenment mode of presentation, and with the assumption that objects alone are enough to engage audiences. Public perceptions of the 'museum', particularly among those who have not visited museums or have had negative experiences there as a child, continue to be dominated by the image of the nineteenth- and early twentieth-century museum: shelves full of dusty, decaying objects accompanied by dry, didactic texts, closed off to the visitor both physically and intellectually. It is true that museums no longer resemble this image to the extent that they did even ten years ago, but, within the British Museum and Natural History Museum, examples can be found of exhibits that have not moved far beyond it. Numerous galleries involve an adaptive reuse of nineteenth-century cases, not so dissimilar from their use in the Enlightenment gallery. Modes of display often continue to be traditional and didactic. Many museum exhibits all over the world continue to offer this *form* of presentation, even if it is supplemented by updated styles of display and interactive terminals.

While the Enlightenment gallery at the British Museum should not be counted among these old-fashioned exhibits, it is unclear how visitors are to differentiate them. Many visitors strolling through the galleries on the Museum's ground floor will not realize that they're seeing something different from what's in the Egyptian gallery next door – that with the Enlightenment gallery, they're not just seeing a museum exhibition, but a representation of a certain *type* of museum exhibition. The danger is that, in representing a historical museum space, the Enlightenment gallery may fulfil people's worst fears about what museums are – long rooms of closely-packed shelves, eighteenth-century cabinets and marble busts, with little interpretation.

The Darwin Centre has a similar problem. The obvious barrier is that jars of specimens are rather boring to the non-specialist visitor; it is only when the history of the taxonomic *system* behind the jars is apparent that they become more interesting. But the system is 'invisible', to borrow Tony Bennett's term.[14] It is not made apparent through looking at objects. As a result, those with knowledge of the system must 'enlighten' those without knowledge. With the recreation of the Enlightenment space the power of the curator, or the museum as a whole, over the visitor appears to be preserved.

However, I do not believe that either the Enlightenment gallery or the Darwin Centre is an attempt to exercise institutional power over visitors. Rather, they are truly Enlightenment spaces to the extent that they challenge the visitor to consider the relationship between objects and systems of thought. In the twenty-first century, this means that they enable visitors to apply different interpretive systems to the objects, and encourage the idea that objects can be aligned with a plurality of coherent conceptual schemes. This, surely, is one institutional motivation behind the recreation of Enlightenment spaces; in providing minimal interpretation, museums invite visitors to relate the objects to systems relevant to themselves, not only to the systems suggested by the museum. Indeed, Neil MacGregor has called the British Museum and museums in general 'communities of interpretation' that are based on the recognition that 'within the same museum object, different histories, meanings and functions may freely cohabit'.[15] This recognition is, I believe, reflected in the Enlightenment gallery, but is complex and perhaps inevitably gives rise to challenges and barriers. With the right interpretation, however, these barriers can be the ideal starting point for visitors to consider what a museum is. If they start out thinking that this exhibition is no different from any other, the interpretation, explaining that the gallery represents an Enlightenment understanding of museum space, might encourage them to consider why these objects were collected, why they are organized and presented in a certain way, and how they can be interpreted and understood. In this way, a visitor's negative perception of the 'museum' can be challenged and, hopefully, changed. Far from trying to reassert institutional power, I believe that with these galleries museums have a progressive aim to open themselves to new audiences, returning to the Enlightenment ideal of democratic participation in learning and knowledge.

I'd like to finish by asking what the future of Enlightenment museum spaces might be – spaces that reflect on the nature of museum representation. In terms of our ways of thinking, we are still broadly in the era of Enlightenment. The question of the relationship between words, concepts, systems and things – the question of representation – continues to dominate philosophy with the same force that it did in Kant's day. Museums continue to be made possible by this space – they continue to posit and question relationships between systems and things. In recreating Enlightenment spaces, I've suggested, museums add a complicating interpretive layer: they bring the question of interpretation to the fore, challenging visitors to reconsider conceptual systems and their relationship to objects.

What is changing, however, is our perception of who should have control over the conceptual systems to be related to objects. More and more, museums invite visitors themselves to control this process, to apply conceptual systems from cultures and backgrounds that are different from the culture in which the museum was created. Visitors are invited to construct their own experience in a way relevant to them. In this way, Enlightenment spaces become networked spaces. Networks are all about *systems*, but, instead of being imposed from above, they are user-led and user-organized. Networks allow for groups and individuals to build systems, rather than discovering or understanding the systems imposed by authority. In this sense they allow for multiple perspectives and multiple interpretations.

155

Networks can be exemplified by the internet and its associated applications – people now routinely build their own collections of music and organize their own content for frequently visited websites. Networks are also exemplified by reality television, which, I believe, has gained such a popular response because it allows viewers to organize their experience and control the outcome of the show. These experiences are more than merely *interactive* – they are actually organizing, system-building experiences. To the extent that museums enable visitors to organize their own experience, to experiment with systems of classification, and to think about how museum representation works, they continue to be 'Enlightenment' spaces in the networked age. The Dulwich Picture Gallery – an Enlightenment space par excellence – has introduced interactive palmtop units for schools, into which the student programmes the artworks he or she finds meaningful, creating an individual learning programme and a personal record of the gallery experience. This model need not be restricted to networking information, but can involve networks of artefacts, experiences, learning, socializing, eating, drinking and shopping – the visitor organizes his or her own museum experience. This is the goal of the small city of Cerritos, California, which is planning a museum that will be networked to the library and to the city's performing arts centre. The city's Experience Library is already a networked experience, with themed rooms networking artefacts, computers and books, and there are queues to get in from all over the surrounding region.

There is a move towards the space of representation being visitor-governed to which today's Enlightenment spaces are already responding. Museum interpretation becomes more and more about including visitors as equal participants in the process of bridging the gap between conceptual systems and things.

Notes

1 At the time of writing, only Phase One of the Darwin Centre has been completed.
2 M. Foucault, *The Order of Things* (trans. anon.), London: Routledge, 1970, p. 130.
3 Ibid., pp. 125–32.
4 I. Kant, 'An answer to the question: "What is Enlightenment?"', in I. Kant, *Political Writings* (ed. Hans Reiss, trans. H. B. Nisbet), Cambridge: Cambridge University Press, 1991, p. 55.
5 K. Sloan, '"Aimed at universality and belonging to the nation": the Enlightenment and the British Museum', in K. Sloan (ed.), *Enlightenment: Discovering the World in the Eighteenth Century*, London: The British Museum Press, 2003, p. 14.
6 Ibid.
7 I. Kant, *Critique of Judgment* (trans. Werner S. Pluhar), Indianapolis, IN: Hackett, 1987, p. 185.
8 L. Syson, 'The ordering of the artificial world: collecting, classification and progress', in K. Sloan (ed.), *Enlightenment: Discovering the World in the Eighteenth Century*, London: The British Museum Press, 2003, p. 115.
9 Foucault, *The Order of Things*, p. 131.
10 Sloan, 'Aimed at universality', pp. 14–17.
11 P. Gates, 'Nature's treasures: the Darwin Centre at the Natural History Museum', *BBC Wildlife Magazine*, special issue published in collaboration with the Natural History Museum, 2002, p. 2.
12 I thank Eilean Hooper-Greenhill for drawing my attention to this point.

13 Interview with Kim Sloan, March 2004.
14 T. Bennett, 'Civic seeing: museums and the organisation of vision', paper presented at the University of Leicester Museum Studies conference on Creative Space, April 2004.
15 N. MacGregor, 'The whole world in our hands', Review, *The Guardian*, 24 July 2004, p. 6.

References

Bennett, T., 'Civic seeing: museums and the organisation of vision', paper presented at the University of Leicester Museum Studies conference on Creative Space, April 2004.
Foucault, M., *The Order of Things* (trans. anon.), London: Routledge, 1970.
Gates, P., 'Nature's treasures: the Darwin Centre at the Natural History Museum', *BBC Wildlife Magazine*, special issue published in collaboration with the Natural History Museum, 2002.
Kant, I., 'An answer to the question: "What is Enlightenment?"', in I. Kant, *Political Writings* (ed. Hans Reiss, trans. H. B. Nisbet), Cambridge: Cambridge University Press, 1991.
—— *Critique of Judgment* (trans. Werner S. Pluhar), Indianapolis, IN: Hackett, 1987.
MacGregor, N., 'The whole world in our hands', Review, *The Guardian*, 24 July 2004, pp. 4–6.
Sloan, K., '"Aimed at universality and belonging to the nation": the Enlightenment and the British Museum', in K. Sloan (ed.), *Enlightenment: Discovering the World in the Eighteenth Century*, London: The British Museum Press, 2003, pp. 12–25.
Syson, L., 'The ordering of the artificial world: collecting, classification and progress', in K. Sloan (ed.), *Enlightenment: Discovering the World in the Eighteenth Century*, London: The British Museum Press, 2003, pp. 108–21.

12

The studio in the gallery?

Jon Wood

Introduction

It is a commonplace that special, privileged access to artistic inspiration and process proves revelatory to the viewer. Even, perhaps, the most sceptical among us have experienced something of the quiet seductions of this ubiquitous belief. We might, for example, find such access in the raw, sometimes diaristic quality of artists' writings, or in the explanations contained in the tape-recorded interview (providing meanings indiscernible in the actual work), or in film footage of artists at work – silently or in conversation, getting on with the business of making art. All these modes of explanation and representation are, of course, merely other kinds of evidence, but all can be seen as affording various kinds of primary access to artists' intentions and thus clues for us to work with, when encountering the actual art work. How often have we stopped to watch an artist painting outdoors, not only comparing the scene depicted with the view at hand, but also looking at the artist him- or herself, examining their clothes, their hands and faces, as well as their palette, brushes and paints? This scrutiny is perhaps especially so when we stop to have our portrait done – when the looking goes both ways and when our nosiness and narcissism becomes the quiet subject of a lousy picture.

The indoor realm of the artist's studio is a place, a space and, in turn, an art-theoretical topos at the very heart of this curiosity and 'accessibility'. The studio has been frequently understood and evoked as the physical surrogate of the artist's mind and has become increasingly mythically so for the last 150 years: from Gustave Courbet to Bruce Nauman, to mention just one recent exemplar. The studio is traditionally perceived as the site of original, unique, authentic and impassioned artistic endeavour, and a space in which viewers become visitors. Visiting an artist's studio, in turn, enables a 'behind the scenes', experiential insight into the artist and his or her work in its correct originary context, prior to the post-studio spaces of the gallery or museum. Studios are thus not only seen as the sites of production for art, but can also give us experience of the background or backdrop to an artist. They might offer up clues and moments of accidental self-portraiture, and thus today have resonance with a contemporary popular mentality that is very literate in the forms and meanings of the physical conditions of private life (evidenced by manifestations such as *Hello!* magazine, *Changing Rooms* and *Through the Keyhole*). The studio is, in turn, to be seen as a place where art and life, and where art-style and life-style, coincide – where pictures are made and lives changed.

The studio of Van Gogh is perhaps one of the most well-known studios of this kind. Today there are hundreds of Van Gogh studios, of which 'Van Gogh's Workroom' in Scarborough is one (Figure 12.1). These Van Gogh studio-photo-booths, in their ubiquity, mobility and accessibility, serve to remind us of the extent to which the idea of the studio has been disseminated and popularized – to the level of minor tourist attraction. It also serves to remind us of a paradox: that the idea of the solitary, creative genius has been both playfully discredited and that it is, in fact, as alive and well as ever. The artist's studio is thus a busy and complex topic, full of contradictions. The ubiquity and multiple meanings of the word 'studio' (as with the French counterpart 'atelier') is a testimony to this richness. It is also an art historical and curatorial subject that has been so frequently overlooked and taken for granted – 'artists, more often than not, have studios, end of story'. So it is this combination of the banal and unfathomable, of the highly private and the highly public, that makes it so compelling to its visitors and its students.

There are many different types of studio, or workshop, and they can be approached, academically and curatorially, in many different ways. For example: the studio can be read through an intellectual history of artistic identity; through a socio-economic history of originality and authenticity – of the studio

Figure 12.1 Van Gogh's Workroom, Scarborough. Photograph by the author.

159

as site of authorship and copyright (as Tony Hughes has done)[1]; through a history of the representation of the studio and through the images of Pygmalion[2]; through architectural history, and through the emergence of the specially designed 'studio-home' (as Louise Campbell is exploring)[3]; through a history of place and a social geography of urban artistic quarters (as John Milner has done of late nineteenth-century Paris)[4]; and through a history of exhibitions and of the material conditions of art's making and display. As a result of all this, I have always tended to think of the studio, in terms of a working definition, in a deliberately open and tentative way. 'The studio' is thus, for me, a complex site of convergence and dispersal for people, ideas and things. About people as much as places, and about the changing relationships between artist, art object and environment. While it is thus a very difficult subject then to make an exhibition about, it is the studio's status and function as an exhibition space in its own right, and as one which finds itself variously transformed and resited in the gallery, that specifically concerns this chapter.

Close Encounters

I would like to start with an exhibition called *Close Encounters: The Sculptor's Studio in the Age of the Camera*, which was held at the Henry Moore Institute in Leeds in 2001–2.[5] The period of the exhibition was the late nineteenth to the mid-twentieth century and looked comparatively at photographs of sculptors' studios in Britain and France, including a mixture of avant-garde and academic, well-known and lesser-known sculptors. The kinds of questions we asked ourselves at the time were: How can we recreate, or re-evoke, the sculptor's studio in the gallery in an informative historical way, without resorting to mock-ups with turntables, tools and stone and sawdust, or without presenting an overly didactic exhibition about sculptural techniques and methods? How could we articulate the importance of the studio in the history of much twentieth-century sculpture and show how black and white photographs of it (as much as written accounts) were crucial to this history? How could we re-enact a kind of studio visit, across a range of 50 or so studios, for the gallery visitor? How ultimately could we show 'the studio in the gallery' without seriously compromising or misrepresenting either place? And, ultimately, was it in fact a good idea to try and put on an exhibition about a place that was (and is) in effect an exhibition site in its own right anyway?

At the Henry Moore Institute, there is a suite of three main galleries. A long first room (measuring 20 by 6 metres), a large and 7 metre-tall second room (measuring 10 by 8 metres) and a third smaller and windowless room (measuring 6 by 6 metres). These three different spaces are excellent for the display of sculpture. We were, however, careful that we didn't over-argue for a rather formulaic beginning, middle and end to this subject, through this sequence of three galleries. Instead, we were keen to offer different ways of encountering the studio in the three rooms, while suggesting both a conceptual development and a synchronicity between them, so that the rooms worked, in a sense, in tandem.

In the first room of the exhibition we showed over 60 framed archive photographs. Half were from our own collections (the Leeds Museums and Galleries collections are particularly rich in studio photographs) and half on loan from elsewhere. These were all arranged from close-up studio photos at the start, to panoramic studio photos at the end – rather than organized by chronology or by genre. We started with the photographic representation of the hand of the sculptor and ended with more hands-off, hands-free studio photo arrangements and ensembles in which the sculptor him- or herself did not figure. The idea here was to evoke, or re-enact, a kind of studio visit (or rather a journey around a number of studios) in which the point of view of gallery visitors was implicitly and poetically allied to that of studio visitors. In this way, it was hoped that the idea of the studio gradually opened out as visitors went along through the gallery.

The exhibition was thus about ways of looking and ways of representing, rather than about social or biographical histories of the studio. The photographs selected (and their subjects, scenarios, compositions and formats) all as a group shared secrets, told stories and quietly shed light on the status and function of the studio and on how the relationship between sculptor, sculpture and studio was constructed in this period. The visitor could compare, for example, a Jacob Epstein studio photograph with an Ossip Zadkine; a Henri Gaudier-Brzeska studio photograph with a Constantin Brancusi; or a photograph taken by a professional photographer with one taken by the artist him- or herself. On the one hand, such photographs give a 'behind the scenes' view of the studio, while, on the other, they are highly staged and self-consciously artificial images – thus ultimately packed with both facts and fictions.

Brassaï's series of studio photographs, published in the surrealist journal *Minotaure* in 1933, represent an extraordinary moment in the history of the studio photograph. The second, large gallery of *Close Encounters: The Sculptor's Studio in the Age of the Camera* was based on this historical moment (Figure 12.2). In this room, a sculpture by each of the six artists who were included in Brassaï's series (Constantin Brancusi, Charles Despiau, Alberto Giacometti, Henri Laurens, Jacques Lipchitz and Aristide Maillol) were positioned in front of large studio photographs in which these same works appear.[6] In this room, the sculptor had disappeared altogether and the gallery visitor was faced with a totally different experience: a large-scale photographic version of an imaginary, composite studio – an 'impossible studio' in the sense that it could never actually be physically frequented, only envisioned and imagined through photography.

The dimensions of this, the largest of the HMI galleries, were perfect for this, since they approximately corresponded with those of a studio of an established modern sculptor. This was, of course, fortuitous and not the original plan of the architects who designed the building and its galleries. Moreover, rather like sculptors' studios, this main gallery was similarly equipped with windows in the roof, which enabled light to come down from above. We used this light source, while also painting the walls light charcoal grey – echoing with the ambiguous

Figure 12.2 *Close Encounters: The Sculptor's Studio in the Age of the Camera*, Henry Moore Institute, Leeds, installation photograph of main gallery. Photograph J. Hardman-Jones, 2001.

time of day evoked in many of Brassaï's photographs and in an attempt to bring the walls in and create a slightly darker, more intimate environment.

Through this installation, the gallery visitor was given the opportunity to compare materials (such as an original studio clay or plaster with a borrowed bronze). It also allowed the visitor to think about the play of different scales between original and copy, and between the sculpture in the photograph and the actual sculpture displayed under the gallery's lighting conditions. The former gave the visitor a chance to walk around a sculpture that was depicted in the photograph and thus, by playful, imaginative extension, to imagine walking into the studio within the actual gallery. We thus tried in a sense here to map the studio on to the gallery, but in a poetic rather than in any 'archaeological' or accurately reconstructed sense. Finally, this conceit was taken a step further in the third and last room, entitled 'The Studio without Walls'. Here, we displayed small sculptures by Henry Moore, Barbara Hepworth, Jean Arp and William Turnbull, which could be read as representing mini-studios: sculptural ensembles were seen as studio ensembles, and the horizontal base of sculpture as a studio floor or a table top. The kind of framing, miniaturization and (trans)portability of the sculptor's studio that could be achieved in a studio photograph was, in turn, taken up by sculpture itself and in three dimensions.

In retrospect, *Close Encounters: The Sculptor's Studio in the Age of the Camera* raises two important issues concerning the problems of presenting and re-presenting the 'studio in the gallery' that I would like now to address. Both

162

deal with the problem of 'the studio in the gallery' from different ends and pull it, in a sense, in different directions: one is historical, the other contemporary; one is retrospective, the other anticipatory. The first concerns the historical and museological problems of reconstructing an artist's studio after the artist's death. The second concerns the way in which a number of contemporary artists self-consciously deal with the question of restaging their own studio – both as a material environment and as a metaphorical shorthand for a way of working and thinking – in the gallery setting. Both these manifestations of 'studios in the gallery' are, it is important to say, highly contemporaneous – both have proved particularly popular in the last 25 years and highly topical in the last 10 to 15 years.

Studio reconstructions: Bacon and Brancusi

For the purposes of this chapter, I will base my observations on the problem of 'studio reconstruction in the gallery' through two recent examples: the reconstruction of Francis Bacon's studio at the Hugh Lane Gallery in Dublin, which opened in 2001, and that of Constantin Brancusi in the new (and second) reconstruction, designed by Renzo Piano, installed outside the Centre Georges Pompidou in Paris in 1997. I will limit my observations to what is at stake here with the material conditions of display and what is afforded the visitor, and will not here deal with the complicated legal conditions of these acquisitions and bequests.

From the outset, it should be said that both these reconstructions are also relocations. Place was, in a sense, sacrificed for space (or at least seen as secondary to it). Bacon's studio was moved from 7 Reece Mews in London's South Kensington to Dublin and Brancusi's studio at 11 impasse Ronsin, a quiet cul-de-sac off rue Vaugirard in the 15th arrondissement, was moved (via the Palais de Tokyo) in 1977 to central Paris and placed outside the Centre Georges Pompidou. Whatever the curatorial and museological strategies later adopted, the original social, economic and geographical contexts of these studios were immediately erased. The studios, dislocated from the fabric and contingencies of their previous urban lives, would, from now on, belong to the art world.

In both cases, the gallery/studio visitor is not able to enter the studio, but invited to look into it (to different extents) from behind glass. In the case of the Bacon studio, visitors approach it via the Hugh Lane's main galleries.[7] Before they get to it, they have to go through an introductory foyer in which is shown – on a loop – Melvyn Bragg's *South Bank Show* interview with Bacon in the Reece Mews studio. Visitors then progress to the studio room itself, painstakingly reconstructed with archaeological precision and immaculately transported across the Irish Sea. Where there was a door there is now a glass window. The visitor can look in from this threshold, examine the mess and clutter in all its authentic/inauthentic glory and marvel at the superhuman effort and sheer brilliance that has gone into creating this 'unique copy', this homage to one man's working quarters. Bragg's film, which prefaces this display, might try to tempt us to imagine Bacon here in it, but this reconstructed studio is such an extraordinary sight in its own right we don't, I think, really need or want to. Walking around the studio in anti-clockwise direction, we then get a chance to view the insides again from different vantage points – first through a peep-hole close to the wall and then looking in through this first-floor studio's window. Visitors are then led into the 'Micro Gallery' which is set up with up-to-date, interactive information technologies that enable us to click on aspects of the artist's biography, his work and this studio's history. This technology is intrinsic to the studio experience, certainly providing information, but also compensating for the fact that we are not allowed in, and for the fact that this is not ultimately Bacon's studio at all but an extraordinary and wonderful simulacrum. Interactive technology tries to provide a 'total visitor experience' for what is effectively unable to be experienced.

In the case of the Brancusi, more or less the whole studio has been provided with glass walls, so that visitors can walk around the plot in its entirety and look in at the works on display.[8] In the earlier 1977 reconstruction, visitors could actually walk into the studio and experience the work close up. These multimillion-dollar sculptures are, of course, no longer out on display in this way – it is simply too risky. Piano's reconstruction is thus, I think, an elegant compromise to an extremely difficult curatorial problem, but for some the new reconstruction does have something of the 'fish tank' about it.[9] By not letting visitors inside, it gives visitors an unreal experience. Brancusi himself of course would have never seen his studio from the outside in. This is important since we are dealing here with a sculptor for whom metaphors of enclosure, interiority and essence were central and quietly echoed his studio environment.

In addition, this reconstruction would also have us believe that all the rooms of the original studio were display rooms. This was, of course, not the case. The last room, shown here, was not a display room, but a junk room: a storage room where bits, bobs and sculptures were assembled by the sculptor. This was not a room a visitor to Brancusi's studio would have ever been shown (it was too much of a mess), but it is nevertheless here on display through glass, as visitors come round to the last part of the studio reconstruction. One thing that can be said, however, is that the contents of the room have been arranged in a manner that closely relates to the way they were left by the sculptor when he died (and his studio was thoroughly documented photographically) in 1957. Like the Bacon studio, despite moments of creative curating, the Brancusi studio is rigorously treated as an 'archaeological' subject, painstakingly recorded and reconstructed piece by piece, work by work to recreate the look and arrangement of the final studio. Despite their inherent impossibilities, these installations do provide some sense of the scale, materials, atmosphere and overall style of things.

If this is what can happen after the death of the artist, might this (we can be forgiven for asking) be taking art's things too far? The journey from working studio to studio reconstruction is, as I have highlighted, a highly problematic and uneven one, and so is this, in fact, a journey too far? Is it a way of making the studio travel posthumously beyond its journey? Does it, for example, merely turn 'live site' into 'tourist trap' with a misplaced nostalgia for the irretrievable, sited conditions of art's making? And what ultimately can we really learn from these reconstructions? Whatever their educational play, I think it is extremely important to be clear-headed about their limitations and about the profound fictions that these reconstructions contain. There will be many a visitor in the years to come who might perhaps need reminding that these places are fabrications. Location, location, location, one might say. If you want to know more about why Bacon's studio was packed full of empty champagne cases (which he often used as palettes), perhaps we should look to Kensington and Soho for answers. And if we want to know why Brancusi lived in his studio in the countrified impasse Ronsin cul-de-sac for 41 years perhaps we should take the walk (as hundreds had done over his lifetime) from the busy metropolitan centre of Paris down this city's longest street to get there. You didn't drop in at Brancusi's on the way to somewhere else, you made a dedicated trip, pilgrimage even, to this rural retreat that was prefaced by Paris itself.

Studio installations: Nelson and Venlet

It is interesting to note that the concept of the 'journey' figures strongly in many contemporary artists' discussion of the actual studio itself. Despite the fact that we are dealing effectively with stasis with the studio – with a single building or room – the image of travelling and journeying is often cast as central to its status and function: central to how it operates metaphorically and literally, in the imagination and in the marketplace. This is neatly articulated in Jason Rhoades's studio-installation called *My Brother/Brancusi* (1995), in which he has surrounded a room (full of doughnut-making equipment) with framed photographs of Brancusi's studio and of a contemporary US home. Rhoades thus playfully compares this modernist studio to a fast-food factory; the production of unique directly carved and finished sculptures to doughnut production. It is telling indeed that this 1995 installation actually includes specific reference to Brancusi's studio: there is an important overlapping of concerns between 1990s' installation art and 1990s' studio reconstruction, and Rhoades here jokes about it and the implied collapse of high and low culture.

The metaphor of the 'journey' is also used by a number of contemporary British artists when asked about what 'the studio' means to them. Artists such as Graham Gussin, Phyllida Barlow, Simon Starling, Keith Wilson and Keith Tyson, for example, have all quietly evoked the idea of the journey when talking about their love–hate relationship with their studios: they can't, it seems, live with them and can't, it seems, live without them.[10] All are alert to the historical baggage of the studio and of its problematic mythic status as the place of genius and creative endeavour. The studio is a place to escape to and escape from, a place to twiddle their thumbs in and have 'brainwaves' in, a place to stop off at (like a layby) and a place of discipline and routine, a place to hide in and a place to be on display in. They can be places of tremendous triumph and achievement, and as dull as ditchwater. In keeping with this sensibility, Bruce Nauman's recent work *Mapping the Studio (Fat Chance John Cage)* is a wonderful recent example not only of taking the studio into the gallery, but also of the casting of the studio as a place at once magical and totally and utterly banal – at once completely under- and overwhelming. This piece, which he showed at the Dia Center in 2001, consisted of wall-to-wall screens showing films of his studio by night (under infrared cameras), populated by mice and the odd cat.[11]

However, two contemporary artists in particular, Mike Nelson and Richard Venlet, raise in very pressing ways the problem of the 'studio in the gallery' and I will conclude this chapter by looking at how they have each offered different responses to this question. Of all the installations Mike Nelson has made, the one he made for the Camden Arts Centre in 1998 was perhaps the most studio-related.[12] The work was actually called *Studio Apparatus for Camden Arts Centre: An Introductory Structure or Temporary Monument*, and its main room was entitled 'The Mysterious Island'. Nelson's installation in Camden was, in a sense, a game of smoke and mirrors, which played with an audience's and the gallery's desire to witness art's making and get privileged access to the 'real' studio work. This 'studio apparatus' is, in effect, 'the behind the scenes' of his art – the jumbled structures, images and iconographies of his practice, and what was going on in his head and studio at the time. We spot objects from earlier shows stuck in new places and next to new and recycled paraphernalia, evocative of multiple peoples, time and places. What you see is what you get, but it is also of course something a good deal more, and the title 'The Mysterious Island' hints at this, celebrating a nomadic artistic imagination in process as a Jules Verne-like journey. Perhaps Nelson himself is offering something that is still very much a mystery to himself or a bundle of secrets and narratives that he is presently keeping from himself, but has put on display anyway because he has got a show to do.

Nelson's work always plays hide-and-seek with visitors' perceptions, with what is real, and what make-believe, and always toys with the poetry of ambiguity, disguise and the impostorous. In this way, it enjoys the same playfulness as many studio reconstructions, but in a deliberately mischievous, obfuscating and self-conscious way. One of strategies that he employs to make his installations so compelling for the visitor is to take himself out of the picture, and to try and make directed installations that privilege the experience of the visitor with the stuff at hand, rather than with him, the artist. Nelson's absence encourages the visitor to think less about the 'artistic persona' of the artist and more about the material environment presented and how it has been constructed, reconstructed and treated. Nelson uses every trick possible to harness the imaginative and self-conscious attention of the visitor and thus attempts to implicate the visitor in his works. Visitors frequenting his work become kinds of imaginary participants, witnessing the aftermath of a mysterious event, like tourists on a film set, after the film has been made but with the camera still rolling. In Nelson's installation *To the Memory of H. P. Lovecraft*, which was staged at the Collective Gallery in Edinburgh in 1999, the gallery has been fitted up and destroyed in such a way that we wonder what kind of gothic monster has been here before us.[13] The walls have been slashed with an axe, but the presence of a dog bowl and large gnawed bone suggest a hound, not a human. What, we wonder, was the cause of the fury? The longer we look the more, I think, it becomes apparent that it might indeed be the white cube gallery itself that is motivating this rage, as if the agent responsible felt caged and imprisoned by it, and so vandalized it, when attempts to escape it became futile. Creative space is here destructive space and Nelson's piece is a strangely beautiful response to a now traditional 'white cube' gallery condition of display.

Compared, finally, to this 1999 piece by Mike Nelson, Richard Venlet's contribution to the 25th Biennale of San Paolo in 2002 offered a much more well-behaved and minimalist form of theatre and subversion.[14] Called *Untitled*, Venlet constructed a room, read as his studio, in the centre of the gallery. The outside walls were mirror panelled and so reflected the gallery's setting – its walls, floors, ceiling and windows. Visitors could enter this studio room and have a look around. On the floor inside and around the edge of the room, he placed a number of cardboard boxes containing A4 photocopies of his own (largely photographic) work. Visitors could take away what they wanted: either one of each and have the whole of Venlet's recent oeuvre in photocopied form, or go away empty-handed. The studio is traditionally seen as the site of artistic production and authenticity and here Venlet subverted this and staged it in the gallery, offering free-of-charge reproductions of his work inside.

The studio, like the gallery reflected in its outside walls, was presented, in a sense, as being 'neither here nor there' – a mirage-like place that was secondary to the ideas that were on offer inside it. So, what was it in the end, if it was not really a studio and not really a gallery? Venlet's master touch was invisible, or rather only visible at the end of the day, when the visitors had left and the lights had been turned off. Hanging down (about a metre from the ceiling and in the middle of this box room) was a large light bulb. Producing a very bright light, the moving shadows of visitors cast on the walls were so striking and remarkable as to be clearly read as an important part of the work. It thus animated the room in collaboration with these visitors. When the light was turned off, however, you could see that Venlet had written in felt-tip pen the dimensions of the room around the bulb. It was a witty, minimalist conceit – at once marvellous and banal – and it says a lot about what 'the studio in the gallery' might be today for many contemporary artists.

If, for Venlet, the studio is about reconstruction, about the transposition of space and about documentation, it is also merely about the interaction between art, the artist, a visitor and a room. It is a cipher, a device and a conceit: on the one hand, Venlet's piece at the San Paolo Biennale punctures and exposes the myth of the studio, while also using it as a way of seducing the viewer (thus the mirrors). The studio is thus a way of harnessing a more heightened, engaged and imaginative kind of visitor attention: studios, after all, make the audience captive. If the light source is connotative of the creative and intellectual energy that can charge the artist – a historical symbol of conception, illumination and the imagination – it is also an energy that closely collaborates with the architecture that frames the work and that houses the visitor. Like moths to a flame, visitors to Venlet's studio-cum-gallery room seeking privileged and revelatory insight into artistic inspiration might well, I think, get it: if you want to know more about his work, turn the light on.

Notes

1 T. Hughes, 'The cave and the stithy: artists' studios and intellectual property in early modern Europe', *Oxford Art Journal*, Vol. 13, No. 1, January 1990: 34–48.
2 M. Peppiatt and A. Bellony-Rewald, *Imagination's Chamber: Artists and their Studios*, London: Gordon Fraser, 1983 and B. Klüver and J. Martin, *Kiki de Montparnasse: Artist and Lovers 1900–1930*, New York: Harry N. Abrams, 1994.
3 L. Campbell, 'Perret and his artist-clients: architecture in the Age of Gold', *Architectural History*, No. 45, 2002: 409–40.
4 J. Milner, *The Studios of Paris: The Capital of Art in the Late Nineteenth Century*, London and New Haven, CT: Yale University Press, 1988.
5 See accompanying exhibition catalogue and essay: J. Wood, 'Close encounters: the sculptor's studio in the age of the camera', in *Close Encounters*, Leeds: Henry Moore Institute, 2001, pp. 8–27.
6 These were: Brancusi's *Danaïde* (c.1918), Despiau's *Bust of Mme Jean Arthur Fontane* (1933), Giacometti's *Spoon Woman* (1926–7), Laurens's *Océanide* (1933), Lipchitz's *Figure* (1926–30) and Maillol's *Ile de France* (1925).
7 For recent publications on the Bacon studio in both Dublin and London, see Hugh Lane Municipal Art Gallery, *Francis Bacon's Studio at the Hugh Lane*, Dublin: Hugh Lane Municipal Art Gallery, 2001 (and the very useful essays by Barbara Dawson and Margarita Cappock), and J. Edwards, 'Foreword', *7 Reece Mews: Francis Bacon's Studio* (photographs by Perry Ogden), London: Thames and Hudson, 2001, pp. 10–13.
8 For a useful and well-illustrated book on the new studio, see M. Tabart, *L'Atelier Brancusi Album*, Paris: Editions du Centre Georges Pompidou, 1997. For a recent reading of the history of the Brancusi studio and its reconstruction, see J. Wood, 'Brancusi's white studio', *The Sculpture Journal*, Vol. 7, 2002: 108–20.
9 A point made by Eric Shanes in 'Brancusi's studio flattened', *Apollo*, Vol. 146, December 1997: 61.
10 These artists all gave talks about their studios at the Henry Moore Institute in October 2001, in a series designed to accompany the exhibition *Close Encounters: The Sculptor's Studio in the Age of the Camera*.
11 Bruce Nauman, *Mapping the Studio I (Fat Chance John Cage)*, Dia Center for the Arts, New York, 10 January–27 July 2002.
12 See also *Mike Nelson, Extinction Beckons* (texts by Jaki Irvine), London: Matts Gallery, 2000, pp. 86–95.
13 Ibid.
14 For further documentation of this display, curated by Moritz Küng, see *Richard Venlet/ 00*, Antwerp: MuHKA, 2002.

References

Campbell, L. 'Perret and his artist-clients: architecture in the Age of Gold', *Architectural History*, No. 45, 2002: 409–40.
Edwards, J., 'Foreword', *7 Reece Mews: Francis Bacon's Studio* (photographs by Perry Ogden), London: Thames & Hudson, 2001, pp. 10–13.
Hughes, T., 'The cave and the stithy: artists' studios and intellectual property in early modern Europe', *Oxford Art Journal*, Vol. 13, No. 1, January 1990: 34–48.

Hugh Lane Municipal Art Gallery, *Francis Bacon's Studio at the Hugh Lane*, Dublin: Hugh Lane Municipal Art Gallery, 2001.

Klüver, B. and Martin, J., *Kiki de Montparnasse: Artist and Lovers 1900–1930*, New York: Harry N. Abrams, 1994.

Mike Nelson, Extinction Beckons (texts by Jaki Irvine), London: Matts Gallery, 2000, pp. 86–95.

Milner, J., *The Studios of Paris: The Capital of Art in the Late Nineteenth Century*, London and New Haven, CT: Yale University Press, 1988.

Peppiatt, M. and Bellony-Rewald, A., *Imagination's Chamber: Artists and their Studios*, London: Gordon Fraser, 1983.

Richard Venlet/00, Antwerp: MuHKA, 2002.

Shanes, E., 'Brancusi's studio flattened', *Apollo*, Vol. 146, December 1997: 61.

Tabart, M., *L'Atelier Brancusi Album*, Paris: Editions du Centre Georges Pompidou, 1997.

Wood, J., 'Close encounters: the sculptor's studio in the age of the camera', in *Close Encounters*, Leeds: Henry Moore Institute, 2001, pp. 8–27.

——, 'Brancusi's white studio', *The Sculpture Journal*, Vol. 7, 2002: 108–20.

13

When worlds collide

The contemporary museum as art gallery

Christopher R. Marshall

In 1716, Filippo Bonnani, then curator of the Museo Kircheriano at the Collegio Romano in Rome, felt compelled to correct a common misconception of visitors to his museum. Bonnani presided over the city's most significant collection of art, natural history and ethnographic material that was comparable in its scope to the great kunst- and wunderkammers of Northern Europe. Yet visitors nonetheless tended to refer to his collection as a galleria. For Bonnani, this diminished the seriousness of his project. As he put it, the term 'galleria' should be used to describe collections 'made solely for their magnificence', whereas for his institution 'One should more properly say *Museo* . . . or, as musaeum alludes, one says a place dedicated to the muses'.[1]

In referring to the Renaissance concept of the locus musus, Bonnani signalled the encyclopaedic aspirations of his museum since, as his readers would have instantly recognized, the muses presided over all aspects of enlightened human activity. He also drew on the long-established spatial distinction between the semi-private Renaissance humanist study-cum-museum and the more expansive, public and transitory space of the gallery. In architectural terms, a gallery was accordingly defined as a semi-open loggia or corridor connecting one area of a palace to another (the Galleria degli Uffizi being the quintessential instance of this in sixteenth-century Europe).[2] Bonnani's complaint thus confirms that, at this stage in its development at least, the transit space of the gallery carried associations of leisure, social communication and aesthetic enjoyment that were to be differentiated, in turn, from the more serious and comprehensive aspirations of the museum.

Museums have, of course, long since ceased regarding themselves as semi-private spaces of arcane contemplation. Conversely, no public art gallery would today identify its mission as not involving a fundamental concern with education and public programming of the broadest and most accessible kind. The continued relevance of Bonnani's distinction nonetheless bears reinforcing at the outset of this discussion. If pushed to formulate an inevitably too simplistic generalization to explain this we might venture that museums constitute inherently projective spaces, whereas art galleries remain committed to the ideal of a more self-contained and reflective space.

Museums generally encompass a greater diversity of objects and/or ideas than art galleries and they allow for a greater degree of spatial interactivity as a result. This is as much true of a sixteenth-century wunderkammer as it is of a contemporary air and space museum. This is not to say, on the other hand, that galleries are not also committed to displaying increasingly divergent art forms and media, particularly those devoted to contemporary art. In relative terms, however, it is nonetheless still striking how little the essential architectural components of the gallery have changed – together with the display regimes that they entail – from the time of Bonnani's baroque galleria through to the museological codification of that space in the early public galleries of the eighteenth and nineteenth centuries and on to today.

Besides their greater diversity museum spaces also project more emphatically than galleries in the ways in which their exhibitionary elements have been knitted together, as it were, in order to reach out beyond themselves to convey an integrated message of whatever broader communications agenda the exhibit is seeking to articulate. This is why museums have traditionally led the field in the development of communications technologies – either through labelling and wall text or, more recently, in the emphasis on interactive displays and multimedia. Much as art galleries might wish to project with all the immediacy and interactivity of contemporary science, nature and social history museums, they are nonetheless bound by an essentially different charter. Their focus, instead, is not so much on the co-ordinated communications message as rather on the autonomy and individuality of the artwork displayed in its own right.

Such an emphasis is accordingly mistrustful of a too overt and heavy-handed emphasis on binding objects together within an overriding didactic programme. Textual interpolation is thus often de-emphasized or presented as somehow secondary to the primary act of viewing. The discrete positioning of room brochures forms one common manifestation of this trend. Further evidence comes more recently in the ways in which information and communication technologies have begun to be integrated into art galleries. Just as these elements are increasingly found in gallery spaces, so too are they increasingly quarantined or minimized in their emphasis relative to the actual artworks in the galleries themselves. The microgalleries in the National Galleries of both London and Washington, DC, for example, are prime instances of this, forming as they do separate zones at either the beginning or the end of the viewer's circulation path.

This essential distinction has created ongoing challenges for galleries that museums, in many respects, have not had to face. We might agree, for example, that a tastefully minimalist and classic white cube installation such as one encounters in Roland Simounet's mid-1980s' renovation of the Musée Picasso, to cite but one of countless examples, runs the risk of decreasing access by virtue of the closed circuit effect that it sets up in the gallery space.[3] Unlike the more outwardly projective spaces of the museum, the display here, beautiful though it undoubtedly is, with its sleek setting and minimal wall text, does not immediately go to the trouble of reaching out beyond its own frame of reference to connect with a non-initiated viewer's experience. Consequently if the viewer does not already recognize Picasso's pre-eminence within the wider traditions of European modernism, together with the mutually reinforcing modernist display regime that his work was constructed for and that the gallery installation further enshrines, then that visitor may well leave this exhibition none the wiser.

This issue, then, of how galleries are to regain the projective space of museums while also continuing to maintain their own divergent emphasis on the individual integrity of the artwork is one that continues to drive their thinking. But while galleries have begun to grapple with this it is interesting to note the extent to which museums have, conversely, themselves been highly attentive to recent developments in contemporary art and gallery design.

An indicative example occurs in Pawson Williams Architects' 1996 redesign of the Geological Museum and the Primates Gallery of the Natural History Museum, London.[4] This project displays two features that are commonly encountered in recent spaces of this kind. First is the use of contemporary art that is often strategically positioned at the entrance to a display or even to the museum itself as a welcoming, non-didactic element. Works of this kind are commonly intended as eye-catching and evocative indications of the exhibition that follows, yet do not require the visitor to stop and read a didactic label. A second feature is the high aestheticization effect that plays a particularly prominent role in the new entrance to the Earth Galleries. In this instance, although it is a natural history exhibit, the entrance displays have been framed through a classic white cube minimalist aesthetic that is highly reminiscent of contemporary art gallery design.

This aesthetic is not applied for its own sake, but rather to underscore the Museum's point of distinction from traditional natural history exhibits. It uses it more specifically as a means of countering the visually deadening serial effect created by the serried ranks of dead creatures, minerals or other such objects in traditional natural history museums. Instead, the designers have focused attention on a smaller number of isolated and strategically positioned elements. Even the pose of the hippo in the Earth Galleries is significant in this respect. By rotating it away from its 'natural' stance the designers have also achieved a more artificial and thus also more artistic effect. The viewer is accordingly asked to contemplate this specimen not as a serial, didactic component but rather as a beautifully framed aesthetic object in its own right. This is, to be sure, a striking and accessible strategy. Yet the art effect is strong, even arguably distracting to a degree, since it reminds us of nothing so much as the work of a certain English *enfant terrible* of contemporary art with his predilection for cabinets filled with mutely suspended sharks, cows and other animals.

Across the Channel this influence seems further accelerated in the splendid redesign of the Muséum national d'Histoire naturelle in Paris.[5] The centrepiece of this redevelopment is the Grande Galerie de l'Evolution. Here the animals have been liberated from their vitrines in a way that helps to overcome the static and tableau-like effect that is a by-product of the traditional diorama. Here the animals act as a dynamic ensemble of inherently projective elements that at the same time also share the viewer's space. Once again though, the art effect is strong and maybe even to a certain degree counter-productive. In the first instance the display has the effect of decontextualizing the creatures, making them appear as free-floating aesthetic elements on a darkened stage. True, they no longer appear as frozen, tableau elements in three-dimensional paintings, this being another of the chief drawbacks of the traditional diorama. Yet the designers have arguably achieved this at the expense of recasting these beautiful examples of the taxidermist's art as a deluxe sculptural ensemble in the round. Perhaps they are not so dissimilar in this respect from the grand sculptural boulevard created by the installation of nineteenth-century public sculpture along the central aisle of the Musée d'Orsay further down the Seine. The result is a spectacular yet at the same time somewhat distancing view that we are encouraged to take in, in a general scene-setting sense, rather than in a more specifically didactic way.

These few disparate examples should have served to introduce a general trend that is evident across all areas of museum practice today. As these and countless other initiatives attest, art and art-inspired elements are increasingly being used to open up recently designed museum spaces to a more experiential and evocative form of communications message that seeks to escape the dead hand of a too overt and traditionally didactic display. At the same time, however, the previous discussion should also have begun to raise the issue of the risks involved in these strategies as the traditional roles and expectations of museum spaces become conflated, at times rather confusingly, with added associations and ideas from art galleries.

If we turn now to look at one example in slightly more detail it is possible to identify a further three key characteristics that initiatives of this kind tend to share. Our case study here is a high-profile Australian instance of the new museology at work, developed in the mid 1990s for the Museum of Sydney.[6] This museum was built over the archaeological remains of the site of the first colonial governor's residence in the city. It was accordingly conceived originally along relatively traditional lines as a reconstructed historic property before being reconceptualized more generally as a museum of the early history of Sydney and its surrounds as viewed from a contemporary pluralist perspective. This new emphasis further encouraged the use of more creative and artistic approaches to exhibition design.

The first feature that this and other museums of this kind demonstrate is what we might term an integrated approach, whereby contemporary art forms part of a broader strategy to draw on a wider palette of innovative features and specializations that attempt to think outside the box of traditional display. In common with other museums of this kind, therefore, the Museum of Sydney accordingly sought the talents of a range of emergent inter-disciplinary specialists. This includes evocative sound installations by the musician and sound artist, David Chesworth, and a video installation by the writer, film-maker and media-theorist, Ross Gibson.

Such innovation is also often partly a product of necessity. This is true of the Museum of Sydney in that it did not possess a rich collection of artefacts with which to tell its stories. Many of its art and design elements were thus deployed as alternatives for the missing objects that were otherwise lacking in a traditional sense. So, another key element of this approach is that it often uses art to bolster the muteness or inadequacy of certain kinds of sites and/or objects to communicate to the viewer in traditional museum displays. Historic houses and other categories of heritage site lend themselves particularly well to this approach. Relatively little remains of the building site upon which the Museum of Sydney is located. The Museum thus needed to reconstruct its narrative on the basis of a fairly meagre archaeological site – meagre, that is, in terms of objects that might be considered 'display worthy' in a traditional sense. So the art elements helped to build up a picture that would otherwise have been almost impossible to develop.

Finally, the art elements in museums of this kind can even achieve such a prominence in the overall design as to take the form of highly ambitious commissioned work. These commissions often stand slightly apart from the exhibits themselves – often again at the entrance – in order to express wider institutional perspectives similar to the role performed by a public sculpture in a prominent civic plaza. Commissioned art of this kind is thus given a major responsibility as regards the projected self-image of the institution in terms of the deeper cultural and ideological values that it seeks to uphold. The prime example of this in the Museum of Sydney is a sculpture and multi-media installation sited at the entrance to the museum – and thus also in this instance literally in the place normally reserved for a civic sculpture. This work is the result of a collaboration between a white Australian artist, Janet Laurence, and an Indigenous Australian artist, Fiona Foley. *The Edge of the Trees* presents a post-colonial perspective on the early history of white settlement in Sydney, as it imagines the Indigenous Eora people of New South Wales standing at the edge of the trees watching Captain Cook and subsequent European colonizers landing on their shoreline. It thus effectively, and also highly evocatively, sets the stage for the narrative of post-colonial perspectives on colonial history that will come in the museum space itself.

The success of these initiatives often hinges, interestingly enough, on the selfsame effects that were previously identified as potentially problematic in the space of the gallery. We noted, for example, that highly aestheticized displays such as that in the Musée Picasso can have an inhibiting effect on the viewer's appreciation of the broader communication objectives the gallery might wish to draw out of the material on display. In fact the opposite occurs in the museum. Museum visitors are programmed to receive didactic messages via a range of often emphatic – and even occasionally hyperactively strained – communication strategies. The aestheticization effect, on the other hand, can provide a breath of fresh air in the museum. It often introduces what we might call slow space into the museum. This emphasis refocuses visitor attention not so much on the relentless drive towards the next interactive, as rather on a more open-ended expression of an evocative idea that is at the same time encapsulated in a work with its own integrity as an object of visual attentiveness in its own right.

174

The introduction of these new elements into the museum is nonetheless not without risk. As we have already begun to see, the new associations and ideas triggered by this process can at times detract from the integrity of the object or idea that the museum wishes to highlight. This might not pose such a significant problem for those museums that are not inherently concerned with maintaining the integrity of their objects or ideas. It may well be the case, for example, in the previously discussed cabinet from the Natural History Museum in London. Where, after all, is the harm in a little Damien Hirst referencing in an entrance exhibit of this kind? Yet for those museums, on the other hand, that do place a particular significance on the authority or artefactual status of either the objects in their collection or the ideas they promote, the stakes are undeniably higher. In these instances, the introduction of art and art-inspired displays can prove disruptive in ways that are in some cases still not fully acknowledged within the very spaces in which they are at the same time most effective.

An especially vivid example of this is provided by the US Holocaust Memorial Museum in Washington, DC.[7] The Holocaust Museum maintains an interesting policy regarding the collecting and display of contemporary art. On the one hand, it is very much in favour of drawing on the creative talents of contemporary artists. Yet, at the same time, it is equally insistent that art must remain separate from the permanent exhibitions. It has specific – and readily understandable – reasons for this, which it explains in the following terms: 'all exhibits should be of authentic documentary character in order to pre-empt attempts by those who would deny that the Holocaust took place from using the Museum as supporting evidence for Holocaust denial.'[8]

To provide a presence for art in the Museum the designers accordingly elected to commission work from established mid-career artists, such as Ellsworth Kelly, Sol LeWitt, Richard Serra and Joel Shapiro. They then positioned these pieces in their so-called transitional spaces between and around the permanent exhibitions. Sol LeWitt's *Consequence*, for example, is sited in one of two 'lounges' designed as reflective spaces, creating momentary pauses in the circuit from one gallery of the permanent exhibition to another. Here the art acts as a kind of 'tonic' or reflective pause in between the relentless conveying of often highly confronting information in the galleries themselves. Effective as this strategy undeniably is, it nonetheless also brings to mind the previously noted tendency of art galleries to minimize information and communication technology elements within their displays. In each instance, it seems, the gallery, or here the museum, seeks to recognize the importance of a new and previously foreign element. Yet at the same time it also remains somehow mistrustful or ambivalent towards the very feature that it seeks otherwise to promote. So art is both welcomed and yet kept at arm's length in the museum space.

Even though art is banned from the galleries in the US Holocaust Memorial Museum, there is nonetheless a sense in which art-inspired concepts and display strategies have continued to play a significant – albeit unacknowledged – role in some of the exhibits. This is strikingly evident in a particularly powerful

175

gallery filled with a heart-rending installation of shoes confiscated from concentration camp inmates. The display is in an important respect documentary, since it bears witness to the suffering of the inmates of Majdanek concentration camp. Yet a more generalized art effect is also evoked through the undeniable reference that it simultaneously creates to Joseph Beuys's use of similar strategies to evoke a contrast between the discarded trace remnants of individuals' lives, and the overloaded symbolic and relic-like significance that he at the same time wanted them to serve – often, in this respect, made via an association with the Holocaust.[9]

A similarly unacknowledged contemporary art reference occurs in a tower of faces that visitors walk through at another stage of the circuit. This displays photographs of an entire Jewish community executed by the SS in the space of two days. Clearly, the aura and archival status of these photographs is fundamental to their effect. And yet, in viewing them one is struck by both their massed display aesthetic, their quasi-religious and ritualistic memorializing effect, as well as by the way in which they, in the end, reinforce not so much a sense of the individuality of these Holocaust victims in particular, but rather a generalized and even collective sense of the anonymity of fadedness and loss. All these features unavoidably bring to mind the work of Christian Boltanski, who has followed similar themes relating to photographs of deceased or missing persons – including Holocaust victims – that he presents in similar ways.[10]

We might be justified in concluding, therefore, that there is something powerfully innovative about the US Holocaust Memorial Museum's deployment of art and art-inspired displays. At the same time, however, their policy remains also somehow ambivalent. Its unresolvedness seems to stem from the institution's admittedly understandable mistrust of the more ambiguous and unresolved emphases inherent within art when applied to their chosen subject area. Yet it is precisely these elements of open-endedness and evocativeness that make the previously mentioned art-inspired displays so effective. The displays constitute a perfect example of the slow space effect mentioned earlier. What makes them so powerful, from the point of view of this visitor at least, is their stark contrast to the rest of the exhibition spaces. Unlike the cumulatively hyperactive, didactically explicit and informationally overloaded displays that characterize the rest of the museum, these two moments make their points with an extreme clarity and efficiency of means.

So while characterizing these exhibits as slow spaces, we might also want to underline that their function is to operate in certain respects as free spaces as well. By this I mean that their mode of communication is arguably more effective precisely because it offers the viewer more space via a more multi-layered and open-ended emphasis that is markedly different from the more linear and traditionally didactic displays elsewhere in the Museum. We need to recognize, of course, that it would not be appropriate for all or even most of the exhibits in the Holocaust Museum to operate in this way. If any museum is going to require didactic, data-heavy modes of information delivery, it is likely to be a museum devoted to this subject matter. Nonetheless, the success of these elements relative to the cumulative overload of the other displays raises the issue of the degree to which the competing effects and associations of art can be resolved – or indeed can even be acknowledged and formally addressed – in museum spaces of this kind.

We are thus reminded, once again, of the importance of the distinction between art galleries and museums that was raised by Bonnani at the outset of this discussion. Much as they have been drawing on the strengths and innovations of art galleries, museums will nonetheless tend to handle the issues here discussed in markedly different terms. A particularly clear demonstration of this can be gained if we compare two directly analogous communications messages framed in two recent, and in fact almost exactly contemporary, displays in Melbourne, Australia: a museum, on the one hand, as compared with an art gallery, on the other.

For many years the Melbourne Museum languished in cramped and run-down quarters that were almost buried under the weight of extensive nineteenth- to twentieth-century encyclopaedic natural and social history collections. A resiting project nonetheless finally enabled this institution to radically rethink its mission.[11] The results are most powerfully evident in an area given over to a permanent exhibition of Aboriginal identity that is maintained semi-autonomously by an Indigenous department. The centrepiece is a cabinet focusing on the disputed legacy of the Anglo-Australian anthropologist, Walter Baldwin Spencer, director of the Museum from 1899 to 1928 (see Figure 13.1). The Spencer cabinet makes manifest the common institutional ambivalence towards such 'father figures' in ethnographic museums founded on colonial collections. It does this by recasting Spencer as a hapless specimen imprisoned within his own display. In so doing, it ritually dethrones its founding father, installing him in a museological form of the stocks. The ritualistic element of the installation is intensified, once again, by the strong art effect that is present in the Museum's decision to depict Spencer not as a realistic effigy but as a marble-like sculpture – and thus as a kind of anti-memorial locked up in the prison of his own former possessions.

There is a certain poetic justice to this role reversal since it locates Spencer's memory in a denigrative form of display, just as Aboriginal people were represented in dioramas until relatively recently. He is also lampooned as an outmoded and ridiculous figure with his whiskers and somewhat puzzled expression in the midst of it all. This impression is underscored by a nearby video display with an actor playing the role of an almost burlesquely ignorant Spencer who is brusquely inducted into some basic Aboriginal understandings by an impressively authoritative elder. A high degree of artistic licence is clearly at work in this portrayal of Spencer as a hapless and hopeless, disembodied ghost, who is both less present and corporeal, ironically enough, than the objects he collected.

The Spencer cabinet is an unforgettable and highly effective act of deliberate provocation against the prevailing emphases of traditional ethnographic museums. To gain some sense of its power in this respect, it might be worth

Figure 13.1 Baldwin Spencer Display, Bunjilaka Gallery, Melbourne Museum.
© Museum Victoria. Photograph courtesy of Design Craft Furniture Pty Ltd.

noting that it would be akin to an institution like the Pitt Rivers Museum in Oxford electing to place a shrunken effigy of Pitt Rivers' own head within one of his former collections of shrunken and tattooed heads. Yet one could argue that this represents an appropriate emphasis in this instance given that this section of the Melbourne Museum is intended as an overtly politicized and impassioned presentation of Aboriginal people's own perspectives that it then seeks to reflect out to the visitor via the displays.[12]

In the end, however, statements of this kind are only as effective as their ability to cross the communications gap between the display and visitors themselves. In this respect, the Spencer cabinet, for all its undeniable power, might at the same time also run the risk of being both overdetermined to a certain degree, and also not as definitive as its designers might have hoped it to be. In the first instance, even though it adopts a broadly artistic approach, its strident communicative mode cancels out any sense of 'free space' such as was noted in the previous examples. In fact, the only free space available to the viewer is created if he or she goes against the grain of the display, so to speak. The exhibit is ostensibly concerned with critiquing the colonial practice of collecting and displaying ethnographic material culture as trophies of possession. And yet it seems simultaneously to undermine this reading through wall text that comments seemingly positively on the collecting process and through the great emphasis it in any event places on the beautifully lit, serried ranks of spears and other indexical artefacts of Indigenous identity.[13]

These comments are intended not so much as a critique of this exhibit in particular as rather a means of illustrating a more general observation concerning the gap that often exists between the on-paper clarity of an exhibition design, versus the often more complex reality of how it is received in the real time of completed display settings. The difficulties that arise from this gap should thus remind us of the importance of one overriding conclusion. That is, that objects and displays interact dynamically with visitors in complex ways that demonstrate their continued ability to evade curators' and exhibition designers' no doubt well-intentioned attempts to regulate and control their meanings. Visitors have the ability to experience displays on their own terms after all. And this obvious point once again highlights one of the great advantages of art and art-inspired displays in contemporary museums. The open-ended and individualized effect of an art element in a museum setting – its ability, in effect, to break free of the museum's institutional voice – is one of its principal strengths. If this can be achieved in a way that also preserves the viewer's freedom to make his or her own connections from the material and ideas on display, then the initiative can be seen to have been highly successful indeed. A clearer sense of this can be gained if we contrast the previous example, by way of conclusion, to an exhibit in another directly comparable Melbourne institution, this time a gallery.

This exhibit occurs in The Ian Potter Centre: National Gallery of Victoria, Australia (NGVA).[14] This institution was formed in 2001 as a result of the splitting into two of the National Gallery of Victoria's long-established and extensive collections of Australian and International art. Like the Melbourne Museum, this relocation also offered the Australian wing of the NGV the opportunity to rehang its collections along more contemporary lines. An emblematic example of this came in its decision to critically reframe one of its iconic colonial pieces. A hundred years earlier the Gallery had itself commissioned a grand commemorative painting of Captain Cook's previously mentioned landing at Botany Bay as a means of celebrating the recent unification of the Australian colonies under the act of Federation.[15] Now, a century later, it was able to restage the commission in a post-colonial setting to coincide with the opening of its new building. It accordingly commissioned the Indigenous artist Julie Gough to create an installation that would respond to this painting as well as to one of her earlier works in the Gallery's collections, *Imperial Leather*, a piece that also interrogates colonial practices of the collecting and stereotyping of Aboriginal identity.[16] *Chase* accordingly evokes a tense and unresolved space between the historical moment and the contemporary situation (see Figure 13.2). The ti trees that hang from the centre of the gallery represent once again the edge of the

Figure 13.2 Julie Gough, *Chase* (2001); ti trees, string, fabric and metal, as installed in The Ian Potter Centre, National Gallery of Victoria, Australia. To the left is E. Phillips Fox, *The Landing of Captain Cook at Botany Bay 1770* (1902). To the right is Julie Gough's *Imperial Leather* (1994). Photograph © NGV Photographic Services.

trees from which the Aboriginal people viewed Cook's landing as well as 'a place that has not been negotiated successfully and so remains our haunted house, our outdoors and indoors, our everywhere', as the artist has recently described it.[17]

In order to make the connection between the historical and contemporary explicit, the artist and the curators decided to take the additional step of removing the frame from the earlier painting. This strategy has two effects. On the one hand, it helps to break down the divisions between the works and to extend the painting out to the space of Gough's installation. *Chase* accordingly succeeds in creating the projective space that was noted previously as often lacking in gallery interiors. There is also a further sense in which the decision to remove the frame from a major late Victorian work constitutes a kind of ritualized debunking that would, of course, have been unthinkable in its own day. The NGVA, via the agency of its commissioned artist, has in effect ritually 'deframed' a painter whom they used historically to hold in the very highest regard. Their intervention is thus directly analogous to the Melbourne Museum's 'dethroning' of its founding father via an Indigenous commentary on colonial collecting. In fact one could argue that the NGVA has gone further than the Melbourne Museum in this regard. For all its overtness, the Baldwin Spencer cabinet enacts its revenge on what is in the end only an effigy of Spencer and his legacy. The NGVA, by contrast, has taken an actual, key historical artefact in its collection and has physically intervened and overwritten it within the context of a contemporary art installation.

It is important to note in this context that it was the artist herself who enabled the NGVA to take this radical step. As non-practitioner, institutional representatives, the curators would have presumably not felt at liberty to implement such an initiative. But the artist acting as a kind of free agent was accorded an artistic licence that enabled her and the institution, in turn, to intervene in a way that extends far beyond the traditional boundaries of curating works.[18] The result is an inherently projective space that makes just as strong and overt a didactic statement as any museum display and yet does so in a way that also remains at the same time powerfully open-ended and evocative.

The foregoing analysis has stressed the processes of risk and ambiguity that have struck this writer as characteristic of all these indicative examples of the temporary conflation of contemporary gallery practices and spaces into the museum environment. The implications of these processes will need to be thought through further by the institutions in question. Museums will need in particular to bear in mind two key considerations that have been highlighted in this analysis. First is the degree to which these initiatives challenge traditional viewing expectations. As museum-goers and professionals alike will know full well, exhibition design remains a constantly developing field. Yesterday's contentious new initiative (think, for example, of the initial debate surrounding the supposed 'dumbing-down' effect of the multi-media interactive) can quickly become either standard fare – or even dated – within a surprisingly short time. In the meantime, however, visitors are often left to grapple with the often uncertain viewing conditions that are created by these shifting parameters of communications, which often exist side by side with earlier or in other respects contrasting communications formats.

Second, and leading on from the previous point, museums will need to address further the extent to which these initiatives match – or rather conflict with – the other communicative strategies employed elsewhere. As one example of this, in the Melbourne Museum the critical approach found in the Baldwin Spencer display appears at odds with the much more positive – even hagiographical – representation of Spencer's legacy that is found in the Museum's own official history. This publication describes the work of Spencer and his collaborator F. J. Gillen as having had 'a profound and lasting impact on European understanding and assumptions; and their systematic collecting yielded a rich and complex harvest of ethnographic material for the Museum'.[19] Visitors to the museum might well be justified in asking which of these two seemingly opposed characterizations is the more accurate.

And yet, as I hope also to have demonstrated, the potentially distracting and even destabilizing elements that are by-products of these new practices are also simultaneously the self-same features that make them so worthwhile. The initiatives here described have the potential to circumvent the anonymity and linearity of traditional didactic modes in order to model instead the kinds of more creative juxtapositions and reimaginings that museums should offer their visitors as a matter of course. They thus open up the tantalizing possibility of a dynamic conjunction between the projective space of the museum, on the one hand, and the reflective space of the gallery, on the other, that might serve as a yet more fertile ground for further synergies between both spaces in the near future.

Notes

1 F. Bonanni, *Notizie circa la Galleria del Collegio Romano*, 1716, cited in P. Findlen, 'The museum: its classical etymology and Renaissance genealogy', *Journal of the History of Collections*, 1 (1), 1989: 60.

2 The classic study remains W. Prinz (ed. C. Cieri Via), *Galleria: storia e tipologia di uno spazio architettonico*, Modena: Panini, 1988.

3 For the Musée Picasso see D. Davies, *The Museum Transformed: Design and Culture in the Post-Pompidou Age*, New York: Abbeville Press, 1990, p. 52 and ff. for illustrations.

4 For this project, see F. Asensio Cerver, *The Architecture of Museums*, New York: Hearst Books International, 1997, pp. 128–35.

5 For the Muséum national d'Histoire naturelle, Paris, see Chapter 7 in this volume together with D. Bezombes (ed.), *La Grande Galerie du Museum National d'Histoire Naturelle, Conserver, c'est transformer*, Paris: Le Moniteur, 1994; Y. Laissus, *Le Muséum national d'Histoire naturelle*, Paris: Gallimard, 1995; H. de Lumley (ed.), *Muséum national d'Histoire naturelle*, Paris: Connaissance des Arts, 1995; J. Maigret, 'Aesthetics in the service of science: the Grande Galerie de l'Evolution in Paris', *Museum International*, 48 (2), 190, 1996: 19–22.

6 For the Museum of Sydney, see S. Hunt (ed.), *Sites: Nailing the Debate, Archaeology and Interpretation in Museums*, Sydney: Museum of Sydney, 1996; and D. Dysart (ed.), *Edge of the Trees: A Sculptural Installation by Janet Laurence and Fiona Foley from the Concept by Peter Emmett*, Sydney: Historic Houses Trust of New South Wales, 2000. For two more critical responses to the Museum, see C. R. Marshall, 'Back in the basilica: the new museology and the problem of national identity in the Museum of Sydney', *Art Monthly Australia*, 100, June 1997: 7–11; and J. Marcus, 'Erotics of the Museum of Sydney', in J. Marcus, *A Dark Smudge Upon the Sand: Essays on Race, Guilt and the National Consciousness*, Sydney: LhR Press, 1999, pp. 37–50.

7 J. Weinberg and R. Elieli, *The Holocaust Museum in Washington*, New York: Rizzoli, 1995.

8 Ibid., p. 29.

9 For associations between Beuys's work and the Holocaust, see M. Biro, 'Representation and event: Anselm Kiefer, Joseph Beuys and the memory of the Holocaust', *Yale Journal of Criticism*, 16 (1), 2003: 113–46, particularly pp. 119–24. For a more critical reading of this topic, see Z. Amashai-Maisels, *Depiction and Interpretation: The Influence of the Holocaust on the Visual Arts*, Oxford: Pergamon Press, 1993, pp. 346 and 501.

10 For associations between Boltanski's work and the Holocaust, see E. van Alphen, *Caught by History: Holocaust Effects in Contemporary Art, Literature and Theory*, Stanford, CA: Stanford University Press, 1997, chapters 4 and 6, 'Deadly histories: Christian Boltanski's intervention in historiography', pp. 93–122 and 'The revivifying artist: Christian Boltanski's efforts to close the gap', pp. 149–75.

11 For the Melbourne Museum, see C. Rasmussen, *A Museum for the People: A History of Museum Victoria and its Predecessors, 1854–2000*, Melbourne: Scribe Publications, 2001.

12 For this emphasis within contemporary Indigenous museum displays, and with a focus also on the Melbourne Museum, see G. Sculthorpe, 'Exhibiting Indigenous histories in Australian museums', in D. McIntyre and K. Wehner (eds), *Negotiating Histories: National Museums Conference Proceedings*, Canberra: National Museum of Australia

in association with the Centre for Cross-Cultural Research and the Australian Key Centre for Cultural and Media Policy, 2001, pp. 73–84.

13 The information panels in the cabinet contain both negative and positive descriptions of collections and the collectors who contributed to the Museum. One panel, for example, notes that 'Until the early 1900s most objects came from small collections. These collections also provided some of the most precious, rare or unusual items.'

14 For The Ian Potter Centre: National Gallery of Victoria, Australia, see P. Goad, 'Enfilade and intrafilament: The Ian Potter Centre: NGV Australia at Federation Square', *Art Bulletin of Victoria*, 42, 2002: 7–15.

15 For E. Phillips Fox, *The Landing of Captain Cook at Botany Bay 1770* (1902), see R. Zubans, *E. Phillips Fox: His Life and Art*, Melbourne: Miegunyah Press, 1995, pp. 97–100.

16 For Julie Gough's *Imperial Leather* (1994), see I. Crombie (ed.), *Flagship: Australian Art in the National Gallery of Victoria, 1790–2000*, Melbourne: The Ian Potter Centre, NGV Australia, 2002, p. 78.

17 The quotation occurs in an artist's statement reproduced as part of the wall text displayed alongside *Chase* during its exhibition in the NGVA from 2001 to 2004.

18 As a postscript to this point it nonetheless needs also to be noted that Julie Gough was subsequently appointed Curator of Indigenous Art at the NGVA two and a half years after the commission here discussed.

19 Rasmussen, *Museum for the People*, p. 140.

References

Amashai-Maisels, Z., *Depiction and Interpretation: The Influence of the Holocaust on the Visual Arts*, Oxford: Pergamon Press, 1993.

Asensio Cerver, F., *The Architecture of Museums*, New York: Hearst Books International, 1997.

Bezombes, D. (ed.), *La Grande Galerie du Museum National d'Histoire Naturelle, Conserver, c'est transformer*, Paris: Le Moniteur, 1994.

Biro, M., 'Representation and event: Anselm Kiefer, Joseph Beuys and the memory of the Holocaust', *Yale Journal of Criticism*, 16 (1), 2003: 113–46.

Crombie, I. (ed.), *Flagship: Australian Art in the National Gallery of Victoria, 1790–2000*, Melbourne: The Ian Potter Centre, NGV Australia, 2002.

Davies, D., *The Museum Transformed: Design and Culture in the Post-Pompidou Age*, New York: Abbeville Press, 1990.

de Lumley, H. (ed.), *Muséum national d'Histoire naturelle*, Paris: Connaissance des Arts, 1995.

Dysart, D. (ed.), *Edge of the Trees: A Sculptural Installation by Janet Laurence and Fiona Foley from the Concept by Peter Emmett*, Sydney: Historic Houses Trust of New South Wales, 2000.

Findlen, P., 'The museum: its classical etymology and Renaissance genealogy', *Journal of the History of Collections*, 1 (1), 1989: 59–78.

Goad, P., 'Enfilade and intrafilament: The Ian Potter Centre: NGV Australia at Federation Square', *Art Bulletin of Victoria*, 42, 2002: 7–15.

Hunt, S. (ed.), *Sites: Nailing the Debate, Archaeology and Interpretation in Museums*, Sydney: Museum of Sydney, 1996.

Laissus, Y., *Le Muséum national d'Histoire naturelle*, Paris: Gallimard, 1995.

Maigret, J., 'Aesthetics in the service of science: the Grande Galerie de l'Evolution in Paris', *Museum International*, 48 (2), 190, 1996: 19–22.

Marcus, J., 'Erotics of the Museum of Sydney', in J. Marcus, *A Dark Smudge Upon the Sand: Essays on Race, Guilt and the National Consciousness*, Sydney: LhR Press, 1999, pp. 37–50.

Marshall, C. R., 'Back in the basilica: the new museology and the problem of national identity in the Museum of Sydney', *Art Monthly Australia*, 100, June 1997: 7–11.

Prinz, W. (ed. C. Cieri Via), *Galleria: storia e tipologia di uno spazio architettonico*, Modena: Panini, 1988.

Rasmussen, C., *A Museum for the People: A History of Museum Victoria and its Predecessors, 1854–2000*, Melbourne: Scribe Publications, 2001.

Sculthorpe, G., 'Exhibiting Indigenous histories in Australian museums', in D. McIntyre and K. Wehner (eds), *Negotiating Histories: National Museums Conference Proceedings*, Canberra: National Museum of Australia in association with the Centre for Cross-Cultural Research and the Australian Key Centre for Cultural and Media Policy, 2001, pp. 73–84.

van Alphen, E., *Caught by History: Holocaust Effects in Contemporary Art, Literature and Theory*, Stanford, CA: Stanford University Press, 1997.

Weinberg, J. and Elieli, R., *The Holocaust Museum in Washington*, New York: Rizzoli, 1995.

Zubans, R., *E. Phillips Fox: His Life and Art*, Melbourne: Miegunyah Press, 1995.

14

Constructing and communicating equality

The social agency of museum space

Richard Sandell

The spaces of the museum have often been characterized, within cultural and sociological analyses, as means through which social inequalities have been constituted, reproduced, reinforced. The hierarchical arrangement of objects, the presentation of partial and biased histories, the marked absence of (certain forms of) cultural difference have been understood as technologies through which museums have contributed to wider social processes of othering, disempowerment and oppression.[1] Recently, however, it is possible to detect a growing confidence among cultural practitioners in articulating goals which might be seen to challenge these perspectives. Against a backdrop of increasing professional concern, internationally, for issues such as the representation of diversity and the inclusion of previously marginalized constituencies, there can also be seen a growing number of specialist museums whose *primary* purpose and rationale is explicitly linked to the combating of various manifestations and causes of social inequity.[2] These museums' socially driven goals are, of course, immensely varied, contingent upon localized, socio-political imperatives, but many are framed by the growing influence of broader, pluralist discourses. These goals may be addressed through a number of means – work with schools and communities, events programmes, research and advocacy – but many seek to use their exhibitions to communicate to audiences specific ideas predicated upon concepts of equality and human rights. It might be argued that museum spaces are being reinvented and, for some, becoming endowed with the potential to effect positive social change – in particular, to promote equality through the combating of prejudices, the reversal of processes of othering and the engendering of pluralist, democratic values.

There is, however, both a paucity of empirical evidence and a lack of theoretical interrogation with which to inform and substantiate these assertions. Indeed, contemporary understandings of audiences – as agents active in the construction and determination of meaning – present a significant challenge to museums that articulate goals around the promotion of equal rights and the combating of prejudice. Within audience studies, the 'dominant text model', in which audiences passively and uncritically absorb the messages they are exposed to, is no longer widely supported.[3] Rather, research suggests that audiences can construct wide-ranging meanings from a museum visit, shaped and informed by a range of personal and socio-cultural factors.[4] Potentially, these meanings might be entirely oppositional to those intended by the museum, exhibiting not tolerant or egalitarian attributes but rather prejudiced (for example, homophobic, racist or sexist) ones. If individual visitors are understood to generate their own highly personalized and variable meanings from the same exhibition encounter, what role, if any, might museums play in constructing spatial forms which communicate notions of equality and enable meanings that combat, rather than enhance, prejudice?

Both theoretical developments and a growing number of empirical visitor research projects lend weight to a constructivist view of the audience–exhibition encounter in which the primacy of the visitor in determining meaning is highlighted. I wish to argue, however, that there are inherent dangers within this perspective. A celebration of audience over media agency should not be appropriated to deny the potential influence (and the concomitant social responsibility) of those who directly shape cultural spaces – curators, architects, designers and increasingly educators and other museum practitioners – determining what is displayed, how and with what purpose in mind. Exhibitions, it will be argued here, contain spatial cues, deploy spatial strategies that, while unable to guarantee a given, preordained response in all visitors, can nonetheless privilege certain readings, and offer ways of thinking that can play a part in tackling prejudice. (Indeed, it might be argued that museums could not function ideologically, as they are claimed to, if they had no influence.) These cues, characteristics, strategies – and their potential influence – it is further argued, must be understood not in isolation but in relation to the individual and social practices of the visitor and the multiple ways in which diverse audiences can draw on them to generate their own (prejudiced? liberal? contradictory?) accounts and meanings.

The chapter is in three main parts. The first draws on analyses of museum spaces that have been characterized as excluding, oppressive and prejudiced to consider the spatial techniques and modes of representation and display deployed to these ends. The second section discusses modes of spatial reorganization that can be identified in many kinds of museum in recent decades. These attempts to accommodate diversity have emerged in response to a range of social, political and cultural factors, including the rise of multiculturalism and the emergence of a politics of difference, calls from increasingly powerful and vocal minorities, and developments within museum practice such as the emergence of the new social history.[5] The final section focuses on museum spaces that have been *purposefully* created with certain (social) intentions in mind. Using examples of museums whose primary purpose is linked to the promotion of equality and the combating of prejudice, this part looks at the particular spatial tactics and modes of display mobilized to achieve these goals. By addressing these issues the chapter also seeks to contribute to broader philosophical debates about the role and responsibility of cultural institutions. More particularly, it raises questions around the extent to which social and power relations, played out beyond the walls of the museum (but also embodied within them), should be more explicitly acknowledged, be 'felt' (and responded to) internally within museum spaces. How might museum spaces take account of, and more proactively engage with, the variously constituted forms of inequality and discrimination manifest within society at large? In what ways might such engagement serve to dramatize and render visible the embodied power relations that exist within displays?

Constructing and communicating otherness

Decisions concerning the allocation, arrangement and utility of museum space have political effects. But what do excluding museum spaces look like? What spatial forms, what display conventions can be found in museums that have traditionally been characterized as reproducing and reinforcing social inequity? My attempt here is not to categorize specific museum spaces as either oppressive, excluding, discriminatory (and thereby attributed with the capacity to reinforce and reproduce prejudice and social inequality) or liberating, inclusive, egalitarian (capable of challenging stereotypes and combating prejudice). Such analyses are both reductive and inappropriate in the light of numerous audience research projects that have pointed to the likelihood of wide-ranging, complex, and often contradictory, audience responses to the same space.[6] Though the potential agency of museum space needs to be understood in relation to the diverse practices (individual and social) of the visitors who inhabit them, it is nonetheless possible to discuss, at least in broad terms, the spatial characteristics and devices that might have political implications and that have attracted fierce criticism from marginalized communities and generated debate within cultural academic discourse.

In many cultural and sociological analyses of the museum's role there is an inherent problematic in the notion of museums as agents of positive (democratizing, empowering, egalitarian) social change. Rather, the museum has been historically linked to processes of exclusion, division and oppression. Tony Bennett, for example, has argued that museums in the nineteenth century were designed to play a part in highlighting distinctions between those who visited and 'the other' in such a way as to reinforce dominant, imperialist power relations:

> Detailed studies of nineteenth-century expositions . . . consistently highlight the ideological economy of their organizing principles, transforming displays of machinery and industrial processes, of finished products and *objets d'art*, into material signifiers of progress – but of progress as a collective national achievement with capital as the great co-ordinator. . . . And this power marked out the distinction between the subjects and the objects of power not within the national body but, as organized by the many rhetorics of imperialism, between that body and other, 'non-civilized' people upon whose bodies the effects of power were unleashed. . . . This was, in other words, a power which aimed at a rhetorical effect through its representation of otherness rather than at any disciplinary effects.[7]

The ways in which anthropological or ethnographic displays, in particular, have served to distance viewer from subject and, in doing so, to exoticize difference has been widely discussed. Henrietta Riegel, for example, states that 'the dominant mode of reproduction in which museums are located denies a shared space between visitors, museum professionals and the people whose cultures are on display. This denial of shared communication is a political act'.[8] Similarly, Ivan Karp and Corinne Kratz discuss the ways in which notions of self and other are constructed within museum displays. In their analysis of ethnographic displays they suggest that often, 'the audience and exhibit makers define themselves as a homogenous entity counterposed to an exotic Other'.[9]

The ways in which museums might constitute and communicate otherness are, of course, many and complex but our concern here is with *spatial* manifestations. What then are the spatial forms most readily associated with the museum as a tool for othering and exclusion?

Three (interrelated) modes of display can be identified. First, and perhaps most clearly illustrated in anthropology or ethnography museums dedicated to the display of different cultures, is the creation (and, sometimes, the relative positioning) of discrete, differentiated spaces (dioramas, exhibition cases or entire galleries) that separate, demarcate and distinguish between different groups. Not only might such strategies be reductive in their exaggeration of difference and exoticization of the cultures on display but they might also be mobilized to suggest superiority of one group over another. For example, Karp and Kratz suggest that the relative placement of these (differentiated, distinct) spaces within the museum building, 'is neither arbitrary nor inconsequential: the invented Other is often placed downstairs from the upstairs domicile of European and American art traditions which museums and exhibits invent and claim'.[10]

Second, and in contrast to the *differentiated* use of space outlined above, museums have been criticized for displaying cultural difference within physically shared spaces but within an interpretive framework that reproduces and reinforces (rather than challenges) social inequalities.[11] For example, overtly colonial interpretations that might use the presence of the conquered, inferior 'savage' as a prop to emphasize the 'civilized' powerful and conquering European. Such displays have generated intense debate and discussion and, in response to angry criticism from communities who have found them offensive, many have now been removed or redisplayed.[12]

In the Royal Museum of the Army and Military History in Brussels, a gallery entitled 'Belgium in the 19th century' has been preserved precisely because it illustrates past approaches to museum displays. The museum's promotional leaflet reads:

> Souvenirs of the first two kings and of the army of a youthful nation, plus reminders of the civic guard and colonial expeditions are displayed in a quaint room, replete with Belgian flags and weapons decorating walls hung with paintings. This gallery is a museum within a museum and gives us an idea of how a Museum used to get furnished.[13]

188

Though it is acknowledged that the gallery is illustrative of past museum practices, the visitor, nevertheless, can encounter a gallery that appears to leave unchallenged the not so subtle representations and present-day implications of past colonial power that many contemporary audiences are likely to find extremely insulting.

The third spatial manifestation of othering concerns the marked absence of (certain forms of) difference from museum spaces. Who is denied access to display space within the museum will, of course, vary from context to context and will change over time. Eilean Hooper-Greenhill considers this issue, drawing on the collections of the first decade of the National Portrait Gallery, London. 'Presented as a display, groups of portraits illustrate relationships with people, demonstrating the importance of certain groups through their exposition and, by implication, the lack of importance of those left unseen.'[14] Increasingly then, those who have found themselves excluded from collections and displays have fought for the right to representation and, in some contexts, museum space has become a highly prized and sought-after cultural commodity. Tony Bennett's comments suggest the factors that have come to shape this perception:

> Demands that representational parity be given to women's art in art galleries or to the histories of subordinate social strata in history museums are thus ones which are generated out of, and fuelled by, the norms of universal representativity embodied in the rhetorics of public art galleries and museums. Earlier collections of valued objects seem not to have given rise to any similar demands – partly, no doubt, because of the limited influence of democratic and egalitarian philosophies but also because principles of curiosity and wonder which governed the constitution of such collections meant that no general political value could be attached to the question of what was included within, or excluded from, such collections.[15]

As different minority groups strive towards equal rights and become more vocal and powerful, museums continue to face new and evolving demands for inclusion within their (limited) spaces.

Spatial trends and transformations

Museums then, have deployed a number of spatial strategies that serve to exclude and marginalize different groups. Though, of course, these modes of display remain in museums today, they are increasingly challenged by new forms of spatial practice driven by attempts to respond to criticism and new demands for inclusion. In recent decades we can identify a process of spatial reorganization and revision unfolding in many museums, mobilized by a broader democratizing project. Specific manifestations vary immensely, but it is nonetheless possible to identify the deployment of some common spatial devices with associated characteristics. Though the intention and aims of these devices are not always fully articulated by the institution, these attempts to accommodate multiple forms of difference, to reflect diversity, can be understood as efforts to begin to respond to some of the criticisms of museums outlined earlier. Many of these have developed out of an increasingly widespread desire among some practitioners and (rather fewer) leaders in the museum sector to develop new forms of practice that enable museums to engage more purposefully with contemporary social issues. In some cases, pressures from governing bodies or increasingly powerful and vocal communities have also influenced these spatial developments. In broad terms, three spatial devices, with associated characteristics, can be identified.

Compensatory

Initiatives that might be described as compensatory (or, perhaps, remedial) are typically small-scale, sometimes temporary interventions within or alongside existing longer-term displays that have generally been perceived as excluding or discriminatory. In some instances, these displays may arise out of internal staff initiatives – attempts by individuals to reflect community diversity and engage groups that are poorly served by the museum. These initiatives may be driven by the personal/political commitment and values of the individuals involved and sometimes develop in the face of indifference or resistance from colleagues. Here, though the displays may be physically marginalized (as a result of organizational resistance or inertia), they nevertheless often provide an important starting point for further institutional change. In other instances, these interventions may be reactive – perhaps responses by the museum to criticisms from communities angered by a lack of positive representation; an attempt to counter displays perceived as offensive or as presenting stereotypical, negative views of a minority; or a tokenistic response to pressure from governing bodies or other constituencies. Here, displays are likely to be short-lived and have rather less influence as a catalyst for future institutional change.

Regardless of underlying motivation and intent, typically a small (possibly temporary) display case dedicated to a specific (differentiated) minority is grafted on to existing displays to which little, if any, modification is made. Sometimes, these interventions may take the form of single 'community show-cases' in peripheral locations within the building – perhaps a corridor or a dimly lit and poorly used corner of a gallery.

Celebratory

Celebratory strategies might typically occupy a more prominent space within the museum. As such they can demand a greater degree of accommodation or organizational change and planning on the part of the museum. Though perhaps relatively temporary (compared to other museum displays), they are generally of higher profile and on a larger scale than initiatives within the former category. Typically, these might be temporary exhibitions, scheduled as part of an ongoing programme of changing exhibitions, and presented within the museum's main exhibition galleries. Such exhibitions, often celebratory in tone, typically focus on a specific, differentiated group. These celebratory initiatives may evolve in response to community concerns over under- or misrepresentation or may be initiated by museum staff who have found that, far from making demands, community groups often have to be convinced to get involved with museums. Some museums have found that it is only once they have approached and worked with one or two groups that others come forward to request space for exhibition, usually to celebrate a particular anniversary or event.

Questions over the efficacy of both compensatory and celebratory displays in conferring and communicating equality might take account of linked spatial and temporal characteristics. Though these approaches are relatively easy for the museum to accommodate, their perceived cultural authority for audiences may well be diminished by their tendency to occupy peripheral locations and for shorter periods of time than their mainstream display counterparts. Sharon Macdonald (drawing on Roger Silverstone) points to the possibility of museum displays – often spatially fixed and in place for many years – holding a greater cultural authority in comparison with other media.[16] Conversely then, displays perceived as less fixed (either spatially or temporally) might also serve to suggest a relatively lesser importance for the groups represented by such transient displays.

Pluralist

The third category of spatial device can be termed pluralist. Here the motivation is to integrate (often several forms of) cultural difference within a unifying interpretive framework, designed to suggest both similarities and also (positive) differences between groups and in ways that aim to challenge rather than reproduce the inequalities of power highlighted earlier by Karp and Kratz. Often, but by no means always, these displays occupy core, 'permanent' galleries and require the most significant degree of organizational change. These changes might include, for example, proactive collecting initiatives, a fundamental redisplay of collections and even radical reallocation of gallery spaces.

Interpretive frameworks commonly deployed to accommodate multiple forms of difference are those based on geographic or thematic narratives. For example, displays that adopt a geographic interpretive framework to tell the story of a particular town, city or other location can be used to accommodate the diversity of communities that live or lived there. Brighton Museum in the south of England, for example, includes an exhibition about associations for which the city is famous, including regency architecture, fishing and the city's renowned lesbian and gay community. Similarly, their displays on the theme of the Body enable a number of diverse perspectives to be incorporated, including, for example, objects and artworks that explore issues around disability and that seek to challenge the discrimination disabled people experience.

Pluralist displays may support the aspirations of some groups to maintain distinct and differentiated identities (that demand recognition, validation and accommodation by the mainstream) but are perhaps more likely to draw upon

191

and emphasize concepts of sameness, in some cases purposefully downplaying difference in order to suggest common and shared experiences, values and beliefs between different groups.

Though each of these three approaches – compensatory, celebratory, pluralist – represents different spatial manifestations of attempts to accommodate diversity, they nevertheless each contain dilemmas and contradictions which continue to challenge museum practitioners. Questions around which groups are allocated space and which continue to be left out will generate different answers in different contexts and over time. For example, while calls for greater representation of women have been debated over a number of years it is only in relatively recent history that museums (and even then a very small minority) have considered the possibility of devoting display space to the representation of lesbians and gay men. Similarly complex and problematic are questions about *how* certain forms of cultural difference are displayed and with what underlying intention in mind. Finally, and not surprisingly, the political implications of these developments have not been uncontested. Attempts to introduce difference can present a challenge to dominant social groups who may object to the museum's perceived validation of alternative, sometimes competing, perspectives and agendas.[17]

Figure 14.1 summarizes the spatial characteristics that can be associated with different display devices. Though the diagram usefully summarizes broad developments in spatial practice, it should not be read to imply discrete and distinct categories of approach. Similarly it is not intended to suggest that all museums are moving along a temporal continuum from compensatory to pluralist. Indeed, individual museums or gallery spaces may simultaneously contain examples of all three approaches. Moreover, as broader societal attitudes shift, museums find themselves facing demands to accommodate 'new' groups that have not previously been represented. Some groups may therefore be represented through

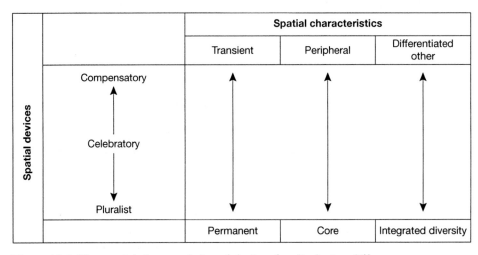

Figure 14.1 The spatial characteristics of devices for displaying difference.

compensatory interventions, whereas, within the same institution, others have become more fully integrated. It is also recognized that different communities will themselves favour different approaches – some preferring to maintain a distinct and differentiated identity, others seeking to be integrated within main-stream displays.

These devices can be observed in many different kinds of museum internation-ally, growing from and being shaped by a myriad of social, political and cultural factors at global as well as local levels. However, against the backdrop of this increasing interest in issues of diversity and representation have emerged a growing number of museums whose socially driven goals constitute the organization's primary rationale. This final part of the chapter draws on two examples of museums with specific social intentions – the Anne Frank House, Amsterdam, Holland, and the St Mungo Museum of Religious Life and Art, Glasgow, Scotland. Though articulated in different ways, both museums can be understood to have goals that are based on notions of equality, the combating of prejudice and promotion of mutual understanding. Though both share a focus on social purpose, they differ in terms of both the forms of inequality and prejudice with which they are concerned and the interpretive and spatial strate-gies they adopt. The purpose here is to look more closely at the spatial strategies that have been deployed in these special instances with a view to illuminating the implications of spatial practice in museums more broadly.

Spatial practice and social agency

> The purpose of the Anne Frank House is to preserve Anne Frank's hiding place and to propagate her ideals, not only in relationship to the times in which she lived, but also in terms of their contemporary significance. The purpose of this organization is further advanced by: combating present-day forms of Nazism, anti-Semitism, racism and xenophobia; and by contributing to the realization of a pluralistic democratic society in which every human being is seen as a unique individual and treated equally under the law.[18]

Visitors to the museum follow a prescribed route through the rooms inhabited by the Frank family while in hiding from the Nazis during the Second World War. Emerging from the house itself, visitors enter a contemporary space, contrasting sharply with the intimate and historic character of the earlier part of the visit and signalling a return to the present day. Positioned here, at the end of the visit, the museum's temporary exhibitions are designed purposefully to explore contemporary issues that relate to prejudice and discrimination. The current exhibition, entitled *Grensgevallen (Out of Line)*, is concerned not only with anti-Semitism and other forms of racial prejudice but also with discrimi-nation on the grounds of sexual orientation, disability, religion and so on. *Out of Line* presents visitors with a series of contemporary, real-life dilemmas in which two basic rights – freedom of expression and the right to protection from discrimination – come into conflict. In each of the scenarios, visitors are invited to make a choice by pressing one of two buttons to indicate which of the rights in question should take precedence. Though, not surprisingly, visitors' responses are diverse, the possibilities for expressing these within the exhibition itself are contained by the museum through the voting format, which permits (and thereby validates) only two possible reactions – the selection of 'the right to freedom of expression' or 'the right to protection against discrimination'. Significantly, both 'choices', framed by the museum and the exhibition-makers, are underpinned by, and predicated upon, notions of equal human rights for all, regardless of gender, race, religion, disability or sexual orientation.

The St Mungo Museum of Religious Life and Art, part of Glasgow Museums, Scotland, 'explores the importance of religion in people's lives across the world and across time. . . . The aim of the museum is to promote understanding and respect between people of different faiths, and none'.[19] This museum makes use of collections, the ways in which objects are positioned in relation to each other and the ways in which they are interpreted, to achieve its aims.[20] When the museum opened in 1993 its thematic approach to the presentation of collections represented a radical departure from traditional, discipline-based modes of display. The museum contains three main permanent galleries (the Gallery of Religious Art, the Gallery of Religious Life and the Scottish Gallery) and a temporary exhibition space.

Within these displays, purposefully designed to achieve the museums' socially driven goals, what spatial strategies can be identified?

Spatial allocation, parity and balance

The allocation of display space for a specific minority within the museum is clearly a political act with differing implications for the organization, its stakeholders, the groups represented and audiences. For some groups, museum space constitutes a highly desirable resource or commodity. The securing of space for display within those cultural institutions perceived to be most prestigious is undoubtedly regarded by some marginalized communities as a form of cultural validation or endorsement, an opportunity to draw on the legitimizing effects of the museum's cultural authority. Unsurprisingly then, the allocation of this commodity is likely to be contested (internally and externally) and may attract fierce controversy. In debates and decisions over the allocation of space, issues of parity and balance emerge as especially significant.

In *Out of Line* at the Anne Frank House, while the majority of visitors have voluntarily elected to visit the house and may therefore be assumed to be (at least partially) receptive to anti-racist sentiments, they may nevertheless find themselves facing issues around other forms of prejudice with which they are less comfortable. For example, the presence, within the exhibition's multimedia presentation, of issues affecting lesbians and gay men, underpinned by an interpretive framework based clearly on equality for all, may be read, by some visitors, as a conferring of rights to homosexuals by the museum. Of course, a whole range of factors can impact upon the extent to which this message might be accepted, rejected or appropriated by visitors. Though oppositional responses might be verbally expressed within or between visiting groups or written in the comments book, significantly there is no opportunity within the voting format of the exhibition to formally register such a view – one which denies or challenges the museum's conferring of equal rights to gays and lesbians. Moreover, it is interesting to ponder the extent to which visitor responses might be framed by the emotionally charged visit to the annex itself. Indeed, many visitors make a connection between the message offered by the first part of the visit (the House itself) and the contemporary exhibition, illustrating the museum's potential to provoke, generate, and perhaps to inform, discussion and reflection.[21]

Issues of spatial parity and balance are very much in evidence at St Mungo's Museum. Within the Gallery of Religious Life, while over 100 religions are represented in the thematic displays, it is the six largest world religions (also the six largest in Glasgow) that receive most attention. Here, efforts have been directed towards ensuring that, as far as is possible, no single religion overtly dominates the gallery display. Moreover, the significance of spatial balance was explicitly expressed by the museum's curator when describing a one-day event designed to provide visitors with the opportunity to find out about a variety of different religions that are practised within Glasgow. Each religious denomination was allocated the same amount of space to present their materials to visitors; attempts by some groups to secure additional space were strongly resisted.[22]

Differentiation and integration

The ways in which forms of cultural difference are displayed as either discrete, differentiated or as integrated alongside others within a unifying interpretive framework generates multiple and complex possible meanings. As Karp and Kratz state:

> Stressing similarities produces an assimilating impression, creating both familiarity and intimacy with representations and their subjects. Assertions of unbridgeable difference, on the other hand, exoticise by creating relations of great spatial or temporal distance, perhaps the thrill of the unknown.[23]

The complex dialectic established by the simultaneous use of these two approaches to display is evident at St Mungo's. In the Gallery of Religious Art Christian paintings and stained glass are exhibited alongside Buddhist statues and Islamic artworks. In the Gallery of Religious Life six equally sized display cases, each dedicated to a single (differentiated) religion, are surrounded by thematic cases in which objects from different religions are brought together to emphasize the shared experience of, for example, childhood or coming of age. These displays support the notion of equal significance and rights for each

195

of the religions represented, but also serve to emphasize sameness and common experience between them. Highlighted differences or unique aspects of a particular religion are, for the most part, positive and non-controversial. (Interestingly one of the most controversial parts of the display – a photograph that shows a young girl being circumcised – avoids attribution of the practice to a specific, named religion.)

Karp and Kratz point out that the construction of 'otherness' is not, in itself, problematic, but rather the ways in which cultural difference has most often been framed through museum displays:

> The problem is that the construction of cultural diversity within Euroamerican cultural traditions has more often focused on what the Other lacks than on the complex dialectic of similarity and difference that operates in all display settings at one the same time. Museums have too often represented cultures in a hierarchy that reproduces inequalities of power.[24]

St Mungo's Gallery of Religious Life deploys a still uncommon approach to display in which spatial integration and differentiation of cultural difference are purposefully combined to confer and communicate notions of equality between the different religious groups represented.

Finally, it is also worth acknowledging that integrated modes of display can also serve to assimilate and hide difference in ways that some marginalized groups will wish to resist.[25]

Audience engagement and participation

A third spatial characteristic evident in these two case studies concerns attempts to directly engage visitors in expressing their opinions and in sharing these through incorporation into the museum's displays or other aspects of the visiting experience. At the Anne Frank House the *Out of Line* exhibition not only encourages visitors to express their opinion through voting for either 'freedom of expression' or 'protection from discrimination' but also displays the collective responses in the form of illuminated bars on the ceiling, which show visitors the results of the vote (among the current room of visitors) in each of the dilemmas presented. The social nature of this experience can be, at one and the same time, uncomfortable, provocative and intriguing.[26]

At St Mungo's Museum, visitors are encouraged to share their thoughts with others on comments cards, which are then displayed as part of the exhibition in the galleries themselves. A comments book located at the end of the museum visit at the Anne Frank House is similarly well used. In both these instances, many visitors take the opportunity to condemn prejudice and intolerance.

Figure 14.2 summarizes the *intentions* (though not the actual audience responses) that might be associated with different spatial tactics in those museums that purposefully seek to communicate notions of equality and combat prejudice.

Figure 14.2 Spatial tactics and intent within displays designed to communicate notions of equality and combat prejudice.

Spatial tactics/processes	Intent
Allocation, parity and balance	Confers equality to represented groups
Differentiation	Counters prior under-representation
Integration	Naturalizes, de-exoticizes, promotes concepts of sameness and mutual understanding
Audience engagement and participation work	Stimulates (non-prejudiced) text and talk

Conclusion

Although it is possible to identify the intentions of specific spatial strategies and to decode their possible meanings, actual audience responses cannot be directly 'read off' from these intended messages. Indeed, as has already been discussed, exhibitions designed purposefully to communicate notions of equal rights and mutual understanding can result in the 'boomerang effect'[27] where intended messages are not simply resisted but turned around by audiences in ways that result in the construction of entirely oppositional meanings. What then might we conclude from this discussion?

Museums remain, for the most part, highly conservative organizations. While there is a growing acceptance of the need to represent diversity in some form or other, this is often confined to specific forms of cultural difference, reflecting dominant social mores and attitudes. Museums that are prepared to deploy their spatial resources to engage with inequalities and prejudices experienced by groups that remain marginalized in society and whose rights to inclusion are more widely contested are much rarer.

Despite growing recognition of the political implications of display there is, nonetheless, a strong resistance to the notion that museums might, in various ways, deploy their spatial resources and their collections in ways that take account of social inequalities. Suggestions of this kind are often simplistically misinterpreted as 'politically correct', policy-led demands that all museums incorporate multiple forms of diversity, regardless of context. It is further argued that this approach deflects museums from the task of caring for and interpreting their collections. Both the St Mungo Museum of Religious Life and Art and the Anne Frank House use their collections to enable audiences to explore their contemporary significance and in ways that acknowledge the collections' social and political contexts. The decisions that are made within museums (including those about the uses to which collections, space and other resources are deployed) should be open to influence from not only academic and aesthetic concerns and agendas but also from the form and nature of social inequalities manifest beyond the museum's walls. This engagement with issues of inequality acknowledges the social agency of museum space and, in doing so, begins to challenge the (apparently) depoliticized, neutral position that many museums prefer to maintain.

Acknowledgements

I would like to thank the staff of the St Mungo Museum of Religious Life and Art and the Anne Frank House for their support and cooperation and, in particular, Jan van Kooten and Harry Dunlop. Many thanks also to Suzanne MacLeod for the opportunity to pursue this line of research. Finally, I am very grateful to Mark O'Neill for his insightful comments on a draft of this chapter and for his ongoing encouragement and advice.

Notes

1 See, for example, T. Bennett, *The Birth of the Museum*, London and New York: Routledge, 1995, and J. McGuigan, *Culture and The Public Sphere*, London and New York: Routledge, 1996.

2 For example, museums concerned with issues around tolerance and human rights. R. J. Abram, 'Harnessing the power of history', in R. Sandell (ed.), *Museums, Society, Inequality*, London and New York: Routledge, 2002, pp. 125–41 describes the origins of the Coalition of Historic Sites of Conscience, which includes the Gulag Museum (Russia), District Six Museum (South Africa) and the Lower East Side Tenement Museum (USA).

3 N. Abercrombie and B. Longhurst, *Audiences: A Sociological Theory of Performance and Imagination*, London, Thousand Oaks, CA, New Delhi: Sage, 1998.

4 E. Hooper-Greenhill, *Museums and the Interpretation of Visual Culture*, London and New York: Routledge, 2000. G. E. Hein, *Learning in the Museum*, London and New York: Routledge, 1998.

5 Steven Dubin describes the new social history as follows: 'Historians have cast their nets in a broader and deeper arc since the 1960s. No longer settling for the exclusive accounts of the highly profiled rich and powerful, they now cast for "history from below".' S. C. Dubin, *Displays of Power: Memory and Amnesia in the American Museum*, New York and London: New York University press, 1999, p. 9.

6 See, for example, R. J. Ohta, '"My eyes have seen the glory": visitor experience at a controversial flag exhibition', *Current Trends in Audience Research and Evaluation*, Vol. 11, Los Angeles: American Association of Museums/Committee on Audience Research and Evaluation, 1998, pp. 48–58.

7 T. Bennett, 'Useful culture', in D. Boswell and J. Evans (eds), *Representing the Nation: A Reader. Histories, Heritage and Museums*, London and New York: Routledge, 1999, p. 339.

8 H. Riegel, 'Into the heart of irony: ethnographic exhibitions and the politics of difference', in S. Macdonald and G. Fyfe (eds), *Theorizing Museums: Representing Identity and Diversity in a Changing World*, Oxford, UK, and Cambridge, MA: Blackwell Publishers/The Sociological Review, 1996, p. 88.

9 I. Karp and C. Kratz, 'Reflections on the fate of Tippoo's Tiger: defining cultures through public display', in E. Hallam and B. V. Street (eds), *Cultural Encounters: Representing 'Otherness'*, London and New York: Routledge, 2000, p. 196.

10 Ibid., p. 194.

11 Ibid., p. 221.

12 For example, I have earlier described the uneasy juxtaposition between military and ethnographic displays within a gallery at Nottingham Castle Museum, which was, after many years, replaced with an exhibit that sought to address these criticisms (R. Sandell, 'Museums and the combating of social inequality: roles, responsibilities, resistance', in

R. Sandell (ed.), *Museums, Society, Inequality*, London and New York: Routledge, 2002, pp. 3–23.). Though, in some countries, many of the most overtly racist displays have been removed, other stereotypical, exclusive and offensive displays nevertheless remain.

13 Royal Museum of the Army and Military History in Brussels, 2003 (unpublished leaflet).

14 Hooper-Greenhill, *Museums and the Interpretation of Visual Culture*, p. 23.

15 Bennett, 'Useful Culture', p. 388.

16 S. MacDonald (ed.), *The Politics of Display: Museums, Science, Culture*, London and New York: Routledge, 1998, p. 5.

17 The controversy surrounding the National Museum of Australia's recent efforts to present Aboriginal perspectives on colonization is a case in point.

18 Anne Frank Stichtung, *Anne Frank House Annual Report 2003*, Amsterdam: Anne Frank Stichtung, 2004, p. 24.

19 Glasgow Museums, 2004. Available at: http://www.glasgowmuseums.com (accessed 28 June 2004).

20 Interestingly, over 95 per cent of the objects on display in the St Mungo Museum were drawn from the existing collections of Glasgow Museums. Mark O'Neill (Director, Glasgow Museums), personal communication with author 5 May 2004.

21 While conducting empirical visitor research in 2003, the following emerged as a typical response:

> The last section where we went in, where it was asking you to vote is a good way of expressing that, in fact, this is one pebble dropped in a stream in 1945 but it's ongoing, it's still with us, you've still got prejudice . . . it's still here, we're still living through that. It's a good conscience-pricker, you come away thinking, 'Well, how should I feel? How would I react if that happened to me?'

22 Harry Dunlop (Curator, St Mungo Museum of Religious Life, Glasgow), personal communication with author 29 May 2003.

23 Karp and Kratz, 'Reflections on the fate of Tippoo's Tiger', p. 198.

24 Ibid., p. 221

25 Ibid., p. 198.

26 On my first visit to the exhibition I recall the discomfort felt at the results of a vote that suggested that, of the ten visitors engaged in voting, I was alone in expressing the opinion that, when a far-right religious group in the US carried banners reading 'God hates fags' at the funeral of a young man whose murder was motivated by homophobia, protection from discrimination should take precedence over the right to freedom of expression.

27 See W. Brooker and D. Jermyn (eds), *The Audience Studies Reader*, London and New York: Routledge, 2003, p. 9 for a discussion of the use of this term within audience studies.

References

Abercrombie, N. and Longhurst, B., *Audiences: A Sociological Theory of Performance and Imagination*, London, Thousand Oaks, CA, New Delhi: Sage, 1998.

Abram, R. J., 'Harnessing the power of history', in R. Sandell (ed.), *Museums, Society, Inequality*, London and New York: Routledge, 2002, pp. 125–41.

Anne Frank Stichtung, *Anne Frank House Annual Report 2003*, Amsterdam: Anne Frank Stichtung, 2004.

Bennett, T., *The Birth of the Museum*, London and New York: Routledge, 1995.

——, 'Useful culture', in D. Boswell and J. Evans (eds), *Representing the Nation: A Reader. Histories, Heritage and Museums*, London and New York: Routledge, 1999, pp. 380–93.

Brooker, W. and Jermyn, D. (eds), *The Audience Studies Reader*, London and New York: Routledge, 2003.

Dubin, S. C., *Displays of Power: Memory and Amnesia in the American Museum*, New York and London: New York University Press, 1999.

Glasgow Museums, 2004. Available at: http://www.glasgowmuseums.com (accessed 28 June 2004).

Hein, G. E., *Learning in the Museum*, London and New York: Routledge, 1998.

Hooper-Greenhill E., *Museums and the Interpretation of Visual Culture*, London and New York: Routledge, 2000.

Karp, I. and Kratz, C., 'Reflections on the fate of Tippoo's Tiger: defining cultures through public display', in E. Hallam and B. V. Street (eds), *Cultural Encounters: Representing 'Otherness'*, London and New York: Routledge, 2000, pp. 194–228.

MacDonald, S. (ed.), *The Politics of Display: Museums, Science, Culture*, London and New York: Routledge, 1998.

McGuigan, J., *Culture and The Public Sphere*, London and New York: Routledge, 1996.

Ohta, R. J., '"My eyes have seen the glory": visitor experience at a controversial flag exhibition', *Current Trends in Audience Research and Evaluation*, Vol. 11, Los Angeles: American Association of Museums/Committee on Audience Research and Evaluation, 1998, pp. 48–58.

Riegel, H., 'Into the heart of irony: ethnographic exhibitions and the politics of difference', in S. Macdonald and G. Fyfe (eds) *Theorizing Museums: Representing Identity and Diversity in a Changing World*, Oxford, UK, and Cambridge, MA: Blackwell Publishers/ The Sociological Review, 1996, pp. 83–104.

Sandell, R., 'Museums and the combating of social inequality: roles, responsibilities, resistance', in R. Sandell (ed.), *Museums, Society, Inequality*, London and New York: Routledge, 2002, pp. 3–23.

Part IV

Creative space

15

Threshold fear

Elaine Heumann Gurian

The nature of our buildings and streets affects our behavior, affects the way we feel about ourselves and, importantly, how we get along with others.[1]

At the small museum, there are no inflated expectations, no pretensions, and no awful waits. The exhibitions may be small and somewhat idiosyncratic, but they mirror the small, somewhat idiosyncratic world we know, close to home.[2]

Members of our museum community write often about inclusion and of the 'new town square', which they wish museums to become. This chapter, entitled 'Threshold fear', contends that there are both physical and programmatic barriers that make it difficult for the uninitiated to experience the museum. The term 'threshold fear' was once relegated to the field of psychology but is now used in a broader context to mean the constraints people feel that prevent them from participating in activities meant for them.[3] To lower these perceived impediments, the fear-inducing stimulus must be reduced or dissolved. There has been little discussion within the museum field about the aspects of museum spaces that are intentionally welcoming and help to build community. There has been, in fact, a disjuncture between museums' programmatic interest in inclusion and the architectural programme of space development – a gap that this chapter tries to redress.

Museums clearly have thresholds that rise to the level of impediments, real and imagined, for the sectors of our population who remain infrequent visitors. The thresholds in question may be actual physical barriers – design ingredients that add to resistance – and other more subtle elements, such as architectural style and its meaning to the potential visitor, wayfinding language and complicated and unfamiliar entrance sequences. Further hindrances include the community's attitude towards the institution, the kind and amount of available public transportation, the admission charges and how they are applied, the organization of the front desk, sensitivity to many different handicapping needs, the security system upon entering and staff behaviour towards unfamiliar folk. My thesis is that, when museum management becomes interested in the identification, isolation and reduction of each of these thresholds, they will be rewarded over time by an increased and broadened pattern of use, though the reduction of these thresholds is not sufficient by itself.

I started with the assumption that most museums wanted to broaden their audiences, that is, they wanted the profile of visitors to include more people from minority, immigrant, school drop-out and working-class groups than was currently the case. I further believed that, in order to achieve that aim, there would need to be a multi-layered approach that would include elements less well known and often untried, because many museums had experimented with programmes alone and had been largely unsuccessful in changing their visitation patterns over the long term. I postulated that, if we worked with theories of city planning and paid better attention to the aspects of space creation and planning that helped build community, museums might be more successful in their goal of inclusion – especially when they combined this work with the elements they were already using – expanded programming, community liaisons and targeted free or reduced admissions. Trying all these options together, museums might finally solve the difficult long-standing problem of the narrow demographics of current museum users.

I sought to look at other institutions I believed served a broader audience, and, while not in exactly the same business as museums, had sufficient similarities to serve as useful examples. The institutions I felt bore further scrutiny were zoos, libraries, for-profit attractions and shopping malls.

Now, after researching the topic, I am less certain that broadening the audience for museums is achievable in general. Museums of real inclusion may be possible only if other competing traditional aspirations are discarded. On a continuum, individual museums can be positioned from cultural icon to home-town club-house with many stops in between. Cultural icons serve very important purposes but these, I have reluctantly begun to realize, may be quite different from, and perhaps even mutually exclusive with, museums focused on community well-being. Sadder but wiser, I will argue that there are certain subtle things we can do related to space and city planning that will help those who are really interested in broadening their visitation. But this prescription probably excludes many museums, and maybe that is just as well. Decisions about space do have a correspondence with mission. That thesis remains intact. However, it is my view that the mission to create a 'temple of the contemplative', for example, has an easier correlation with both traditional and contemporary architecture than does the mission to create a welcoming inclusionary museum.

That many museums do not really wish to become more inclusionary institutions is the subject for a different paper. Let me preview that elusive next paper as follows. We know a lot about the amalgamated profile of current museum users. The typical visitor is well educated, relatively affluent and generally has a wage earner who is white collar or professional within the family unit. Many museums, like good commercial product marketers, are programmed to satisfy this niche market – their current users.[4] Many museums, especially the more notable ones, are important elements of the tourism infrastructure of the metropolis that surrounds them, and tourism is primarily a middle- and upper-class activity. These same institutions are described in the 'quality of life' bumf that is intended to elicit more managerial-level interest, an aspiration intended to enlarge the financial base. Finally, and perhaps not surprisingly, visitors and non-visitors alike may not wish museums to change because most citizens separate their belief in the value of museums from their actual use of them.

I will postulate that, to become truly inclusionary, a museum must provide services seen by the user as essential, available on demand, timely and personally driven. The definition of essential has to do with the personal impulsion to transform an internal inquiry into action. Thus going to the library to get a book on how to fix the leaking sink makes the library an essential place. To change an institution from 'nice to have' to 'essential' is difficult. For most museums, concentrating on being the storehouse of the treasures of humanity may seem like virtue enough regardless of the use visitors make of them. I will consider some of the space elements that can either help or hinder the mission of the museum, focusing on those elements that foster inclusion – should the museum wish to add space to their programmatic arsenal for just that purpose, understanding that many may not.

For architects, designing a museum is among the most coveted commissions of the day and iconic architecture frequently turns out to stimulate increased attendance. It is the typical affluent educated museum-goer who is much impressed with the current architectural emphasis of museum buildings. Thus the creation of new architecture will increase, at least for a limited time, the quantity of users without necessarily changing its demographics.

But, when architects do not care about the needs of the visitor – as happens more often than I care to report – especially if visitor needs are seen to interfere with artistic vision, architects create museums that are difficult to use. These inhospitalities reinforce the non-welcoming nature of museums overall and add to the discouragement of the tentative user. That is a problem of both new buildings and the augustly overwhelming museums of the past.

If the architect wants to combine a really interesting building with one that is welcoming to the novice user, then, I would contend, he or she must be interested in hospitable and less intimidating spaces, a plethora of easily locatable human amenities and wayfinding that is easy to understand. The grand museums assert monumentality and make their presentation as revered but not necessarily comfortable icons. Very few new buildings of note have been reviewed as friendly and comfortable. There are exceptions of course: the Picasso Museum in a historic building refurbishment in the Marais in Paris and the I. M. Pei-designed Herbert F. Johnson Museum of Art of Cornell University come to mind.

With these thoughts in mind, in the following sections I will draw upon a number of architectural planning theories, in order to consider some of the spatial and the related organizational problems of the museum. This will lead to a list of suggestions as to some of the small changes museums might make to become more inclusionary.

Congregant spaces

The populace needs and has many congregant public spaces at its disposal. There are theoreticians who believe that, in order to maintain a peaceful society, people need access to three kinds of spaces – spaces for family and friends (our most intimate relationships), places for work and places where it is safe to interact with strangers.[5] The last category has important meaning beyond the functions they overtly serve. That these places exist and are available to strangers reassures the public there is order and well-being to be found in populated centres. Whenever these places are considered unsafe for any reason they are abandoned, sometimes permanently, and society becomes more Balkanized.[6]

The congregant places organized for strangers fall into a surprisingly long list. They include (but are not limited to):

- Transportation hubs, such as railway stations and airports and the transportation vehicles themselves.
- Religious gathering places, such as churches, mosques and synagogues.
- Places of commercial transactions large and small, such as shopping malls, markets, public streets lined with shops and the shops themselves.
- Places organized for eating and socializing, such as restaurants, pubs and bars.
- Places used for recreation, such as bathing beaches and parks.
- Civic buildings that are organized to do the people's work, such as judicial courts and town halls.
- Places that hold access to information and/or present experiences. These include libraries and archives, theatres and concert halls, athletic arenas, schools and public spaces used for celebrations like parades and pageants.

It is to this last segment – those sites that hold access to information and experiences – that museums, historic houses, zoos, botanic gardens and historic sites belong.

All civic spaces used by strangers have some commonalities, and many kinds of civic spaces have more in common with certain museums than with others. There are elements of libraries, zoos, shopping malls, attractions, stadiums and train stations that can become models for museums. It has been unfortunate that museum personnel have often felt that associating themselves with the kinds of congregant spaces on this list is a disservice to their own uniqueness and status. I would suggest the contrary.

The city planning theory of Jane Jacobs and her followers

Architectural theorists and city planners refer to physical spaces offering a variety of services often co-located with residential areas as 'mixed-use space'. Mixed-use spaces can be small, found within one strip mall, one city street and one building, or so large so that they encompass whole sections of cities. It is these mixed-used spaces that particularly interest such theorists as Jane Jacobs.[7]

Studies of these spaces have had a profound effect on the development of planned communities and the refurbishment of downtown cities. The theorists have postulated that the broadest array of users inhabit locations that house a multitude of offerings, products selling for a wide band of prices, a combination of useful services (shoe repair, pharmacy, etc.) mixed with more exotic specialties, open hours that are as close to around-the-clock as possible, residential units, public amenities such as seating and, most importantly, reliance on foot traffic.

They go on to postulate that these mixed-use spaces are perceived as safe to use because they are busy, lighted and have many people present all the time, including 'regulars' and 'lurkers' who are vigilant and proprietary but also welcoming, exemplifying a peaceful and even friendly code of behaviour that can be easily perceived by strangers.[8]

Since the 1970s, in addition to an explosion of new museum buildings and commissions for high-profile architects, museums have also become keystones to economic revival plans in urban settings recognized as having positive fiscal impacts for the city. In addition, a change in the economic base of museums from philanthropic and governmental support to an emphasis on earned income through the creation of larger and more prominent retail activities within the museum has profoundly revised the architectural programme needed for museums and has changed museums (inadvertently) into mixed-use spaces.

Museums now offer mixed-use spaces providing exhibitions, programmes, restaurants and cafés, shopping and party spaces under one roof. Museums often either incorporate or are adjacent to public transport and other services (child care, schools, performance spaces, parks and additional food and shopping opportunities). As they incorporate or align themselves with such services, they become a thoroughfare for a broader population, who may have different motivations for entering and different stay-lengths, and who use the facility during different times of the day. This quality of mixed-use can also be seen in zoos, libraries and shopping malls.

Architectural programme planning

There has been little overt discussion within the museum field about the spatial considerations that might assist in increased service to a wider community. There has often been a disjuncture between the museums' professed programmatic interest in inclusion and the resultant architectural programme of space development. I have often found that, prior to embarking on construction of a new expansion or building, the senior museum personnel have not understood the architectural process sufficiently, so that they did not understand the relationship between programmatic intention and physical planning. This has allowed the museum's strategic direction and its architectural development to diverge.

Architectural writing, beginning in the 1960s, is full of humanistic philosophy, behavioural design and a keen interest in the creation and sustainability of 'livable' cities.[9] Finding this disjuncture between many contemporary museum buildings and the philosophy espoused, I conclude that the people involved (on both the architectural and museum teams) did not realize that the new architectural literature could positively affect building plans (or were not sympathetic to the theories espoused).

My extensive experience working with architects and museums on architectural programme planning is illuminating. First, most museum staff do not know that a process called architectural programme planning exists; they think in terms of blueprints and do not know that there is a prerequisite step that focuses on volumes and adjacencies, which is driven by the articulated programmatic needs of the museum. They are often not coached by the architect about the process and do not do a thoroughgoing job in stating their philosophy, their specific programmatic needs or their future aspirations. One cannot hope to have a building that corresponds to the philosophic aspirations of the museum leadership without first divining the strategy directions of the museum and translating those into binding architectural terms. Second, some, though certainly not all, architects are happier to gloss over this planning stage because without it the architect is left with much more artistic freedom. Finally, senior officials are often blinded by the aspiration to build a museum that will enter the world stage by virtue of architectural excellence and novelty. So they come to believe that putting programmatic or even budget constraints on the architect will only point out their own philistine-like nature. And some architects are happy to capitalize on that fear.

These three situations work against having an architectural programme plan of any specificity or rigour. When a museum lacks a specific guiding programmatic document, it becomes difficult to judge all subsequent designs against the plan as the museum's basic evaluation tool. In this regard, it does not matter if we are talking about new building, refurbishment of existing structures or even just rearrangement of the current fit-out. My advice to my many clients is that the architectural programme plan is the most critical element in the building process.

Location on neutral ground

City planners, imbued with the theories of Jane Jacobs and the other communitarians, are increasingly interested in enriching the services and liveliness of neighbourhoods by enhancing one's ability to walk around, expanding public transport and creating easily accessible parking in an off-site location. There are some institutions that are seen to be on neutral ground, equally available to all people, and others that seem intentionally isolated and relatively unavailable. Location and placement often create, overtly or inadvertently, turf boundaries where citizens believe that the spaces in question are reserved predominately for a small segment of society. I am old enough to remember the protests and legal action over the then legal segregation of swimming pools and playgrounds in my country. Ending legal segregation did not necessarily end de facto segregation. Some of these very same swimming pools are still almost exclusively used by either blacks or whites because the area surrounding the pool, while no longer legally segregated, is virtually so. The creation of such non-neutral space can be unintentionally thoughtless or intentionally off-putting.

Museums must look at their own locations with care. It seems axiomatic that the more accessible the location, the more likely will be a heterogeneous group of users. What constitutes site 'ownership' is not always apparent. The regular clientele of one local pub may be a clique established by custom despite the fact that there may be many to choose from within a close proximity.

Museums on once neutral ground can become segregated by changes in resident patterns in the surrounding neighbourhood. Similarly, non-neutral space can be turned into more inclusive space by the acceptance and even encouragement of public activities taking place inside and outside that change the perception of use. The Brooklyn Museum of Art, finding their forecourt used by skateboarders, invited them to continue rather than having them ousted. Turf ownership, therefore, while seemingly entrenched, turns out to be mutable.

The common understanding by potential visitors of how safe or dangerous the surrounding neighbourhood will be becomes an important factor in deciding to visit. New Yorkers' perception of the safety of any borough other than middle and lower Manhattan makes visiting museums in the other boroughs adventurous and seemingly fraught with danger for Manhattanites. It is interesting to watch the visitor's hesitation when getting off the subway and trying to locate the Museum of Modern Art now that it is in its temporary location in Long Island City, Queens. The reverse is true when the decision is made to visit the Metropolitan Museum of Art by a Queens' resident. That is also an activity of some adventure. I know, I grew up in Queens.

Learning the resources before visiting

Civic sophistication can sometimes be measured by the ease that citizens have in using available resources. In effect, research management occupies part of everyone's daily transactions. 'Which shop will have the specific material we might need?' and 'Is the owner reliable?' Much of the most readily available information comes by talking to trusted intimates. Thus word of mouth and street credibility has much to do with use.

In the museum world, we are more reliant on previous satisfied users than we understand. Most of our new users are people who know and trust someone who has already been there. So if we do not pierce the many strata of our community – economic, cultural, educational, etc. – we are, perforce, limiting access to whole segments of users. Spending more time cultivating adventurous pioneers by giving them reliable sources of information, and developing positive street credibility, are essential tasks for institutions who wish for wider attendance.

Getting there

In Britain (as in many countries) there is an increased reliance on automobile transportation. A study reports that over 50 per cent of all children's trips involve riding in a car, and there is a much-decreased use of the bicycle.[10] This means that children can go to fewer places on their own. For the parents it means that those things that can be done within walking distance of one parking stop are easier to contemplate than several errands each needing its own exclusive parking. Hence the growth of the shopping mall and the increase of pedestrian traffic associated with convenient parking.

Here again, museums embedded within public walking thoroughfares can more easily become casual visits and even multiple visits – an ingredient often seen in the more 'essential' institutions, such as libraries, which accommodate short, focused and efficient visitation. The monumentality of the large museum set off by itself, with its need to accommodate the parking of its patrons in a sea of black top, or with the added cost of a parking garage, mitigates against casual use.

In the UK, there is a series of fascinating websites that look at social exclusion and its relation to public transportation. One study in particular looks at both the issues of the interconnectedness between public transport availability and the knowledge required for using transport to unfamiliar sites.[11] It seems all too evident that lack of available public transport coupled with inexperience makes it less likely for the non-user population to visit. However, if the motivation is high enough, such as 'seeing the doctor' or 'going for a job interview', the person will brave the trip if possible.

Once public transport is in place and experienced users ride along with the inexperienced, visitation increases to certain places. Yet, there is only occasional interest in the museum sector to view public transport as an essential ingredient towards enlarged public use.

Entering

Once potential visitors have made it to the front door, it seems easy, on the surface, to enter a museum, without the potentially uncomfortable task of revealing too much personal information. Actually, visitors need to reveal quite a lot. They need to demonstrate that they can afford the price of admission, by paying. If they visit during weekday hours, assumptions will be made that they are on holiday, unemployed, retired, a student or somehow not in the workforce. Visitors must dress and behave superficially 'normally' in order to be allowed to remain in the building. Most of these assessments, and any anxieties they may engender, rest within the potential visitors' minds, of course. But this mental projection is very real to the novice user and impossible to ameliorate except by training our museum personnel to become sincere, but not effusive, welcomers.

Much of the initial person-to-person engagement begins at the admissions desk. Because this is a direct interpersonal transaction, the collection of charges, I believe, is the single biggest disincentive for entering. Charges make visits to the museum an 'outing' rather than a useful casual drop-in errand. A look at the free museums located on pedestrian ways often shows a steady stream of users who are pursuing short-time or casual activities. By eliminating charges, the museum eliminates personal scrutiny from staff. I contend this will go a long way towards the reduction of threshold fear.

Unfortunately eliminating charges itself does not seem to change the demographic make-up of visitors. Many museums in the UK have gone from free to charges and back to free again. In the process they learned that the total number of visitors falls precipitately when charges are inserted and rise again when that is reversed, but the demographics of their users do not appreciably change.[12]

It is helpful if the novice visitor can figure out the process of entering by passive watching from an anonymous location. A large lobby, or one visible from the outdoors, helps. Large railway stations allow for such decoding.

More recently, because of perceived security needs in many countries, the encounter that precedes admissions is the most threatening of all – security checking, requiring surveillance by a police-like person. I look forward to the day when museums will eliminate security in their entrance sequence. Passing a security checkpoint is a very high threshold for anyone. That is why few libraries and fewer shopping malls use overt security screeners in their entrances. I am convinced that they are just as vulnerable as museums, but remain more anxious to serve their public.

Malls and other animals

A review of the organization of shopping malls in most countries gives credence to the rightness of the Jacobs philosophy. Shopping mall design intentionally includes the ability to enter anonymously, and the possibility of sitting and strolling without committing to organized activity. These amenities allow 'lurkers' – unfamiliar users – to figure out the services and customs required without drawing attention to themselves. Malls offer simple access to easily understood facilities such as toilets, and there are plenty of opportunities to socialize while eating. Finally, they welcome multi-generational groups and increasingly try to understand packs of adolescents who find strolling and meeting in the mall their main avenue of socializing. Museums, though they currently don't think so, might be lucky if they found themselves with this problem. While museums have many of the same amenities as the mall, the use of them requires passing an entrance sequence described above.

The lobby of a museum, like the strolling spaces of malls, can become a meeting place for people who may not intend to visit the exhibitions. What mall designers understand is the notion of 'impulse buying' (if you are there anyway, you might discover you need something). I believe museums must begin to value impulse visiting, that is, savouring a small segment of the museum for a short segment of time. All of that will require museums to think of themselves differently.

It is sometimes surprising to find out the reasons why some civic spaces are more popular than others. Zoos provide venues for picnicking with food brought from home. Therefore they allow groups (those that have dietary restrictions or who do not trust food from strangers) to come to a public place and inadvertently socialize with others. In a community meeting I held recently in Israel, it was for these reasons that the zoo was the last remaining neutral public space in Jerusalem used by family groups who were otherwise fearful of each other. Jerusalem's Bloomfield Science Museum decided that it too could arrange for picnic tables and refrigerators, so that, in the hopeful future when a more tentative peace might emerge, they too could be a location for social interaction between strangers.

Learning from Disney and other attractions about the importance of customer service, there are now customer-friendly hosts in many museums. These hosts, if they represent the community and are sensitively trained, make the experience more understandable and less alien for the novice. In Jacobs' terms, visitor service personnel act as 'regulars', offering reassurance and knowledge on the one hand and demonstrating the behaviour norms required on the other.

There are other space considerations that can be learned from the other institutions I have suggested as models – malls, zoos, attractions and libraries, and that could increase use by a wider population:

- Create spaces for small group interaction and for private contemplation. See that they don't interfere with each other.
- Have help staff available who are posted in a physical location that can be seen, but without requiring interaction from anyone.
- Train visitor services staff not to be intrusive but still welcoming.
- Fight for public transportation to the door, and look for physical reorientation of the building that minimizes the necessity for cars and parking lots and is directed towards public transportation and foot traffic.
- Introduce more visitor amenities such as seating, toilets, cafés and baby spaces with easy access to all.
- Watch for the ways the public actually uses the building, and then formalize these unexpected and even serendipitous uses.
- Revamp systems to focus on avenues of self-directed learning, such as browsing in the library. This probably means visible access to the collections themselves or at least access to collections information without intercession of staff.
- Set the hours of operation to suit the neighbourhood rather than the staff.
- Accept behaviour, clothing choice, sound level and styles of interaction that are consistent with norms of courtesy in the individual's community.
- Trust the visitor so that intrusive security can be minimized. Organizing for the best in people is a risk worth taking.

- Finally, and most importantly, understand the importance visitors place on 'seeing the evidence' and so encourage interaction with three-dimensional experiences. Our special legitimacy remains visual access to physical things.

The repair of the dead mall and other conclusions

When a mall begins to lose income or even 'dies' there is an economic imperative to fix it, tear it down or re-purpose it. A website run by Los Angeles Forum held a competition to fix 'dead malls'.[13] The winning entries offer fascinating glimpses of what architects and merchants think is needed to enhance the usage of moribund shopping centres.

One entrant used the following four categories for redesign into useful spaces: (1) big box cathedral – gathering, (2) global vortex – raving, (3) elastic bazaar – wandering, and (4) smart mobs – swarming. Even the words chosen for the categories intrigue me. Imagine if there were museums that wished for raving and swarming. I think these word choices (and the rest of the website) foretell of the kinds of spaces needed for increased museum use.

Museums remain one of the important congregant spaces in any community. To encourage use by all citizens we need to be more sensitive to the space requirements that make it clear the visitor is welcome. It is my hope that, as we readjust the way we build, repair and reinstall museums, we will invite more citizens to join us. I once said I wished museum audiences to be as diverse as those to be found at any given moment in Grand Central Station. Mindful that some do not share my vision, I hope for that more today than ever.

Notes

1 Becket, M. G., 'Foreword', in C. M. Deasy, *Designing Places for People: A Handbook for Architects, Designers, and Facility Managers*, New York: Whitney Library of Design, 1985.
2 R. Chew, 'In praise of the small museums', *Museum News*, Vol. 81, January/February 2002: 36.
3 See, for example, 'Gypsies and travelers in Belgium', an online interview. Available at: http://home2.pi.be/tmachiel/educati2.htm (accessed 16 August 2004).
4 'Our visitor profile and demographics demonstrate why Museum sponsorship is an ideal way to magnify your company's image.' Museum of Science, Boston, website enticing corporate sponsorship by pointing out that 74 per cent of visitors have a college degree or higher and a median income of $82,000 per annum. Available at: http://www.mos.org/doc/1026 (accessed 16 August 2004).
5 R. Oldenburg, *The Great Good Place*, New York: Paragon House, 1989.
6 Currently there are no seemingly neutral spaces in Israel. Much of the economic distress in the country is because there are no spaces that are considered neutral and businesses that were formerly frequented by a mixed group of clients cannot survive with only part of the population prepared to go to any particular location.
7 J. Jacobs, *The Death and Life of the Great American Cities*, New York: Vintage Books, 1961.
8 See E. H. Gurian, 'Function follows form: how mixed-used spaces in museums build community', *Curator*, Vol. 44, No. 1, January 2001: 87–113 for a fuller discussion on mixed-use space and its effects in building community in museums.

9 See, for example, C. Alexander, *A New Theory of Urban Design*, New York: Oxford University Press, 1987; C. Alexander, *Notes on the Synthesis of Form*, Cambridge, MA: Harvard University Press, 1964.

10 *National Statistics of Great Britain*. Available at: http://www.statistics.gov.uk/STAT-BASE/ssdataset.asp?vlnk=3661 (accessed 16 August 2004).

11 Households without a car, in a society in which household car ownership is the norm (peri-urban and rural areas), are socially excluded within our definition of the term, since they cannot fully participate, i.e. behave as the vast majority of society behaves. See *Social Exclusion and the Provision of Public Transport: Summary Report*. Available at: http://www.dft.gov.uk/stellent/groups/dft_mobility/documents/page/dft_mobility_50679 4-05.hcsp#TopOfPage (accessed 16 August 2004).

12 'Research conducted to determine the impact of free entry to museums and galleries throughout London shows that increase in visitation has been greater among the AB social group. Although free entry was introduced to encourage visitation from all social backgrounds, this has not been reflected in the visitor profile.' From *Maritime Museum UK Report: Comparative Visitor Profile 1999–2001*. Available at: http://www.nmm. ac.uk/uploads/pdf/Comparative_visitor_profile.pdf (accessed 16 August 2004).

13 Los Angeles Forum, 'The dead mall competition'. Available at: http://www.laforum.org/ deadmalls/index.html (accessed 16 August 2004).

References

C. Alexander, *Notes on the Synthesis of Form*, Cambridge, MA: Harvard University Press, 1964.

——, *A New Theory of Urban Design*, New York: Oxford University Press, 1987.

Becket, M. G., 'Foreword', in C. M. Deasy, *Designing Places for People: A Handbook for Architects, Designers, and Facility Managers*, New York: Whitney Library of Design, 1985.

Chew, R., 'In praise of the small museums', *Museum News*, Vol. 81, January/February 2002: 36.

Gurian, E. H., 'Function follows form: how mixed-used spaces in museums build community', *Curator*, Vol. 44, No. 1, January 2001: 87–113.

'Gypsies and travelers in Belgium' (interview). Available at: http://home2.pi.be/tmachiel/ educati2.htm (accessed 16 August 2004).

Jacobs, J., *The Death and Life of Great American Cities*, New York: Vintage Books, 1961.

Los Angeles Forum, 'The dead mall competition'. Available at: http://www.laforum.org/dead-malls/index.html (accessed 16 August 2004).

Maritime Museum UK Report: Comparative Visitor Profile 1999–2001. Available at: http:// www.nmm.ac.uk/uploads/pdf/Comparative_visitor_profile.pdf (accessed 16 August 2004).

Museum of Science, Boston. Available at: http://www.mos.org/doc/1026 (accessed 16 August 2004).

National Statistics of Great Britain. Available at: http://www.statistics.gov.uk/STATBASE/ ssdataset.asp?vlnk=3661 (accessed 16 August 2004).

Oldenburg, R., *The Great Good Place*, New York: Paragon House, 1989.

Social Exclusion and the Provision of Public Transport: Summary Report. Available at: http: //www.dft.gov.uk/stellent/groups/dft_mobility/documents/page/dft_mobility_506794-05. hcsp#TopOfPage (accessed 16 August 2004).

16

From cathedral of culture to anchor attractor

Peter Higgins

Originally perceived as an opaque compartmented box, as a secret treasury, the museum housed surprisingly varied collections, marvels, curiosities, antiquaria, libraries – the natural world alongside art and sculpture. It was in the first half of the nineteenth century that they became increasingly specialized in their subject matter: art, archaeology, the natural sciences, handicrafts. At the same time, the central architectonic theme of the museum was perfected: lateral windows, overhead skylights, cupolas and lantern lights provided natural light, while vestibules and grand staircases provided entry to the contemplative container.

Although arguably among the most spectacular examples, Berlin, Munich and Vienna merely reflected a wider trend in the development of the nineteenth-century metropolis in which the museum as a recent building type came to play a prominent role. So prominent in fact, that scholars have argued that the often-invoked metaphor of the museum as cathedral for the arts is not simply a facile comparison.[1]

At the beginning of the twentieth century, just as in all of the arts, the rupture spurred by the avant-garde was reflected in museums both as institutions and as spaces where modern art collections could be exhibited. The unimpeachable status of the previously preferred classic temple, suitable for banks, town halls and law courts, was at last threatened. The mood was best captured by Jean Cocteau, who described the Louvre as a morgue.

The modern movement challenged the opaque box and the solidity was lost with more open and flexible floor plans. There was an absence of mediation between the space and the objects to be exhibited. The art became an autonomous object within the museum, detached from its setting.

More recently, there has been an obsession with museums configured as singular organisms, as extraordinary phenomena, as exceptional occurrences, as unrepeatable occasions. These tend to crop up in well-established urban contexts in which the building stands in radical contrast to its surroundings in an effort to create a shock effect. It follows the trail blazed by Frank Lloyd Wright's Guggenheim Museum in New York (1943–59), designed in response to the city's staggered skyscrapers. Wright paved the way for the museum as an artistic environment, as a vast sculpture inspired by organic shapes, as an extraordinary container within the urban context.[2]

The idea of museum architecture as monumental and spectacular is encouraged by the continuing ambitions of the Guggenheim Foundation, where Thomas Krens as director demanded that Bilbao should match the power that Chartres Cathedral wielded over Europe when it was completed in 1257. The rise of superstar architects has resulted in the architecture overpowering the art inside. In an interview by Jeffrey Hogrefe for the *New York Observer* with Charles Desmarais, commissioning director of Zaha Hadid's Contemporary Arts Centre in Cincinnati, it became clear that the pre-publicity focused on the architect much more than the work inside. Over in Los Angeles, Gehry's Walt Disney Hall has been celebrated first as a building to promote the city, rather than as a building to support high-quality performance.

Many commentators defend the skill and need for the architect to lead the team. In the preamble of the exhibition projects of the 8th Venice Architectural Biennale, Max Hollein claims that the architect is responsible for the grandiose solutions through scale, distribution of space and language of forms, but that primarily it is a matter of gesture. He claims that it is also the architect who consistently moulds the way in which the installed works are received, as 'product', and, in consequence, that museums may be freely compared to shopping centres and yes . . . cathedrals.[3]

Others argue that such organicists as Gehry have the ability to place the widest possible range of spaces within a large architectural museum complex, to house the widest range of formats found in contemporary art. The artist's studio is evoked in the giant hall, or corners and passageways provide unique spaces for photography or video installations.[4]

In a superbly robust article in the *Observer* in which Deyan Sudjic took the architectural 'bull' by the horns, he complained that the search for the architectural icon has become a ubiquitous theme of contemporary design:

> Competitions that require an icon lead to architecture that looks best reduced to a logo on a letterhead.

> A cultural building, designed with a heavy subsidy from public funds, built with the express purpose of getting previously obscure cities into the pages of in flight magazines.

> London Docklands, where architects tried hard to be interesting, and produced a lot of exclamation marks but not much prose.[5]

Somewhat more formally, Herman Hertzberger reminds us of the importance for architects to have something to say that rises above the obscure jargon that architects share with one another:

> Every new step in architecture is premised on disarming and outspoken ideas that engender spatial discoveries. To concentrate the essence into a

concept means summarising in elementary form all the conditions of a particular task on a particular site as assessed and formulated by the architect. Trusting on the insights, sensibility and attention he accords the subject, the concept will be more layered, richer and abiding and not only admit to more interpretations but incite them too. The idea encapsulates the DNA, so to speak, containing the essence of the project and guiding the design process from start to finish. The concept, then, is the idea translated into space – the space of the idea, and bearer of the character traits of the product as these will emerge upon its development.[6]

When Hetzberger goes on to challenge what sense of purpose or idea that architecture represents and what, finally, is the issue it seeks to resolve, he is heavily supported by artist/practitioner Donald Judd: 'Forms for their own sake, despite functions are ridiculous. One reason art museums are so popular with architects and so bizarre, is that they must think there is no function.'[7]

It was the spirit of the Enlightenment that saw the museum as the focus for instruction, a universal centre of education that was to transmit academic taste and the new values of progress to the people as a whole. This is a perfect starting point for our twenty-first-century status. Then, European culture began to define itself in relation to the phenomenon of the museum; now, the museum has to respond to rapidly changing needs of a pluralist world suspended in the information age, with many alternative competitive delivery mechanisms of knowledge, information and experience.

Surprisingly, the nomenclature of the 'new museum' rarely defines the precise tasks and functions of this ubiquitous building type. It has become even more complex in the UK as we have enjoyed an absurdly accelerated distribution of funding to add to the confusion. Now we bundle such things as art, science, sport, transport, ecology, the war, the sea, social history and natural history into the convenient 'museum' typology. In Manchester an initiative conceived to investigate the concept of the city avoided any object collections but enjoyed its title, 'Urbis: a museum of the modern city'.

Commercial pressures have enforced diversity of activity reflected in the need for museums to generate revenue 'blockbuster' temporary exhibitions, food and beverages, and significant retail facilities typified by the Louvre's spectacular underground shopping mall. Ultimately the one concept that draws them together is their desire to provide informal learning environments that can be experienced by anybody, at any level, at any time. The primary perception of the museum may be of sublimely lit pieces of art, but now a carefully sequenced timeline, a random collection of interactives representing scientific principles, or a sensitive immersive audio-visual about genocide are the sort of imposters that wreck these preconceptions. The 'new museum' is an emerging beast that has to survive the ferocious leisure marketplace at all costs.

What we have seen in the UK, in the wake of the lottery roller-coaster, are mysteriously appointed executive officers and project managers who often form the client team. As these people have little experience of commissioning architecture, design or communication media, the process can naively start with a seductive 'landmark' building that inevitably treats the internal function as a secondary activity, both conceptually and financially. Alternatively, existing converted buildings are rarely fit for the purpose even though it is the popularity of its content that will ultimately determine the long-term economic sustainability of the project. In many cases there is no duty of care for the dislocated interpretive content.

Local, global, virtual

Patrick Geddes, biologist and geographer, undertook a fascinating project that challenged the concept of the museum as monument and, in fact, turned the whole city that it surveyed into a museum of itself. His thesis is that we should not do away with the past, but relate it to the present in a way that would actively participate in the future. History, he stated, 'is the very essence of our growing sociological re-interpretation of the past to see its essential life as continuous into the present, and even beyond'.[8] His concept for a new museum followed the purchase of the abandoned Outlook Tower in Edinburgh (complete with camera obscura) where he aspired to activate history as an organic part of a universal geography. The concept hinged around the spectacular view of the city as a starting point from which the extended narratives unfold as the visitor descends through the building. Disparate subject matter, including astronomy, the city of Edinburgh, Scotland, and English-speaking countries, was threaded together with a continuing leitmotif of place, work and folk. As a museum then, the Tower was a kind of historical-geographical astronomical instrument, appropriately described by Alessandra Ponte as a 'thinking machine', a kind of modern Wunderkammer or theatre of memory.[9]

A more contemporary view of the evolution of the museum as container was taken by the Centre Pompidou client, Pontus Hultan, who encouraged Renzo Piano and Richard Rogers (via Archigram and Cedric Price) to create a multi-purpose, multifunctional, populist cultural centre, where the viewing of the art became simply one of a variety of activities to choose from alongside an ambitious temporary exhibition programme, mediatheque facilities and, more recently, extensive retail opportunities. The building's massive scale and colour and dynamic movement systems indicated a total break not only with the urban syntax of Paris, but also with the traditional museum. Its high-tech exterior embodied the concept of the 'cultural factory', emphasizing processes of production and consumption, rather than quiet contemplation.[10]

At the hugely ambitious New Metropolis in Amsterdam, the commissioning director, James Bradburne, drew our attention to the broader concept of informal learning. He prefers bottom-up, or user-driven, learning, where the user is considered as the starting point for all effective learning. Rarely do science centres allow visitors to actively shape the nature of enquiry. They focus almost exclusively on principles and phenomena rather than processes, they misrepresent the nature of scientific activity and they show the science out of context –

science defined top down by scientists, rather than as experienced by visitors. Rarely do the centres put science and technology into a social context.

Bradburne goes on to differentiate between two distinct institutes of informal learning: the library and the collection. The library is a resource and puts its accent on use, especially use directed by the users themselves. The library is rooted in its community of users and is global, in terms of the resources that it makes available. A library is not exhausted by a visit. On the contrary, it is refreshed by it. A library is used as long as it provides resources and experiences – real or virtual – that are needed by its users. The collection, on the other hand, is meant to be displayed and its identity is bound to the collector or, more recently, the curator. The organization of the collection is a function of the message that its organizers wish to communicate.

Bradburne contemplated a learning platform built upon that which is unique to a specific locality, on what cannot be found or done elsewhere. This platform must put a premium on local culture, local practices and local experience and must be firmly rooted in its local conditions and use them to build a community commitment to the institution. Now we can link local to global through the virtual domain. Global information networks allow for the first time real, virtual institutions open to visits from around the world. Exhibits can be designed that can be actively enjoyed by international virtual participants, as well as local users, and the participation of the virtual community can actively change the state of the local activity. In consequence, the local centre does not have to be a major capital investment, merely a portal.[11]

What are the intellectual shifts that are required to redefine the potential function of museums within the urban masterplan? To paraphrase Claire Fox's article 'Brave new museums', we need to move away from fixed museums in fixed places for fixed hours and integrate their educational role with real life. She goes on to say that, without connecting artefacts with people's lives, the past seems distant and irrelevant.[12]

Knowing men in suits

In the UK it is important to establish some criteria that will help to inform the debate that considers the concept of the potential of 'the new museum' as a building type and to inform a broad base of powerful stakeholders that are responsible for the all-important hubs of our built environment. These champions may include city councils, government agencies (such as English Partnerships, Regional Development Agencies, Heritage Lottery Fund, English Heritage, DCMS), town planners, private developers, architects, landscape architects, engineers and, occasionally, leisure/tourism consultants. Their collective perception of what constitutes a 'new museum' will be surprisingly varied.

As a redevelopment of an existing asset, local government culture/leisure departments will see it as an important social/heritage legacy that can build on nostalgic value within the community. But, as a new initiative, it will often be considered as a dangerous venture inviting revenue leakage and major scrutiny from the media. Government agencies are also understandably cautious and encourage precedent models that apparently negate any concept of risk. Town planners and engineers always seem to adopt a two-dimensional empirical view that is driven by the zoning diagram, traffic engineering and car parking, while architects (hopefully not tempted by iconic tendencies) are able to provide a much more emotional input involving three-dimensional massing, city context and a sensitive response to such issues as materials, sunlight, topography and scale. Private developers have an understandably monocular vision driven by rentable value where non-revenue-generating activities are an anathema. Leisure/tourism consultants can present highly tuned business advice streaming out SWOT data but often work without the most critical piece of information: what is it going to be?

Supremo developer Stuart Lipton, writing in the *Independent on Sunday*, warned us of the potential danger of meeting the demands of the current growth of public capital spending. He goes on to say that there is a stifling fear of failure that knocks ambition and limits innovation on so many UK projects. He suggests that the lesson is that the bean counters and all knowing men in suits must not be allowed to prevent the development on the basis of crude investment analysis. Fear of the National Audit Office can often cause public agencies to lose sight of the bigger picture and needlessly channel their energies into unsustainable cost-cutting exercises.[13]

Prototype processes

Working with Locum Destination Consulting, Land have developed two projects that investigate the concept of the convergence of the cultural and the consumable. In both cases, the projects would only have been possible if we could have convinced a diverse collection of stakeholders that we could add extraordinary value to a prime retail development and provide an entirely sustainable vision.

At the White City development in West London we worked closely with the architect and developer to consider the possibility of embedding a new 'BBC Experience' into the main body of the 600,000-square foot retail complex. The project was to create a visitor experience that would present the extraordinary history of the BBC (both TV and radio), and incorporate a significant object collection, with a strong focus on the process of programme making and investigation into the ambitious new media and communication futures. It soon became evident that it would be possible to incorporate the added value of this high-profile corporate showcase into the aspirations of retail and catering activities located within the heart of the development. In consequence, a media hub was conceived where the brand experience would naturally attract compatible commercial activity, such as multiplex cinemas, synergy retail, bookshops, software, music, communication technology and themed cafés and restaurants. A live studio running local radio, broadcast and webcast would have provided a spectacular dynamic focus.

At the time the incumbent (now theatrically departed) director general of the BBC felt that the main focus of the corporation should be on programme making and not on what could only be conceived as a visitor centre. This observation failed to acknowledge that a carefully constructed real-time experience would have extended their communication strategy in the same way that BBCi has developed its virtual presence. In the meantime this collection and a complementary collection held by the British Film Institute lay dormant in suburban warehouses.

The Hysel Plateau in Brussels is one of the most visited mixed-use destinations in Europe, attracting in excess of eight million visits per annum. Among other things it comprises exhibition pavilions, a trade mart, the national football stadium, the 1958 World Fair Atomium, and a large cinema complex called Kinepolis. The paradox is that even with this apparent diversity it fails to deliver depth and a range of experience that the increasingly sophisticated consumer demands. Our consortium devised an unusual mix of retail and leisure incorporating a significant cultural component.

The key feature of this informal learning environment was to create the concept of 'Tomorrow's World', which would investigate themes contained within the site and proposed commercial development. Here, themes such as sport, health, lifestyle, science and technology, media, environment and transport would

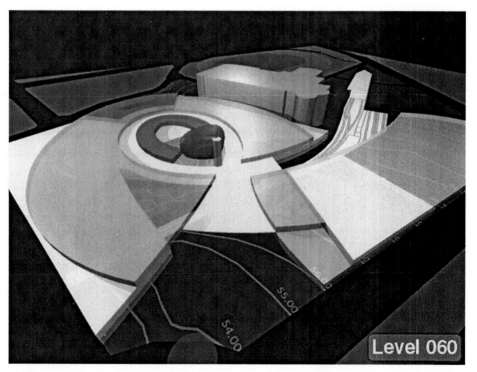

Figure 16.1 Concept of 'Tomorrow's World', a mixed-use destination. © Land Design Studio/Locum Destination.

221

become distinctive interpreted modules referring directly to aspects of the adjacent retail offer and adjacent activities. The centre would need to be supported by a programming/authoring facility that would continue to maintain topicality and even presentation events (subsequently we may reference the superb precedents of the Darwin Centre at the Natural History Museum, or the recently completed Dana Centre at the Science Museum, London). The breakthrough would have been the concept of empowering the consumer where authoritative independent institutions (museums, science centres) could begin to help demystify fascinating consumer issues. We could explain important aspects of nutrition and well-being, the science of perfume or sports injuries, the science behind your mobile phone, or simply the social history of a conservation quarter, before you set off on your city walk. How would all of this affect the adjacent participating retail tenants? It would clearly charge them to consider their buying strategy very carefully, becoming an embryonic centre of excellence with a point of difference and a sense of geographical place.

Though not in an urban city context, the National Maritime Museum Cornwall, set on the waterside in Falmouth, presents a realized project that demonstrates how a cultural facility can activate an energy in a community primarily through its diverse narrative content, while at the same time draw together many architectural 'loose ends' that have accumulated as a result of circumstantial and laissez-faire situations. The extended brief for the architects to masterplan

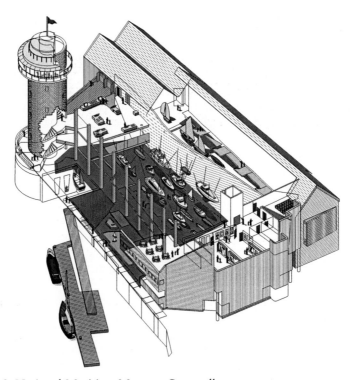

Figure 16.2 National Maritime Museum Cornwall. © National Maritime Museum Cornwall.

adjacent commercial initiatives and an events square has had significant impact on the success of this initiative.

For our company it was an unprecedented opportunity for interpretive designers to collaborate with architects Long & Kentish from the very inception of the project, encouraging the built form of the museum to have an uncanny sense of place and purpose. The introduction of a volumetric spine through the length of the building was collectively exploited. As an organizing principle it provided an immersive audio-visual experience, a dramatic north-lit 'Flotilla' gallery and an ideal starting point for the environmental control of the building. The elegant timber treatment of this symbolic wall has the resonating presence of a ship's hull past which 25 small boats are sailing. The periodic rehang of the gallery acknowledges the all-important need to attract repeat visitors.

Other features continued to reflect this powerful symbiotic relationship between different design disciplines. Sunlight, daylight, views, object display and media were optimized in respect of a preferred narrative sequence. Ramps provided movement and ideal viewing facilities and interpretive galleries were stacked at one end with a conscious control of potentially distracting views to help internalize the visitor's focus. The iconic tower is used to interpret both the estuary at high level and the tide below water level. All ancillary facilities, such as auditorium, library, workshop, café, education and administration, have been carefully incorporated.

Architect M. J. Long summarized the outcome of a very enjoyable and fruitful process:

> The collaboration with the exhibition designers enabled us to design a building which had positive architectural character throughout. The building has in fact become a player in the exhibition story. We developed the building as a series of very different environments, each a unique place related to the exhibition space. This is not a museum which could be anywhere else, it is essentially connected to its location and in that sense it is an authentic part of it.[14]

In a small way these three precedent models challenge the traditional episodic approach in incorporating culture into the conceptual masterplanning process. As noted earlier, typically, collections of material culture, valuation of real estate, funding initiatives and planning protocols are strung together in an unimaginative way, fulfilling the needs of local or national political agendas. The order of these activities may be shuffled but one thing that is always missing is any holistic understanding of a conceptual masterplan that is able to provide real substance to bond civic, commercial and cultural activities. It is perfectly normal for us to be handed a brief that has fundamental weaknesses concerning the central philosophy, the potential connectivity with other initiatives, an understanding of user profile within the extended marketplace, economic sustainability and the fundamental notion of 'fit for purpose' architecture.

223

I would go further and suggest the need for the critical involvement of a new breed of thinkers who understand the narrative of environments through an awareness of social context and material culture, and who are able to incorporate high-end information and communication skills within sympathetically designed architectural space. The proposition is that such masterplanning requires conceptual thinking that helps provide a broader framework for a destination rather than the developer's ersatz photoshopped visual showing video walls, fountains and people having fun. A response to these needs has encouraged the University of the Arts London to introduce a masters' course titled 'Creative Practice in Narrative Environments'.

The time has come to consider ways to fulfil the imperatives of the current British government, and to make business and culture speak the same language, by actively exploiting their mantra of empowerment, inclusiveness, diversity and customer satisfaction. We have to nurture a more creative way to integrate any informal learning environments into the urban matrix. The classical portal of learning should not just be conceived as tangible, but virtual. It is now important to understand how we can integrate, rather than demote these activities to isolated, peripheral leftover sites, or ambiguously titled 'cultural quarters'. New Labour thinkers Charles Leadbetter and Kate Oakley wrote that 'art, culture and sport create a meeting place for people in an increasingly diversified, fragmented and unequal society, meeting places that were once provided by work, religion or trade unions'.[15] This can only happen if mentors and practitioners of the 'cultural industries' are at the top table. However, we must remember that, if successful, these prototypical informal learning environments require inspired leadership, with a keen knowledge of the leisure and tourism marketplace, a pragmatic view of operational and revenue issues, events programming, PR and marketing, and a clear understanding of emerging new media alongside the clear prerequisite of a coherent understanding of the structural narrative.

If it is ever possible to establish the importance of *genius loci*, entrepreneurial leadership and the fundamental importance of local context, then it may be possible to engage with the next development stage, which will use this tangible launchpad to experiment with broadcast, webcast and virtuality underpinned with an important sense of authorship and origin.

Notes

1 J. Pedro Lorente, *Cathedrals of Urban Modernity: The First Museum of Contemporary Art 1800–1930*, Aldershot: Ashgate, 1998, p. 1.
2 J. Montaner, *Museos para el nuevo siglo*, Barcelona: Gustavo Gili, 1995, p. 12.
3 M. Hollein, 'Monumentality and its discontents', *Next, 8th International Architecture Exhibition 2002*, New York: Rizzoli, 2002, pp. 70–3.
4 Montaner, *Museos para el nuevo siglo*, p. 18.
5 D. Sudjic, 'Landmarks of hope and glory', *The Observer*, 26 October 2003, p. 6.
6 H. Hertzberger, *Space and the Architect: Lessons in Architecture 2*, Rotterdam: 010 Publishers, 2000, pp. 100–1.
7 Hollein, 'Monumentality and its discontents', p. 71.

8 P. Geddes, *Cities in Evolution: An Introduction to the Town Planning Movement and to the Studies of Civics*, London: Williams & Norgate, 1915, p. 372.
9 A. Ponte, 'Thinking machines: from the Outlook Tower to the City of the World', *Lotus International*, 35, 1982: 46–51.
10 M. Giebelhausen (ed.), *The Architecture of the Museum*, Manchester: Manchester University Press, 2003, pp. 6–7.
11 J. Bradburne, 'Dinosaurs and white elephants: the science center in the 21stC', *Public Understanding of Science*, 7, 1998: 237–53.
12 C. Fox, 'Brave new museums', *Museums Journal*, Vol. 101, No. 1, 2001: 41.
13 S. Lipton, 'We're on our way to Wembley, and our knees have gone all trembly', *Independent on Sunday*, 26 May 2002, p. 25.
14 M. J. Long, *National Maritime Museum Cornwall: The Architect's Story*, London: Long & Kentish Architects, 2003, p. 24.
15 C. Leadbetter and K. Oakley, *The Independents*. Available at: http://www.demos.co.uk/theindependents_pdf_media_public.aspx (accessed 19 August 2004).

References

Bradburne, J., 'Dinosaurs and white elephants: the science center in the 21stC', *Public Understanding of Science*, 7, 1998: 237–53.
Fox, C., 'Brave new museums', *Museums Journal*, Vol. 101, No. 1, 2001: 41.
Geddes, P., *Cities in Evolution: An Introduction to the Town Planning Movement and to the Studies of Civics*, London: Williams & Norgate, 1915.
Giebelhausen, M. (ed.), *The Architecture of the Museum*, Manchester: Manchester University Press, 2003.
Hertzberger, H., *Space and the Architect: Lessons in Architecture 2*, Rotterdam: 010 Publishers, 2000, pp. 100–1.
Hollein, M., 'Monumentality and its discontents', *Next, 8th International Architecture Exhibition 2002*, New York: Rizzoli, 2002, pp. 70–3.
Leadbetter, C. and Oakley, K., *The Independents*. Available at: http://www.demos.co.uk/theindependents_pdf_media_public.aspx (accessed 19 August 2004).
Lipton, S., 'We're on our way to Wembley, and our knees have gone all trembly', *Independent on Sunday*, 26 May 2002, p. 25.
Long, M. J., *National Maritime Museum Cornwall: The Architect's Story*, London: Long & Kentish Architects, 2003.
Lorente, J. Pedro, *Cathedrals of Urban Modernity: The First Museum of Contemporary Art 1800–1930*, Aldershot: Ashgate, 1998.
Montaner, J., *Museos para el nuevo siglo*, Barcelona: Gustavo Gili, 1995.
Ponte, A., 'Thinking machines: from the Outlook Tower to the City of the World', *Lotus International*, 35, 1982: 46–51.
Sudjic, D., 'Landmarks of hope and glory', *The Observer*, 26 October 2003, p. 6.

17

The vital museum

Stephen Greenberg

Changing audience expectations and an explosion of new technologies, and the consequent increased media literacy, mean that there has never been a more challenging and a more exciting time in which to be devising creative spaces. These spaces are inevitably becoming more dynamic and experiential, changing and theatrical, rather than monumental and static. To make these kinds of spaces we have to change the way we work. This chapter will describe how we can draw on contemporary theatre to challenge current discourse in space making. It will suggest also that, as in a performance, creative space in a museum or cultural environment is primarily the audience's space. It is a space that resonates with them and their lives, a space where they can learn, explore and be inspired, a space as much in the audience's mind as it is physical.

Experience making, as I am going to explore it within museums, is a recent phenomenon, which perhaps began only in the 1970s with the inclusion of monitors in display spaces and performance and installation art in gallery spaces. To begin with, monitors were hidden away, or became useful dumping grounds for everything a curator couldn't fit on to a graphic panel. However, it has taken us a while to realize that, as soon as a monitor is placed in a space, the space becomes mediated – the monitor is the display. In a nineteenth-century context this kind of mediation was unimaginable. Museums were object buildings filled with objects in cases, about which the curators knew less than we can now learn from the Discovery Channel, and the audiences knew even less. Exquisite installations and displays they may have been, but in the end the notion that the 'object must speak for itself, unmediated' became not only culturally and institutionally enshrined, but also a way of secreting knowledge. Access, engagement and connection were not on the menu.

Similarly, every eighteenth- and nineteenth-century building type had its typology. Durand produced an encyclopaedia of types, and as recently as the 1970s the architectural historian Sir Nikolaus Pevsner was writing confidently about typology. Building typologies are changing rapidly; we can do anything in a big-span 'shed' or a multi-storey frame 'loft' building: manufacture, shopping, storage and sport in a shed; homes, offices, hospitals and laboratories in frame buildings. A curious anomaly here is the art museum, whose typology and liturgy remain largely unchanged, and where the building is clearly an iconic artefact that can have its own abstract existence. Museums are not so straight-forward, particularly museums of science and industry, and natural and social history. Everyone knew what a museum was, but not any more.

Just think how our ordered assumptions about buildings and spaces are being overturned, when a surgical operation can be performed remotely on a laptop personal computer. We are still absorbing the shock-wave from the invention of the desktop PC as a way of manipulating information. Surfing and scrolling, juggling information, and text messaging still and moving images and sound have transformed our behaviour. Through digital media our access to content is breathtaking. Not only do we watch the film on the DVD, but also the out-takes, the making, the storyboarding. The production values contemporary audiences are exposed to are incredibly high. A new generation of audiences come to a museum not just with pre-knowledge from the internet, the learning cable channels and DVDs, but with expectations for high editorial and produc-tion values from MTV and pop videos. They are gadget literate, and segue from text and image messaging on their mobiles and PDAs, from the real to mixed reality, to virtual without hesitation, and they can make their own multi-media presentations on their laptops with ease – science fiction to most middle-aged museum directors, who first visited museums in the 1950s and 1960s.

New technologies mean we can make high-quality transitory environments; it has changed our view of permanence. It is a revolution in which creative spaces are moving away from static architectural spaces towards dynamic mediated experiences. One only has to go to Selfridges or Nike Town to see this at work in retail environments – to see shopping as theatre. But there are other factors driving it as well, such as our exposure to outdoor cityscapes like Tokyo, filled with images and information printed in gigantic formats, projected or displayed on large-format screens that work in broad daylight. These are the materials of the future.

As a consequence, more and more twenty-first-century environments, and not just museums, will be made out of and transformed by a range of media. Media-literate audiences will expect high production values and consummate editing of content when they come to a museum. They will want to make connections between artefacts and their stories, just as documentaries do. It is for these reasons that the expectations of museum audiences must lead us to focus on the primacy of the visitor's experience. This is a shift in where we start from, which neither curators nor architects find easy. Curators have traditionally been object-based – they have coveted objects but not stories or audiences. And so as a general rule have architects and designers, whose education and discourse is biased towards object making. Simply put, architects see space with objects within it, whereas the audience sees it the other way round; in perception terms it is like diametrically opposed readings of a Rorschach test. Nonetheless, the shift towards a more holistic experience, where artefacts and architecture are suffused as part of that, will take place whether we like it or not; it is a process that we need to accept and to work with, rather than resist.[1]

So how do we learn to make these experiences? And who are these experiences for and how do we judge their success or their failure?

To make the mediated experience I have described, we have to change our thought patterns. We need to think of spaces in a different way, leaving behind our old habits of monumentalism and permanence, in both buildings and their content, and think instead of dynamic performance spaces. However, the language of design is of little use when thinking about environments, especially museums, as complete experiences; architecture and design monographs focus on form, on object making, rather than experience. Of far greater use is the literature on twentieth-century theatre where the kind of shift described above took place from the 1960s. For me, this is best represented in the work of the remarkable director Peter Brook. A recently published book called *The Open Circle* by Andrew Todd and Jean-Guy Lecat describes Brook's theatre environments – his creative spaces.[2] Lecat has been responsible for finding the spaces in which Brook's company has performed all round the world: tram sheds, quarries, factories, cloisters and an assortment of theatres. Many of these, such as the famous Bouffes Du Nord in Paris and BAM in Brooklyn, were derelict, and have now become the venue of choice. All these spaces have memories, past lives and patinas of inhabitation that set them apart from new buildings. The whole experience, from arrival to departure, is part of the performance sequence. Design must walk a tightrope, as Brook says: 'the great danger comes when the architect proceeds either from practical considerations or from purely abstract ones.'[3] He is quite clear that they are not cathedrals:

> one has to say that a theatre cannot be and must not be considered as a temple; a theatre is a temporary, practical place, which should have the capacity to inspire and be uplifting. For an architect to be carried away – as Denys Lasdun was with the National Theatre – and so try to build a theatre as noble and as permanent as a temple is going too far one way. If, however, one says, 'This is just a working space, so let's just follow the requirements and nothing should go beyond basic functionality', then the architect won't have done his job in the other direction.[4]

In this vein, I would argue, even though a theatre audience is not a museum audience, that a museum space is primarily a performance space, and as such requires the same kind of thought and perception; what Brook says about the design of theatres can apply equally to the design of museums. Most inspiring is how Brook and his collaborators make a creative space enhance the bond with the audience; this is because they have broken out of the frozen frame of the proscenium and made both a real and a metaphorical 'open circle' with the audience. The stalls and orchestra pit of a conventional nineteenth-century theatre are in-filled as a level floor where performance takes place in an amphitheatre surrounded by the balconies, with the proscenium providing what Brook has called a double-depth stage: 'as for myself, I had gradually moved from two rooms to one, from stage and auditorium to a shared experience.'[5] The barrier between actor and audience is removed and the performance is taken out of its picture frame. The nineteenth-century museum has created a similar distance between viewer and artefact, because it was built as an ornate cabinet, full of other cabinets, and drained of curiosity.

For Brook, rethinking the creative space is only half the story, the other half being the nature of performance itself. For him there are four kinds of theatre: the conventional, the vulgar, the vital and the holy. One can think of museums that fit each of these categories, but also of museums and visitor experiences that embrace all four. There is a place for each: for the conventional encyclopaedic museum, for the vulgarity of a theme park, and for the holiness of a museum with a clear moral or social message. It is harder to think of museum experiences that live up to Brook's 'theatre of the vital spark'.[6] The 'vital museum' demands much more of us, if we are to make a transforming visitor experience that combines imaginative interpretation and display with a resonant architectural setting. The importance of a text like *The Open Circle*, therefore, is that it provides an alternative language and discourse to that of design and museology with which to frame and articulate creative space making, for audience studies and for creating a methodology for evaluating projects.

Figure 17.1 Permanent Holocaust Exhibition, Imperial War Museum, Lambeth, London. Audio testimony, home movies, archive film, photography, exhumed artefacts, information, maps and facsimile documents are seamlessly integrated into one 'layered' presentation. © DEGW. At Large. Nick Hufton.

These are new trends. My first experience of them was in working with the Imperial War Museum and its team, and my co-designer Bob Baxter, to produce the Holocaust Exhibition.[7] This was conceived as a completely integrated experience in space using every available medium; in a typical space you can find a seamless fusion of artefact display, home movie, testimony, newsreel, audio, cartography and biography and interior architecture. In devising this exhibition we used the techniques of film-making and storytelling. The Holocaust story falls into the classic shape of a three-part drama. It is a shape that Aristotle first defined and it is a shape that is still followed by most of the films – including all Hollywood blockbusters – that have reached the biggest audiences. By underlining the three-act shape we could find a structure that every member of the audience would recognize (even subliminally) and – more than that – it meant that we could access the power inherent in this structure.

As a consequence, it isn't just the story that is structured, but also the exhibition landscape that is conceived as a series of layers, which when plotted on paper are akin to an opera production; but in this case a production that integrates layers of text, personal testimony, archive and newsreel film and photography, alongside pacing and drama, alternating the principle mode of delivery in each space, the audio-visual plot and the lighting plan. Given the gravity of the subject, and its effect on the emotions of each member of the audience, we also identified another layer we called 'space to imagine'. And on top of this was the visual language of spaces or displays that were predominantly white or black, representing the experience of victim or perpetrator; these worked like a visual expression of the images in a Shakespeare play, e.g. blood and darkness in *Macbeth*. This combination of physical and content layering allows the exhibition to be subject to both simple and also complex readings and interpretations, and for it to appeal to the intellect and intuition, to be both visceral and vital. And because the exhibition is conceived as a 'film in space' rather than a film in two dimensions, each visitor can explore and edit at their own pace and in their own creative space. But the approach is 'filmic' in another way as well, largely because the exhibition was low on iconic artefacts but very high on impact. And here we had to unleash the power inherent in certain artefacts, and discovered that they could become 'social actors'. In one space there is only one artefact – an ordinary Adler typewriter of the period, a basic tool of the bureaucracy. It sits in a space bounded by an organization chart of the whole Nazi chain of command from Hitler down. This is printed in white out of black behind glass, so that visitors see their own reflection mirrored in the black perpetrator space, as they stand on a white floor, in victim space. Beside the typewriter a series of words and phrases are presented whose meaning was deliberately altered during this period of history; a few will recognize their source as George Steiner's *Language and Silence*.[8] This single artefact has become a social actor engaging with the audience in a shared creative space.

In our work at Metaphor, principally in exhibition design and masterplanning, we start every project using the tools of film and TV programme making. We have a professional writer in our team, who develops treatments, narratives and scripts. The script fixes and structures the story for all the members of the creative team before we start and enables us to check that the experience is working before we began to visualize it. Now here's an interesting point. Architects aren't comfortable with this approach; it's totally alien to their way of thinking, because with words the vision remains a shared one in people's minds. And nor are curators, because – I suspect – it cuts through what they do. It diminishes the primacy of the building, the artefact and the content as separate entities. For object-based designers conceiving the creative space as audience space represents a massive transformation in thinking. In many mediated museum environments the building could become secondary or even tertiary to the experience: object, setting, building – not building, setting, object. But even so the scriptwriting technique is very revealing. I would argue that many major projects would have been altered with its use. The entrance and courtyard sequence of the British Museum (BM) Great Court would not have survived the 'script' treatment. In filmic terms, it needed an 'establishing shot', which with the truly inspired inclusion of artefacts would be far more than its architecture. The Great Court was conceived as a covered urban square, not as an extraordinary display of artefacts, a simulacrum for the BM's mission to illuminate world cultures. Instead, as Charles Saumarez-Smith put it so

Figure 17.2 Imperial War Museum North, Trafford. The original masterplanning model illustrates the concept of a dramatic installation suffusing Daniel Libeskind's building into the display. The architects' curved floor, or 'earth shard', becomes the stage on which the complex story of people's experience of conflict is structured through the changing media of each epoch. The architecture supports the content rather than becoming the narrative itself. © DEGW. At Large. Andrew Putler.

succinctly when the Great Court opened, 'everyone was overwhelmed by the architectural experience – the sweep of the roof and the sensational sense of scale. Now I hear more complaints that it sucks the life out of the galleries'.[9]

While working on the Holocaust Exhibition, Bob Baxter and myself devised the original exhibition masterplan for Imperial War Museum (IWM) North. The final display has retained the four components of the original installation – a time line, thematic silos, symbolic artefacts and programmable space – but it has been executed with limited means and therefore without the structure layers of the Holocaust Exhibition. These are replaced with a picture show that periodically engulfs the whole building – a cinematic not a theatrical experience. As Brook notes:

> the cinema is by its very nature overwhelming; its images and sound invade every corner of the brain, washing away all sense of distance, making our identification with the action complete and irresistible. In the theatre, a line of verse, a song, a dance, even a leap in the air are often all that is needed for the most secret of meanings to appear.[10]

What has also happened in IWM North is that the architectural sequencing and the elements of the display are disconnected experiences, and they don't make a narrative arc – not surprising given the limited budgets and easily remedied in the years ahead, but this raises another issue. IWM North is important because it is a pathfinder for museums as performance spaces, and buildings that will become *programmable* (i.e. changeable) spaces in which film, audio and artefacts are seamlessly woven together to create an experience in which the architecture is just one more enriching element.[11]

A frequent albeit anecdotally received comment from those who don't want to repeat their visit is because they feel they've seen it all. I would suggest that this response is because Daniel Libeskind's object-making vision has overwhelmed the experience and has taken precedence over the story and the characters in that story. IWM's story is a profound one – people's experiences of conflict. Libeskind rises to this epic with a building that is based on the shards of a shattered globe. He has stated how the visitor should experience the disorientation of war through the broken pieces of the building and its geometry of deconstruction. But unless this is part of an intense and layered visitor experience it remains a scenographic response; an opera set without the libretto, the score and the performers. In Peter Brook's terms, twentieth-century conflict is on the scale of his legendary production of the Mahabarata. But for Brook the purpose of a performance is transformative, to 'make you feel better, consoled, relieved, or, ideally, more courageous, given new vitality' – not to 'go back out into an already rotten world feeling more angry, more depressed, more frustrated'.[12] Libeskind's vision is personal and it eschews any closure or reorientation for the visitor, whereas in the Holocaust Exhibition, the closing and harmonious oval-shaped space provides a humane place of safety and contemplation. From here visitors can look back into the blackness of the exhibition they have experienced, while they test their emotions against testimony from survivors about trust, faith, memory and rebuilding their lives. For the visitors, many of whom are in bits by this point, this is not a redemptive experience, but it is transforming. The testimony answers the questions in their minds and they are left in awe of other human beings and their courage. IWM North has yet to make the audiences' creative space in the same way.

In a number of our projects, my colleagues and I at Metaphor have continued to explore how to make vital creative spaces that integrate challenging architecture, artefacts and rich mediated content. They all work from the premise that the physical experience is a complete installation at the building scale, and that it is structured through a series of layers, pathways and themes through which displays and mediated content are woven from the macro to the micro level – with the building as the background layer. An example of the installation at the building scale would be the Natural History Museum in Paris. The visitor sees what God and Noah would have seen – all of the animal kingdom in one panoptic sweep – something that the visitor can experience nowhere else, and certainly not in nature, in the wild. Another example at the building scale was the installation as originally conceived for IWM North – a panoptic view of twentieth-century conflict.

An example of a series of structured mediated layers would be the Holocaust Exhibition. The challenge is to make an installation that traverses the macro and the micro and integrates the building as well.

'Identities' is the working title for a creative space which will be included in a new mixed-use iconic building (yet to be designed), which will be the centrepiece of the Heart of Slough project. 'Identities' is about multiculturalism and communities who have migrated to the UK. Slough, with its proximity to Heathrow and with its many communities, provides a natural dynamic for the project and a natural constituency. It is also within the creative corridor that stretches from the BBC in Acton to Ealing Studios, a partner in the project, and on to the M4 Silicon Valley corridor. The project is organized around four themes: beginnings, childhood and adolescence, adulthood and working life, and futures.

The important point here is that the concept masterplan has been produced before the icon architect has been appointed. The building (which is conceived like a Rubik's cube that visitors explore) comes out of the exhibition concept, what Charles Samaurez-Smith describes as the 'theatricality of display', and not vice versa.[13] Visitors arrive by one of four lifts into one of the four thematic areas. The lifts are part of the experience, and the level at which they arrive is set by the 'fuzzy' logic of the lift, arriving in programmable spaces. The point of all this is that from each thematic area visitors can see and move into others. This reflects an experience that is not a sequential narrative, but a condition of being migrant. No two visits will be the same. Added to this, many of the artefacts, and much of the mediated material, are already being made by the communities 'Identities' represents. Mixed reality technologies will be used within the spaces to bring communities together across continents.

Figure 17.3 'Identities', Heart of Slough. This is a concept model for a visitor experience that explores identity of minority and migrant cultures across generations. It is structured like a Rubik's cube. The four themes representing aspects of the condition of being a migrant are represented by four colours, between which visitors move freely, in one state but aware of the other. Visitors circulate between floors in large lifts – rooms with programmed displays that move up and down and are a part of the migrant journey. Within this bold structure, the experience will be programmable, and include artefacts, film, audio and immersive spaces. © Metaphor.

Another of our studies is for a museum to house the video art of New York-based artist Nam June Paik, set in a park within Kyongii Cultural Museum, Suwon, South Korea. His most famous work uses installations of TV monitors. For us, this was an opportunity to take the changing rhythm and patterns of the programmable artworks and make a programmable space for them, and beyond that to programme the whole visitor experience. In the park, the building has no conventional elevations; it is buried beneath a landscape of light boxes that visitors can walk between – containers for an ever changing concert of Nam June Paik's work. Inside, the flowing spaces can be subdivided

Figure 17.4 Nam June Paik Museum, Suwon, South Korea. This competition design for a museum for the work of video and performance artist Nam June Paik is conceived as a series of display cases or light boxes in the landscape, programmable and displaying the rhythms and patterns of the artist's ever changing light and projection-based installations in an electronic garden. The building becomes a fusion of landscape, exhibition making and installation art that visitors explore. © Metaphor.

as the artist sees fit. The building structure is a test rig with hollow towers above the display spaces that make light and dark conditions that respond to the various light media, lasers, monitors, holograms and fluorescent tubes that are used in the installation. The concept is a fusion of landscape, architecture, exhibition design and installation art.

In the competition to masterplan the Victoria and Albert Museum the short-listed architects went for the usual heavyweight solutions, such as roofing in the central courtyard. In contrast, few adopted the opposite approach.[14] We avoided monumental thinking and instead started with an exploration of the visitor experience that led us to a new map that was about way-finding and 'the mind of the museum'. It was starting from how the visitor experiences the museum that prompted us to think of it as moving and filmic, rather than static and monumental, and to realize that other media, film, graphic design, video art and installations could be more effective than capital-intensive interventions. We asked the client to think about the Museum, which stretches across 12.5 acres, as a city with quarters, and to formulate the guide as a city guide not a museum catalogue. Only then did we identify over 50 projects, and a flexible ten-year implementation plan, that would use many different kinds of designers: interior, exhibition, graphic and landscape – the antithesis of the classic architect-driven project. The first ten are under way.

The core idea in the V&A masterplan is to put the visitor and their experience first – to make the museum their space, and their creative space. As a new approach to masterplanning it was a breakthrough. Its success is that it has been intellectually robust enough to both frame and change the discourse within the museum and to have enough flexibility to survive the vicissitudes of a complex multi-headed institution. The lesson here is to solve the intellectual challenges first, by starting with the museum's assets: its content, artefacts and collections.

In this shift that I have outlined we will need to think of a creative space as a place of vital engagement, as audience space, as an experience and not as a static object. These spaces will need creative directors to bring all the different elements together so as to orchestrate the experience. We will have to develop a deeper understanding of how different visitors experience these new spaces, their different learning paths and what they need from them, and then respond with tools that frame the discourse and evaluate a creative space or a visitor experience.[15] Above all, creative space has to be collaborative space – it must bring together a range of creative disciplines. How much more exciting and vital the next generation of museums will be if the architecture is integral to this experience and the architects share in this collaboration and dialogue.

Notes

1 Object- or artefact-based does not automatically mean that an experience is story-poor or context deficient; object-rich can illustrate better than audio-visual.
2 A. Todd and J-G. Lecat, *The Open Circle*, London: Faber, 2003, p. 250.
3 Ibid.
4 Ibid.
5 P. Brook, *Threads of Time: A Memoir*, London: Methuen, 1999, p. 220.
6 R. Eyre and N. Wright, *Changing Stages: A View of British Theatre in the Twentieth Century*, London: Bloomsbury, 2000, p. 360.
7 The Permanent Holocaust Exhibition at the Imperial War Museum 1996–2000 and Imperial War Museum North 1996, designed by Stephen Greenberg, then of DEGW and now of Metaphor, and Bob Baxter, then of Amalgam and now of At Large.
8 G. Steiner, *Language and Silence: Essays on Language, Literature and the Inhuman*, New York: Atheneum, 1967.
9 C. Samaurez-Smith, 'Opinion', *Museum Practice*, spring, 2004: 11. This perception of a major museum space mirrors Brook's on too many architects of theatre spaces:

> they see only as far as the vessel: they do not understand that what they do is necessarily incomplete in the case of a theatre. In some cases there seems to be a rigidity, a fear, in the spaces – a refusal to accept the need for openness in their forms; a retreat into inflexible and deadening materials and structures. As a consequence, there are many modern spaces that reject almost all attempts to breathe life into them.

(Todd and Lecat, *The Open Circle*, pp. 194–5)

10 Brook, *Threads of Time*, p. 201.

11 In museums of this kind we will also need to reconsider the business model, and specifically the capitalization of exhibition space as against the building fabric, as the refreshment rate for this kind of experience is shorter than a more traditional permanent gallery.

12 Todd and Lecat, *The Open Circle*, p. 250.

13 Samaurez-Smith, 'Opinion', p. 11.

14 V&A Masterplan 1999–2001, won in competition by Stephen Greenberg while a partner at DEGW and completed by Metaphor.

15 My thanks to Robert Barnett, previous Vice President Gallery Development at the Royal Ontario Museum for his comments and contribution to this chapter.

References

Brook, P., *Threads of Time: A Memoir*, London: Methuen, 1999.

Eyre, R. and Wright, N., *Changing Stages: A View of British Theatre in the Twentieth Century*, London: Bloomsbury, 2000.

Samaurez-Smith, C., 'Opinion', *Museum Practice*, spring, 2004: 11.

Steiner, G., *Language and Silence: Essays on Language, Literature and the Inhuman*, New York: Atheneum, 1967.

Todd, A. and Lecat, J-G., *The Open Circle*, London: Faber, 2003.

Index